PERSON–CENTRED COUNSELLING

IN ACTION

Third Edition

Dave Mearns *and*
Brian Thorne

SAGE Publications
Los Angeles · London · New Delhi · Singapore

First published 1988
Reprinted 1990, 1991, 1992, 1993, 1994, 1995, 1996, 1997
Second edition published 1999
Reprinted 2000, 2001, 2002, 2003, 2004, 2005, 2006
Third edition published 2007

SAGE Publications Ltd
1 Oliver's Yard
55 City Road
London EC1Y 1SP

SAGE Publications Inc.
2455 Teller Road
Thousand Oaks, California 91320

SAGE Publications India Pvt Ltd
B 1/I 1 Mohan Cooperative Industrial Area
Mathura Road, New Delhi 110 044
India

SAGE Publications Asia-Pacific Pte Ltd
33 Pekin Street #02-01
Far East Square
Singapore 048763

British Library Cataloguing in Publication data

A catalogue record for this book is available from the British Library

ISBN 978-1-4129-2854-0
ISBN 978-1-4129-2855-7 (pbk)

Library of Congress Control Number: 2006937727

Typeset by C&M Digitals (P) Ltd, Chennai, India
Printed in Great Britain by The Cromwell Press Ltd, Trowbridge, Wiltshire
Printed on paper from sustainable resources

PERSON-CENTRED
COUNSELLING

7 DAY
BOOK

SAGE COUNSELLING *IN ACTION*

Series Editor: WINDY DRYDEN

Sage Counselling in Action is a series of short, practical books developed especially for students and trainees. As accessible introductions to theory and practice, they have become core texts for many courses, both in counselling and other professions such as nursing, social work, education and management. Books in the series include:

Sue Culley and Tim Bond
Integrative Counselling Skills in Action, Second Edition

Windy Dryden and Michael Neenan
Rational Emotive Behavioural Counselling in Action, Third Edition

Michael Jacobs
Psychodynamic Counselling in Action, Third Edition

Diana Whitmore
Psychosynthesis Counselling in Action, Third Edition

Patricia D'Ardenne and Aruna Mahtani
Transcultural Counselling in Action, Second Edition

Ian Stewart
Transactional Counselling in Action, Second Edition

Petrūska Clarkson
Gestalt Counselling in Action, Third Edition

Tim Bond
Standards & Ethics for Counselling in Action, Second Edition

Peter Trower, Windy Dryden and Andrew Casey
Cognitive Behavioural Counselling in Action

This third edition is dedicated to Elke and Christine in gratitude for their support and inspiration.

Praise for Previous Editions

'An important book .... a most sophisticated text. Mearns and Thorne have written a book for all counsellors and psychotherapists. The reader will be left both grateful and hungry for more.' – *British Journal of Guidance and Counselling*

'The discussion of empathy, acceptance and congruence is central and should be required reading for all trainees working to understand the richness of these core concepts ... outstanding.' – *Counselling and Psychotherapy*, The Journal of the British Association for Counselling and Psychotherapy

'The first systematic, comprehensive text about this approach since Carl Rogers' own *Client-Centred Therapy* ... outstanding.' – *Counselling*, The Journal of the British Association for Counselling

'Without doubt the clearest description of the person-centred approach to counselling that I have read, apart from Carl Rogers' own writings. I felt that I had got to know both Dave Mearns and Brian Thorne through their offering the reader their own congruence and I found this aspect of the book at times quite moving.' – *Social Work Today*

'Gives real insight into person-centred counselling ... This is a gentle book; an absolute delight to read (I couldn't put it down) as it held me in the realm of my own feelings. I would like to thank both authors for sharing so much of their intimate selves. I recommend this book to trainee counsellors, trained counsellors, clients and those involved in the helping professions. It is a book that has influenced me and that I would not want to be without.' – *BPS Counselling Psychology Review*

'Excellent "all rounder" for practitioners to learn and build upon counselling skills with young offenders.' – lecturer, Guidance, Youth and Youth Justice, Nottingham Trent University

'An excellent text. Student friendly and covering all main issues.' – lecturer, Psychology Swansea Institute of HE

'Stimulates a re-exploration of the doctor–patient relationship.' – *British Medical Journal*

'I felt understood by this book!' – Ann Weiser, PCA Letter Network

'This book could very sensibly be placed on the reading lists of all counselling trainers and trainees … this is the most informative and useful book I have read in a long time and I have no doubt that if Carl Rogers were still alive today, he would not only agree but also acknowledge experiencing some envy.' – *Changes*

'The skilful conveying of tenderness and building of trust are well explained and described with lots of case study examples.' – *Guidance Matters*

'Excellent book – a useful and practical way to underpin current emphasis on humanism in nursing.' – lecturer, West London NHS Mental Health Trust

'Continues to be an excellent, easy introduction but with depth. Deserves to be a bestseller!' – lecturer, Preston College

'The book conveys the profound respect for the person, for his/her autonomy and uniqueness, which is inherent in the Rogerian approach.' – *British Journal of Medical Psychology*

'A marvellous book; highly recommended. Someone has finally written an easily accessible book about the theory and practice – mostly practice – of the kind of therapy that makes the most sense to many focusers. Hurrah!' – *The Focusing Connection*

'Truly allows the reader to enter the world of the person-centered counselor.' – *Contemporary Psychology*

'*Person Centred Counselling in Action*, written by Dave Mearns and Brian Thorne was originally published in 1988 about a year after the death of Carl Rogers. It has helped to maintain and stimulate interest in this approach and has become a best-seller in the Counselling in Action series.' – *The Journal of Critical Psychology, Counselling and Psychotherapy*

Contents

Acknowledgements

Our indebtedness to our original trainers and close colleagues remains as profound as ever and most particularly, of course, to Dr Carl Rogers without whose life and work our own personal and professional lives would have been very different. In more recent times we have been enriched and stimulated by the contributions of other younger practitioners and we particularly wish to acknowledge the influences of Mick Cooper, Judy Moore, Margaret Warner and Peter F. Schmid.

As always, we are grateful to the editorial and marketing staff of Sage Publications whose support and efficiency have been exemplary and who succeed in making the writing of books a pleasurable as well as a challenging activity. Finally we wish to acknowledge the patient and meticulous work of Tessa Mearns on the word processor. She has been a constant source of encouragement and her longstanding and intimate knowledge of both authors has made us feel secure while at the same time, putting us on our mettle.

Preface to the Third Edition

It is now almost 20 years since the first edition of *Person-Centred Counselling in Action* appeared. During that period there has been a remarkable burgeoning of the practice of counselling and psychotherapy and a comparable development within the particular domain of person-centred counselling. In 1988, apart from the writings of Carl Rogers himself, there was little literature available to assist the aspiring person-centred counsellor and the first edition of this book brought both substance and discipline to an orientation which was in danger of becoming anarchic. Indeed, it was not uncommon at that time for practitioners to appropriate the label 'person-centred' for themselves without any firm grasp of either the theory or the practice of what is, in fact, one of the most demanding approaches to therapy to emerge in the twentieth century. Ironically, the inappropriate and ill-informed use of the term person-centred is still to be found in government literature especially in the context of NHS provision where the emphasis on putting the patient at the centre of treatment is buttressed by terminology which has nothing whatsoever to do with the theory and practice of person-centred counselling as we understand it. It is, indeed, difficult to avoid the mischievous thought that if the NHS were really undergirded by a genuine person-centred philosophy we would be living in a very different culture to the target-driven, efficiency-obsessed, surveillance monitored environment prevailing in so many professional fields at the present time.

This third edition appears against the background of the profound changes that have occurred in the person-centred world during the last two decades. The approach is now well established in Britain and is embraced by thousands of practitioners. Several high-quality training courses exist and person-centred practitioners, scholars and researchers are to be found in prestigious universities – most notably in the Universities of Strathclyde and East Anglia – where the current authors have been responsible for the development of Centres that have achieved international recognition. The approach has also been well served in the professional literature and there are several person-centred authors whose books are widely read and appreciated (e.g. Merry, 1995, 1999; Keys, 2003; Tolan, 2003; Wilkins, 2003; Sanders, 2006; Tudor and Worrall, 2006). Two flourishing professional associations exist, the British Association for the Person-Centred Approach (BAPCA) and its sister organisation, the Association for Person-Centred Therapy (Scotland). The approach is now also admirably served by PCCS Books Limited of Ross-on-Wye who, under the inspirational leadership of Pete Sanders and Maggie Taylor-Sanders, are almost entirely devoted to the publication of person-centred books and have become the primary publisher of person-centred material not only in Britain but in the world. At the same time, Sage (UK) have continued to play a central role in the publication of books (like this one) which have proved to be trail-blazers in the person-centred tradition. More recently the World Association for Person-Centered and Experiential Psychotherapy and Counseling has been established and its journal *Person-Centered and Experiential Psychotherapies* currently has two thousand subscribers worldwide.

The rapid spread and consolidation of the approach in Britain and other parts of the world has also ensured its vitality. New schools of thought have emerged which, while remaining faithful to the core elements of the approach, have embraced different emphases and opened up fresh therapeutic possibilities. The current authors welcome such developments while remaining alert to deviations that threaten to abandon key elements of the approach. They have also been assiduous in continually reviewing the theoretical basis of person-centred work to see where it needs extending or elaborating. In this respect Dave Mearns has been especially active and his work on configurations and ego-syntonic process has proved to be particularly illuminating and of considerable clinical importance. Both of us have embraced the concept of relational depth as an unusually helpful notion in evaluating counsellor competence and therapeutic efficacy. For Dave Mearns it has proved a valuable concept in addressing the challenge of existential despair while for Brian Thorne it has provided a context for exploring the quality of presence and the movement into spiritual experience. From the outset of our 32 year friendship and collaboration, the fact that Dave is a humanistic atheist and Brian an Anglican Christian of the liberal catholic persuasion has proved to be an unexpected strength and has endowed our work with a creative energy which seems to appeal to a wide readership. It perhaps also reflects the fact that person-centred practitioners tend to be fairly evenly divided between those who declare themselves agnostic or atheist and those who hold a religious or spiritual belief system which postulates some kind of higher power or universal meaning.

Against this background we have been at pains in this revised text to produce a book which both in context and style will commend itself to practitioners whose level of experience may vary significantly. Those who are new to the approach and may be embarking on the first stage of training will find in its pages a clear exposition of key aspects of theory and practice. They will also gain first-hand knowledge of the challenging and sometimes dramatic day-to-day experience of being a person-centred counsellor. We believe, however, that well-established practitioners and even seasoned scholars of the approach will find much here to interest and stimulate them. In an earlier book, *Person-Centred Therapy Today* (Sage, 2000), we attempted to explore new frontiers in both theory and practice and an introduction to that work has been incorporated into the present volume. We are proud, however, to belong to a tradition that remains constantly open to new insights and possibilities and there are moments in this new edition when we take tentative steps into, as yet, little explored terrain. Readers of the first two editions have been generous in their praise of a book that they found both clear and compelling, accessible and yet conducive to profound reflection. They also commented frequently on the pleasure of being accompanied by two authors so evidently different in temperament and yet united in values and purpose. The first two editions have sold 130,000 copies. Perhaps we are insane to produce this radical revision in the third edition, adding 20,000 words and tripling the references. Yet we believe that this new edition will have lost none of the clarity and accessibility of its predecessors and that its content will be sufficiently compelling to retain the loyalty of old readers while welcoming new enquirers. Of one thing we are sure: we have not grown bored with each other's company and have not lost the ability to startle each other by our differing but complementary perceptions of the fascinating arena of a therapeutic approach which we believe has much to offer a desperate world. Above all it can contribute to the restoration of confidence in the capacity of human beings to move, against all the odds, towards a more constructive future.

Professor Dave Mearns, University of Strathclyde, Glasgow
Professor Brian Thorne, University of East Anglia, Norwich

Introduction

On 8 July 1997 in Lisbon the World Association for Person-Centered and Experiential Psychotherapy and Counseling was founded and three years later in Chicago its Statutes were agreed by consensus at a General Assembly. These events would probably have astonished Dr Carl Rogers, the pioneering originator of person-centred counselling, and might even have horrified him for he had an almost instinctive dislike of associations and organisations. For Rogers they tended to lead to a form of entrenched professionalism where all too easily the needs and insights of clients could be obscured by forms of expertise which served to bolster the self-importance, prestige and power of therapists. For person-centred practitioners throughout the world, however, the formation of the World Association marked an important milestone in the evolution of an approach to counselling and psychotherapy which had its origins in the work of Rogers and his colleagues in the 1930s and 1940s. It offered the possibility of a firmer identity and a more powerful voice at a time when, as now, the prevailing Zeitgeist was less than favourable to many of the principles which have from the outset underpinned the theory and practice of person-centred counselling.

The central truth for Rogers was that the client knows best. It is the client who knows what hurts and where the pain lies and it is the client who, in the final analysis, will discover the way forward. The task of the counsellor is to be the kind of companion who can relate to the client in such a way that he or she can access their own wisdom and recover self-direction. The various names under which the approach has been identified over the years bear witness to the primary principles. Rogers began by calling his way of working *non-directive* counselling, thereby emphasising the importance of the counsellor as a non-coercive companion rather than a guide or an expert on another's life. Because critics interpreted non-directivity as a kind of mechanical passivity on the counsellor's part, Rogers subsequently described his approach as *client-centred* and in this way placed greater emphasis on the centrality of the client's

1

phenomenological world and on the need for the counsellor to stay accurately attuned to the client's experience and perception of reality. Many practitioners throughout the world continue to call themselves 'client-centred'. They argue that when Rogers himself first used the expression *person-centred* he was concerned with an attitudinal approach to activities outside the counselling room such as group work, educational processes and cross-cultural understanding. They maintain that the expression 'person-centred approach' should continue to be reserved for these non-counselling contexts. While respecting this point of view we have opted for the expression *person-centred counselling* and employ it throughout this book. Both of us are committed members of the World Association and it seems wholly appropriate that we should adhere to the description which features in the Association's title.

Our decision to employ the term 'person-centred' does not rest, however, simply on a desirable alignment with the World Association's terminology. There are at least three other powerful reasons. In the first place, it is not true that Rogers himself always confined the expression 'person-centred approach' to non-counselling activities. There are clear instances where he used the terms client-centred and person-centred interchangeably and he was altogether happy to be associated with training courses which aimed to train person-centred counsellors and psycho-therapists. More importantly, however, a second reason lies in our belief that the description 'person-centred' more accurately conveys the dual emphasis on the client's phenomenological world and on the state of being of the counsellor. Our therapeutic activity is essentially the development of a relationship between two persons; the inner worlds of both client and counsellor are of equal importance in the forging of a relationship which will best serve the needs and interests of the client. The concept of relational depth has great significance in the pursuit of therapeutic efficacy and the counsellor's ability to meet the client at depth is dependent on her own willingness to enter fearlessly into the encounter. Person-centred counselling is essentially a relationship between two persons, both of whom are committed to moving towards a greater fullness of being.

The third reason for opting for the term 'person-centred counselling' concerns the development of Rogers' work since his death in 1987. When we were working on the first edition of this book Rogers was still alive and there were only limited opportunities in the UK for training in any depth in this approach. The result was a situation, which we lamented with considerable feeling, whereby many practitioners with inadequate or even minimal understanding were prepared to label themselves 'person-centred', bringing the approach into disrepute by their superficial, muddled or misguidedly anarchic practice, which had no solid foundation in genuine person-centred theory. In a second edition some ten years later we reported that, although elements of the 1980s situation remained which still fuelled our exasperation, there were now a number of specialised training courses in place with an established track record. In brief, it was increasingly possible to identify a growing cohort of practitioners who had received an in-depth training in the approach. At the same time there had been a burgeoning of literature on the approach, the establishment of professional associations and a number of academic appointments in British universities. It was now much more difficult to sport the label 'person-centred' spuriously or to claim ignorance of the 'real' thing in the face of the growing development of the approach through training institutes and scholarly activity.

In more recent years the situation both here and in other countries has taken another turn which, while rendering the field more complex has, if anything, strengthened the case for retaining the term 'person-centred'. As is perhaps inevitable after the death of a leading figure, those who have been most influenced by his or her work began to follow their own paths, developing aspects of the original work while abandoning others. In Rogers' case this was an almost predictable outcome for he had himself always insisted on the provisionality of theory and had remained remarkably open to fresh experience and new research findings throughout his life. The title of the World Association is again revealing. Incorporation of the word 'experiential' indicates that the Association invites under its umbrella those practitioners who have been profoundly influenced by the work of Eugene Gendlin and his focusing-oriented psychotherapy, as well as those who emphasise the client's process of experiencing and see the counsellor as a skilled facilitator of process, while preserving a stance of non-directivity as far as content is concerned. Such offshoots from the main branch of what might be termed classical client-centred counselling are evidence, we would suggest, of a healthy state of affairs. They demonstrate an approach which is not moribund and where practitioners are open to new practical and theoretical developments in the light of experience. At the same time an attempt has been made by such writers as Lietaer (2002), Schmid (2003) and Sanders (2000) to elucidate the irreducible principles or criteria of person-centred work so that it is possible to identify those developments that remain true to the core concepts against those that have deviated so far from the approach's origins as to be no longer what Margaret Warner (2000b) has described as 'tribes' of the person-centred nation. For us, person-centred counselling serves as an appropriate umbrella term for all those 'tribes' that subscribe to the primary or irreducible principles of the approach; it is our hope that what follows will be valuable to practitioners or practitioners in training whether they conceptualise themselves as 'classical' client-centred counsellors or prefer to identify with one or other of the more recently evolved person-centred tribes. For our own part, while situating ourselves, by temperament and experience, at the 'classical' end of the continuum we have been keen to develop and refine many of Rogers' original theoretical constructs and this work is incorporated in what follows. Person-centred counselling, as we view it, is neither set in theoretical tablets of stone nor confined to one particular and exclusive form in practice.

Where the book is intentionally limited is in its primary focus on practice informed – as this is – by what we trust is a clear exposition of theory. It makes no pretence to offer a detailed exploration of research studies or to engage in research analysis. As a result much of the painstaking work of American researchers of past generations goes unacknowledged as does the more recent work of eminent European researchers. Readers who wish to remedy this deficiency are invited to consult Goff Barrett-Lennard's monumental history of the approach (Sage, 1998), which gives, inter alia, a comprehensive account of the approach's embeddedness in research. PCCS Books (a publishing house dedicated to the person-centred approach and founded in the early 1990s) has also published a collection of papers from the Chicago international conference of 2000 including accounts of recent research studies to that point (Watson, Goldman and Warner, 2002). Since 2002 the international journal *Person-Centered and Experiential Psychotherapies*, currently in its sixth volume, represents the major vehicle for reporting new developments in the approach.

As with past editions we hope that *Person-Centred Counselling in Action* is written in such a way that it will prove useful to practitioners and trainees in Europe, America and other parts of the world where the person-centred approach is flourishing. There are two issues, however, which are perhaps peculiar to Britain and need elucidation for readers in other countries. Firstly, there are several references to the work which a counsellor does with her *supervisor*. This emphasis on supervision reflects the British setting, where continued accreditation as a counsellor with the British Association for Counselling and Psychotherapy requires life-long supervision, a condition which, as far as we know, is not obligatory in most parts of America and continental Europe. Secondly, it should be understood that as far as the person-centred approach is concerned the activities of counselling and psychotherapy are usually considered indistinguishable because the *processes* involved between practitioner and client remain the same irrespective of the name given to the activity. For American readers the situation is rendered even more confusing because in Britain the word counselling tends to be used much more generally in contexts which in America might well warrant the term *psychotherapy*. In this book we have stayed consistent with the spirit of the series by referring to what we do as 'counselling' and by confining ourselves to relatively short term therapeutic relationships. None of the cases we present progressed beyond a year.

In Britain we now have, to our minds, the regrettable situation where female counsellors and trainees considerably outnumber male practitioners. Partly for this reason, but mainly to simplify the text, we refer to counsellors as female and clients as male, except where the context clearly demands otherwise. This convention on our part should in no way detract from our absolute belief in the uniqueness of persons and no literary artifice which inadvertently appears to demean individuals because of their gender or for any other reason is intended.

The book, as in its previous editions, attempts to invite the reader into the living experience of person-centred counselling. It seeks to engage practitioners and would-be practitioners at an emotional as well as an intellectual level. Above all it seeks to convey the excitement – sometimes allied to anxiety and risk – of relating to another human being in depth. We hope, too, that the book will be read by some would-be clients and more particularly by those who may have had the unfortunate experience of encountering helping professionals who, either by temperament or through training, have been reluctant to meet them as persons. The opening chapters present a contemporary overview of the major theoretical constructs of the approach and of the demands placed upon the counsellor in terms of her own awareness and disciplined attitude to the self. Thereafter, the reader is plunged into the moment-to-moment challenges of the person-centred counsellor at work with all the dilemmas these inevitably present. Attitudes and skills are closely explored, especially where these foster in the counsellor the ability and the temerity to enter into relational depth with persons who may previously have been gravely wounded within the context of relationships that proved treacherous or abusive. A substantial part of the book is devoted to the experience of one particular therapeutic relationship and this is greatly enlivened by the client's willingness to be fully participant in the process of reflecting on her therapeutic journey. The book concludes with the two co-authors having an enjoyable time responding to questions often thrown at them by trainees, new practitioners, seasoned practitioners and curious or hostile counsellors from other orientations. We welcome the opportunity to face these queries, which can so often occur at the end of an exhausting lecture or workshop when we are longing for a gin and tonic.

Our hope is that readers will be encouraged to reflect on their own therapeutic journeys – whether as counsellor or client – and that they may catch something of the excitement that we invariably experience as we attempt to put into words the beauty and mystery of the person-to-person encounter that we call counselling. We know, of course, that the attempt must fail because only poetry at its most richly expressive can truly capture such beauty and penetrate the heart of the mystery.

THE PERSON-CENTRED APPROACH: A CONTEMPORARY REVIEW AND BASIC THEORY

The Current Zeitgeist

In 1988 when the first edition of this book appeared there was plenty of evidence to suggest that person-centred counselling was at odds with the prevailing culture. Its insistence on the uniqueness of persons, on the need for assiduous attention to process, on the trustworthiness of the human organism seemed wildly out of kilter with a rapaciously materialistic culture where the profit motive, short-term goals, technological efficiency and sophisticated surveillance techniques governed the lives of the vast majority of citizens in Britain as well as those of most of the developed world. In the years since then the momentum of this increasingly depersonalised culture has intensified to the extent that a whole generation is growing up that knows nothing other than the freneticism of a brutally competitive society where quick answers, briefly adulated experts, technological wizardry and the dominance of market forces is accepted as the inevitable backdrop to so-called civilised existence.

The situation has taken an even more sinister turn in the closing years of the last millennium and the opening years of this. Terrible conflicts in Rwanda, Somalia, Bosnia, Kosovo and Chechnya have been followed by the so-called War on Terror, embarked upon since the attack on the World Trade Center and the Pentagon in 2001. The desperate plight of Afghanistan and Iraq continues while the Middle East conflict between Israel and the Palestinian authority remains unresolved. Rumblings in Iran and North Korea promise more instability ahead. If this were not enough, the increasingly dire effects of global warming are everywhere apparent and the meteoric advance of the economies of India and China have added immeasurably to the pollution inflicted upon the planet through human folly. The net result of these catastrophes is to induce panic and an almost global sense of impotence. In such a context governments inevitably develop defensive policies and become obsessed with security, surveillance and draconian measures to ensure survival. A psychological world has been created where trust is in very short supply, anxiety breeds suspicion, individual liberties are curtailed in the interests of corporate security and impulsive solutions are imposed upon the proliferating problems engendered by a society under threat.

It is difficult to imagine a more unpropitious setting for the reception of the values that underpin the person-centred approach. The current culture does not place a high value on the uniqueness of the person and on the importance of his or her subjective reality. It is not a culture that endows human nature with the ability to move towards the creative fulfilment of inherent potential. It certainly does not seek to affirm the personal power of each individual or place supreme importance on the fostering of relational depth between parents and children, husbands and wives, friends and partners, colleagues in the workplace or teachers and students. On the contrary it is a culture that has grown deeply suspicious of personal autonomy and attempts to regulate almost all areas of interpersonal involvement. We live increasingly in a regulated nightmare where teachers are afraid to exercise compassion towards children in pain, nurses no longer have the time or even the inclination to relate to patients and counsellors and psychotherapists can find themselves mentally ticking off paragraphs in the ethical codes of practice of their professional associations before responding to the distress of a particularly difficult client.

Strangely enough, in what appears to be an increasingly bleak world, we do not feel despair. On the contrary, we believe that the situation is now so dire that we may be approaching the crunch time when a paradigm shift will occur and the world will come to its senses. In some ways we are encouraged in this hopefulness by our clients and our trainees. They are often people who have experienced the full rigour of the cultural forces we have described and yet they discover in the context of the person-centred counselling milieu a new source of strength and inspiration. Most particularly they come to know – perhaps for the first time – what it means to have a sense of self-worth and to access their own thoughts and feelings. They are increasingly conscious of their own personal power. With that consciousness comes a new freedom to take decisions and to gain a sense of purpose. Perhaps most transformational of all is the escape from loneliness which comes with the experience of being received in relational depth by someone who makes no demands on them but simply insists on being fully human in the consulting room.

The reader would not be altogether mistaken to detect a slightly evangelical tone in these last comments. It is indeed the experience of living out the tenets of the person-centred approach in both our professional and personal lives which enables us to grasp a hope that seems to lie beyond despair. When we encounter the dismissive attitude towards person-centred counselling which seems still to characterise some academic quarters, or when we witness yet again the dubiously motivated affirmation of cognitive behaviour therapy in both government and medical circles, we are no longer too dismayed. Thanks to our clients and trainees we find daily confirmation of the power and efficacy of the approach we embrace. We are aware of its solid base in both theory and research and, above all, we know something of the discipline required of waiting on the process and the importance of the readiness of the client for counselling. Our culture, we believe, is fast approaching a crisis point where the human spirit will no longer tolerate the sterile predicament in which we have currently landed ourselves. It is then, we believe, that there will be a greater readiness to embrace the key concepts of the person-centred approach and to find in them the resource for an altogether more positive and hopeful way of relating to self, to others and to the whole created order. It is to those concepts that we now turn.

The Self-Concept

Distrust of experts runs deep among person-centred practitioners. The person-centred counsellor must learn to wear her expertise as an invisible garment in order to be an effective counsellor. Experts are expected to dispense their expertise, to recommend what should be done, to offer authoritative guidance or even to issue orders. Clearly there are some areas of human experience where such expertise is essential and appropriate. Unfortunately, all too many of those who seek the help of counsellors have spent much of their lives surrounded by people who, with devastating inappropriateness, have appointed themselves experts in the conduct of other people's lives. As a result such clients are in despair at their inability to fulfil the expectations of others, whether parents, teachers, colleagues or so-called friends, and have no sense of self-respect or personal worth. And yet, despite the damage they have already suffered at the hands of those who have tried to direct their lives for them, such people will often come to a counsellor searching for yet another expert to tell them what to do. Person-centred counsellors, while accepting and understanding this desperate need for external authority, will do all they can to avoid falling into the trap of fulfilling such a role. To do so would be to deny a central assumption of the approach, namely that the client can be trusted to find his own way forward if only the counsellor can be the kind of companion who is capable of encouraging a relationship where the client can begin, however tentatively, to feel safe and to experience the first intimations of self-acceptance. The odds against this happening are sometimes formidable because the view the client has of himself is low and the judgemental 'experts' in his life, both past and present, have been so powerfully destructive. The gradual revelation of a client's *self-concept*, that is, the person's conceptual construction of himself (however poorly expressed), can be harrowing in the extreme for the listener. It is with this revelation that the full extent of an individual's self-rejection becomes apparent and this often proves a stern challenge to the counsellor's faith, both in the client and in her own capacity to become a reliable companion in the therapeutic process.

The brief extract in Box 1.1 captures the sad and almost inexorable development of a self-concept which then undermines everything that a person does or tries to be. There is a sense of worthlessness and of being doomed to rejection and disapproval. Once such a self-concept has been internalised the person tends to reinforce it, for it is a fundamental tenet of the person-centred viewpoint that our behaviour is to a large extent an acting-out of how we actually feel about ourselves and the world we inhabit. In essence what we do is often a reflection of how we evaluate ourselves; if we have come to the conclusion that we are inept, worthless and unacceptable it is more than likely that we shall behave in a way that demonstrates the validity of such an assessment. The chances, therefore, of winning esteem or approval become more remote as time goes on.

Box 1.1   The Evolution of the Poor Self-Concept

Client: I don't remember my parents ever praising me for anything. They always had something critical to say. My mother was always on about my untidiness, my lack of thought about everything. My father was always calling me stupid. When I got six 'A' passes in my GCSEs he said it was typical that I had done well in the wrong subjects.

Counsellor: It seems you could never do anything right in their eyes no matter how hard you tried or how successful you were.

Client: My friends were just as bad. They kept on at me about my appearance and told me that I was a pimply swot. I just wanted to creep around without being seen by anyone.

Counsellor: You felt so awful about yourself that you would like to have been invisible.

Client: It's not all in the past. It's just the same now. My husband never approves of anything I do and now my daughter says she's ashamed to bring her friends home in case I upset them. It seems I'm no use to anyone. It would be better if I just disappeared.

Conditions of Worth

Fortunately the disapproval and rejection which many people experience is not such as to be totally annihilating. They retain some shreds of self-esteem although these may feel so fragile that the fear of final condemnation is never far away. It is as though they are living according to a kind of legal contract, and that they only have to put one foot wrong for the whole weight of the law to descend upon them. They struggle, therefore, to keep their heads above water by trying to do and to be those things which they know will elicit approval while scrupulously avoiding or suppressing those thoughts, feelings and activities which they sense will bring adverse judgement. Their sense of worth, both in their own eyes and in those of others who have been important to them, is conditional upon winning approval and avoiding disapproval, and this means that their range of behaviour is severely restricted for they can only behave in ways which are sure to be acceptable to others. They are the victims of the *conditions of worth* which others have imposed upon them, but so great is their need for positive approval that they accept this straitjacket rather than risk rejection by trespassing against the conditions set for their acceptability.

Sometimes, though, the situation is such that they can no longer play this contractual game and then their worst fears may be realised as they experience the disapproval and the growing rejection of the other person (see Box 1.2).

Box 1.2   Conditions of Worth

Client: Everything was all right at first. I knew that he admired my bright conversation and the way I dressed. He liked the way I made love to him, too. I used to make a point of chatting when he came in and of making sure that I was well turned out even after a busy day at the office.

Counsellor: You knew how to win his approval and you were happy to fulfil the necessary conditions.

Client: Yes, but that all changed when I got pregnant. I wanted to talk about the baby but he wasn't interested it seemed. He obviously didn't like what was happening to my figure and I used to feel so tired that I hadn't the energy for the sort of love-making he wanted. He got more and more moody and I felt more and more depressed.

Counsellor: You were no longer acceptable to him or to yourself.

The Organismic Valuing Process

Carl Rogers believed that there was one motivational force that determined the development of the human being. He called this the *actualising tendency*. It was the actualising tendency which despite every kind of opposition or hindrance-would ensure that an individual continued to strive to grow towards the best possible fulfilment of their potential. Those who were fortunate enough to have a loving and supportive environment during their early years would receive the necessary reinforcement to guarantee the nourishment of the actualising tendency. They would also be affirmed in their ability to trust their own thoughts and feelings and to make decisions in accordance with their own perceptions and desires. Their *organismic valuing process*, to use Rogers' terminology, would be in good order and would enable them to move through life with a sense of satisfaction and fulfilment.

Those not fortunate enough to have such supportive relationships but who, on the contrary, suffered from the imposition of many punitive *conditions of worth*, would soon discover that they had an overwhelming *need for positive regard*. So great is this need in all of us that its satisfaction can, not infrequently, take precedence over the promptings of the actualising tendency and as a consequence create gross confusion for the organismic valuing process (see Box 1.3). This conflict between the desperate need for approval and the wisdom of the individual's organismic valuing process lies at the root of much disturbance and often leads to an inner bewilderment which undermines confidence and makes effective decision-making impossible.

Box 1.3   Early Confusion of the Organismic Valuing Process

Child: [*Falls over and cuts his knee: runs crying to his mother for comfort or assurance.*]

Mother: What a silly thing to do. Stop crying and do not be such a baby. It's hardly bleeding.

Child: [*Thinks: it's stupid to fall over; it's wrong to cry; I shouldn't want mummy's support but I need it. But I wanted to cry; I wanted mummy's cuddle: I wasn't stupid. I don't know what to do. Who can I trust? I need mummy's love but I want to cry.*]

The loss of trust in the organismic valuing process and the loss of contact with the actualising tendency which informs it can result in the creation of a self-concept that is forced to suppress or deny altogether the promptings that emanate from the deepest parts of the person's response to experience. A person who is told repeatedly, for example, that it is wrong and destructive to be depressed may arrive at a point where he says of himself, 'I am a person who never feels depressed', or, just as disastrously, 'I am a person who deserves to be punished because I am always feeling miserable.' In the first case the intimations of depression have been repressed from consciousness whereas in the second they are a cause for self-condemnation and guilt. In both cases the resulting self-concept is far removed from any sense of trust in the reliability of the organismic valuing process as a guide to assessing direct and untrammelled experience. One of the most rewarding moments in a counselling process comes when the client discovers or re-discovers the dependability of his organismic valuing process however temporary or partial this may be (see Box 1.4). Such a moment can do much to strengthen the counsellor's faith in the client's ability to find his own way forward. It also points to the resilience of the actualising tendency, sometimes against all odds, to survive despite all the obstacles to its healthy functioning. At the deepest level, it would seem, the yearning to become more than we currently are is never completely extinguished.

Box 1.4   The Organismic Valuing Process is Restored

Client: I feel very sad: it's an overwhelming feeling.
Counsellor: As if you have no option but to give yourself to the sadness.
Client: That sounds very frightening – as if I shall lose control. But I never lose control. [*Suddenly bursts into tears.*]
Counsellor: Your tears speak for you.
Client: But big boys don't cry.
Counsellor: Are you saying that you are ashamed of your tears?
Client: [*Long pause.*] No … for the first time for years I feel in touch with myself … It feels OK to be crying.

It would be incomplete to leave the discussion of the organismic valuing process there. Human beings, because they are essentially relational creatures, are deeply affected not only by the responses of significant others to them during the course of their lives but also by the societal and cultural norms of the milieu in which they find themselves. The organismic valuing process is inevitably affected by these norms and is indeed permeated by them in such a way that the individual is sometimes prevented from behaving in ways that could be foolhardy or even self-destructive. What we have come to term *social mediation* is an important factor for the counsellor as she encounters a client who is struggling to determine a course of action in light of the promptings of the organismic valuing process. A response to those promptings – which seem to be demanding growth at all costs – may need the moderating influence of social mediation to forestall disaster. The actualising tendency and organismic valuing process sometimes require the compassionate brake of social mediation to ensure that the client listens to a voice which whispers that, in this instance and at this time, no-growth is the more prudent option. This is not to deny, of course, that very often the norms of society or of the prevailing culture impede the functioning of the organismic valuing process rather than informing or enhancing it. It is not always easy by any means to distinguish between social mediation as the compassionate brake and social conditioning as the vehicle of pervasive conditions of worth which stifle creativity, undermine confidence and condemn persons to half a life. A more detailed exploration of this and some of the other complex issues arising from recent developments in person-centred theory as they affect the actualising process is to be found in the next chapter.

The Locus of Evaluation

The person who has been unlucky enough to be surrounded by those who are sharply critical and judgemental will have been forced to resort to all manner of strategies in order to achieve a modicum of approval and positive regard. In most cases this will have entailed a progressive alienation from the organismic valuing process and the creation of a self-concept divorced from the person's innate resources and developed wisdom. The self-concept is likely to be poor but in some cases the person establishes a picture of himself that enables him to retain a degree of self-respect through a total blocking off from all significant sensory or 'visceral' experience. In all such cases, however, the organismic valuing process has ceased in any significant way to be a source of knowledge or guidance for the individual. He is likely to have great difficulty in making decisions or in knowing what he thinks or feels. There will probably be a reliance on external authorities for guidance or a desperate attempt to please everyone which often results in unpredictable, inconsistent and incongruent behaviour.

Psychologically healthy persons are men and women who have been fortunate enough to be surrounded by others whose acceptance and approval have enabled them to develop self-concepts that allow them for at least some of the time to be in touch with their deepest feelings and experiences. They are not cut off from the ground of their being and they are well placed to move towards becoming what Rogers has described as 'fully functioning' persons (Rogers, 1963a). Such people are open to experience without feeling threatened and are consequently able to listen to themselves and to others. They are highly aware of their feelings and the feelings of others and they have the capacity to live in the present moment. Most importantly, they display a trust and confidence in their organismic valuing process which is manifestly lacking in those who have continually had to battle with the adverse judgement of others. Such trusting is most evident in the process of decision-making and in the awareness and articulation of present thoughts and feelings. Instead of searching for guidance from outside or experiencing an internal confusion or blankness, the fully functioning person holds their source of wisdom deep within and accessible. Rogers has described this self-referent as the internal *locus of evaluation* and, for the counsellor, one of the most significant moments in therapy is the point at which a client recognises this reference point within himself perhaps for the first time (see Box 1.5).

Box 1.5   The Internal Locus of Evaluation

Client: I suppose I went into the job to please my father. It seemed to make sense, too, in terms of having some sort of career structure.

Counsellor: It was important to please your father and to feel OK in conventional career terms.

Client: Yes – and I have a feeling I married Jean because I knew my parents liked her. I certainly wasn't in love with her.

Counsellor: You married her to please them, really.

Client: And last night I knew that I can't go on. I hate the job and my marriage is a farce. I've got to find out what I want, what makes sense to me, before I waste the whole of my life trying to please other people. And I think I'm beginning to get some glimmering of what I must do. It's very frightening to hear your own voice for the first time.

Creating the Conditions for Growth

The person-centred counsellor believes that all clients have within themselves vast resources for development. They have the capacity to grow towards the fulfilment of their unique identities, which means that self-concepts are not unalterable and attitudes or behaviours can be modified or transformed. Where development is blocked or distorted this is the outcome of relationships which have trampled upon the individual's basic need for positive regard, and which have led to the creation of a self-concept and accompanying behaviour that serves as a protection against attack and disapproval. The counsellor's task is to create new conditions of relationship where the growth process can be encouraged and the stunting or warping remedied. In a sense the counsellor attempts to provide different soil and a different climate in which the client can recover from past deprivation or maltreatment and begin to flourish as the unique individual he or she actually is. It is the nature of this new relationship environment and the counsellor's ability to create it that is central to the whole therapeutic enterprise.

It is possible to describe the nature of the growth-producing climate briefly and clearly./Rogers believed that it is characterised by three core conditions. The first element focuses on the realness, or genuineness, or *congruence* of the counsellor. The more the counsellor is able to be herself in the relationship without putting up a professional front or a personal façade the greater will be the chance of the client changing and developing in a positive and constructive manner. The counsellor who is congruent conveys the message that it is not only permissible but desirable to be oneself. She also presents herself as transparent to the client and thus refuses to encourage an image of herself as superior, expert, omniscient. In such a relationship the client is more likely to find resources within himself and will not cling to any expectation that the counsellor will provide the answers for him. The second requirement in creating a climate for change and growth is the counsellor's ability to offer the client a total acceptance, a cherishing, an *unconditional positive regard.* When the counsellor is able to embrace this attitude of acceptance and non-judgementalism then therapeutic movement is much more likely. The client is more able to feel safe to explore negative feelings and to move into the core of his anxiety or depression. He is also more likely to face himself honestly without the ever-present fear of rejection or condemnation. What is more, the intensive experience of the counsellor's acceptance is the context in which he is most likely to sense the first momentary feelings of self-acceptance. The third element necessary in the therapeutic relationship is *empathic understanding.* When this is present the counsellor demonstrates a capacity to track and sense accurately the feelings and personal meanings of the client; she is able to learn what it feels like to be in the client's skin and to perceive the world as the client perceives it. What is more, she develops the ability to communicate to the client this sensitive and acceptant understanding. To be understood in this way is for many clients a rare or even a unique experience. It indicates to them a preparedness on the part of the counsellor to offer attention and a level of caring which undeniably endows them with value. Furthermore, when a person is deeply understood in this way it is difficult to maintain for long a stance of alienation and separation. Empathic understanding restores to the lonely and alienated individual a sense of belonging to the human race. These three elements in the therapeutic relationship are summarised in Box 1.6. They are often referred to in the person-centred literature as the *core conditions* and were constantly reiterated by Rogers (1951, 1961, 1974, 1979, 1980a).

Box 1.6   The Core Conditions

The creation of a growth-producing climate in a therapeutic relationship requires that the counsellor can:

1 be genuine or congruent
2 offer unconditional positive regard and total acceptance
3 feel and communicate a deep empathic understanding.

The core conditions are simple enough to state, but for a counsellor to develop and maintain such attitudes involves a lifetime's work and demands a commitment that has profound implications not only for the counsellor's professional activity but for her life as a whole. Much of this book, indeed, is devoted to an exploration of the complex issues involved when a counsellor attempts to be congruent, accepting and empathic. The words can trip off the tongue but their significance is little short of awe-inspiring.

2

RECENT DEVELOPMENTS IN PERSON-CENTRED THEORY

The Actualising Process

There has been considerable person-centred theory development since Rogers' death in 1987. In this chapter we shall weave together Rogers' original theorising on the actualising tendency and the creation of disturbance (Rogers, 1951, 1959, 1963b) with Mearns' efforts to extend Rogers' theory (Mearns and Thorne, 2000; Mearns, 2002) and Warner's developmental contributions (Warner, 2000a, 2002a, 2006).

The starting point is Rogers' motivational concept, the *actualising tendency* which he describes as:

> … the tendency of the organism to maintain itself – to assimilate food, to behave defensively in the face of threat, to achieve the goal of self-maintenance even when the usual pathway to that goal is blocked. We are speaking of the tendency of the organism to move in the direction of maturation, as maturation is defined for each species. (1951: 488)

In his personality theory the actualising tendency was Rogers' only motivational concept. It described a human being's basic drive to maintain, develop and enhance their functioning. In a sense it is a fundamental 'life force' that does not abate but constantly urges the person towards development. The actualising tendency drives the person to make the best they can of their circumstances. Some critics who do not understand the concept see it as evidence of Rogers' over-optimistic view of human nature – that people continue to develop in a positive fashion. However, the concept is not actually linked to values like 'positive' or 'negative', it is simply a force towards continuing development which may be affirmed or condemned depending on different perspectives. Consider Sheila and Nigel below.

> *SHEILA* is unsettled in her relationship with Maureen. The relationship has lasted fifteen years despite the considerable age difference (Sheila is 35 and Maureen 54). But during the past couple of years Sheila is placing less value on the security the relationship has always offered and is craving a more exciting lifestyle.

> *NIGEL* was a prisoner of his father's physical and emotional abuse throughout his first 14 years. His father would ceremonially tie him up and beat him once a week on some pretext – the slightest piece of disobedience could bring out his father's belt. Nor were the beatings only physical – when Nigel showed signs of doing well at school he became subject to a torrent of insults. Nigel survived by 'going underground' as a person. Now, at 22, he runs a drug dealing operation involving 40 people. He tightly controls his operation and the people in it, exerting his authority at times with considerable public cruelty. He gained supremacy in the gang wars partly through violence but also due to his intellect.

Both Sheila and Nigel show evidence of the action of the actualising tendency. While security was of prime importance to Sheila earlier in her relationship with Maureen, she is moving on from that to seek development in other ways. This may well be viewed as 'positive' by Sheila and her friends, but perhaps not so enthusiastically by Maureen, unless she too is moving. Nigel survived his childhood, but he had to 'go underground' to do it. Yet, he still shows evidence of the actualising tendency's pressure by making the best he can of, literally, tortuous circumstances. He did not remain a 'victim' but he used his intellect to find ways to express himself and to develop, albeit within the confines of his subculture. As he said, 'There are not many people from my school who become millionaires by the age of 22.' Many readers would be disinclined to view Nigel's development as representing anything 'positive'. But the actualising tendency is not directional in terms of society's values. It is directional only in the sense that it will urge the person to make the best job they can of survival, development and enhancement.

Also, of course, the actualising tendency does not stop. Attaining security was necessary for Sheila at an earlier point in her development, but now she yearns for diversity and later, will be driven towards different goals. Nigel's present position represents a developmental success in a psychological if not societal sense. But he will be pressured by his actualising tendency towards continuing his development. That pressure does not necessarily result in immediate development – perhaps Nigel will become stuck for a while and be unable to move on in any direction he sees as 'forward'. Sometimes frustration and depression kick in as secondary motivators (see Rogers' sixth theoretical 'proposition', 1951: 492–4). Perhaps Nigel's continuing development will see him applying his intellect and management skills to legal enterprises, or perhaps he will become an even more effective criminal.

Rogers published three main theoretical papers on his theory of personality (1951: 481–533, 1959, 1963b). In the 1951 and 1959 accounts his concept of the actualising tendency in relation to the creation of disturbance was broadly consistent. However, there was a marked change in his lesser known 1963 paper, as he acknowledges:

> I have gradually come to see this dissociation, rift, estrangement, [between self-structure and experience] as something learned, a perverse channeling of some of the actualizing tendency into behaviors which do not actualize … In this respect my thinking has changed during the past decade. Ten years ago I was endeavoring to explain the rift between self and experience, between conscious goals and organismic directions, as something natural and necessary, albeit unfortunate. Now I believe that individuals are culturally conditioned, rewarded, reinforced, for behaviors which are in fact perversions of the natural directions of the unitary actualizing tendency. (1963a: 19–20)

This represents a considerable change of view from his previous writings. Now he has introduced a negative value judgement in respect of the social forces that might work against the expression of the actualising tendency. In 1963 when this paper was published Rogers was ending the period of his life that had been devoted to psychotherapy. The bulk of that work had been undertaken in Chicago, with a clientele that both he and Bill Coulson (1987) described as 'Chicago neurotics'.[1] A typical 'neurotic'

---

[1] Present day readers are cautioned against seeing this as a pejorative term. In the clinical context of 1960s USA it was simply descriptive of the client group, distinguishing them from 'psychotics', 'psychopaths' and others.

disturbance would find the actualising tendency opposed by powerful injunctions introjected from parents, for example: *don't trust your feelings*; *your self-expression is dangerous*; *be careful rather than spontaneous*; and similar sentiments. Relative to this clientele, Rogers' 1963 judgement on the forces that restrict the actualising tendency is understandable. But it has the unfortunate effect of classifying *all* the influences that would challenge the actualising tendency as negative. There is no place for a 'normal' social restraint: any social restraint is seen as a negative influence. It was this change in Rogers' framing of his theory that also won him great popular appeal, marked by his move to California. He became a champion of the 1960s counterculture that challenged the restraint on self-expression emphasised by previous generations.

A critic of this new value position of Rogers was Bill Coulson (1987). A more detailed account of this criticism is given elsewhere (Mearns and Thorne, 2000: 179–80), but, briefly, Coulson suggested that much social restraint is indeed 'normal' and represents a reasonable accommodation between the person and their social world. Coulson's challenge, from someone so close to the centre of the movement (he worked with Rogers in Wisconsin and went on with him to California), was regarded as heresy by many of Rogers' colleagues, though not, in Coulson's view, by Rogers himself (Coulson, 2000). Viewed simplistically by his opponents, Coulson was merely representing the repressive forces of parental socialisation. This response depicts an understandable defensiveness on the part of the new movement, but it is a narrow view that we can now re-consider from a position of greater security. For Coulson, social contexts, especially the family, represent not an inhibiting force but the opposite. They offer a rich environment for self-expression and self-development. Being attentive to the dialogue with partners in the social world serves chiefly to enhance the actualising opportunities for the person.

Rogers' immersion in the 'neurotic' socialisation process had narrowed his perspective on the social environment. His observations on the harmful effects of socialisation were important and useful, but the short-term effect was to help the pendulum swing too far in the opposite direction – to a point where all social influence was to be regarded as unwelcome. It is interesting to see how this same process is recapitulated in clients within counselling. Once they escape from incapacitating social restraint they often, for a time, swing in the other direction and can become 'impossible to live with' as they reject normal social influence. Fortunately, in due course, the pendulum attains a more realistic balance.

However, in terms of Rogers' theory, the defensive and judgemental position in relation to social influence inhibited its development and potential application to other cultures and belief systems where the individual is seen as embedded in their social environment and inseparable from it – where the notion of *actualisation* only makes sense in the context of that embeddedness. An example of this can be found in present day Japanese culture. Although the country is heavily 'westernised', the fundamental sense of the importance of *community* prevails and is interwoven into modern structures. So, for example, the person-centred school counsellor trained in Kyusyu Sangyo University in Fukuoka will seek to work not just with the individual student, but will also go to his home to talk with his mother and grandmother, before returning to the school to meet his home-base teacher and even his friends. In many other parts of the world school counsellors might be alarmed by the wide boundaries operating in this way of working and would be concerned about confidentiality. But their tightly boundaried way of working is not better or worse – it is merely different, in a fashion that reflects their own culture. In Japan, the student client would expect his counsellor to work with his whole community because, as a person, he is not only a part of his community, his community is a part of him (Ide, Hirai and Murayama, 2006; Morita, Kimura, Hirai and Murayama, 2006). There are many similar contemporary opportunities for the person-centred approach to apply itself to cultures and subcultures and numerous challenges to do so (Balmforth, 2006; Boyles, 2006; Chantler, 2006; Khurana, 2006; Lago, 2006; Lago and Haugh, 2006; Sembi, 2006; Shoaib, 2006). We also witness striking attempts at dialogue, such as Inayat's articulation of the Islamic concept of the self in relation to psychological theories (2005). These highly significant developments show that the theory, as far as Rogers took it, needs adjustment and amplification to move it from 1960s California towards a modern world view.

When Rogers was writing about the actualising tendency he said: 'Finally, the self-actualisation of the organism appears to be in the direction of socialization, broadly defined' (1951: 488). This concession to the social dimension is insufficient and does not reflect the clinical experience of working with a range of clients with varying forms of disturbance, nor work that engages a broad range of the world's cultures. Human beings are profoundly social animals and most of their avenues for development are social in nature. Our relationships with friends, colleagues, partners and children represent most of the potential contexts for our own growth and development. Therefore, in a development of Rogers' theory, we introduce the notion of *social mediation* (Mearns, 2002; Mearns and Thorne, 2000: 182–3) as a buffer to the actualising tendency. As well as the individual's drive towards maintenance and development (the actualising tendency), we hypothesise a restraining force, also within the person, which seeks to artic-ulate with the person's social contexts. In other words, the force towards growth is not allowed to promote its own enhancement without some kind of check or 'mediation'. By that means the person not only enhances their own development but maintains sufficient social contexts that, in turn, pro-vide the bases for further growth. We use the term *actualising process* to describe this articulation between the forces of the actualising tendency and social mediation. Elsewhere, we say:

> In this revision of the theory the central concept becomes the *actualising process* which is described by the homeostasis of the imperatives of the actualising tendency and social mediation within different areas of the per-son's social life space and the reconfiguring of that homeostasis to respond to changing circumstances. (Mearns and Thorne, 2000: 184)

In other words, the person *takes other people in their life into account* in the course of their own maintenance and development. In his time, Rogers might have been wary of this kind of statement because so many of the clients he and colleagues worked with in his main Chicago base dis-played a neurotic valuing of the wishes of others over their own needs. According to the new theory, their actualising process had become imbal-anced, resulting in a relative over-emphasis on the forces of social media-tion and an undervaluing of the promptings of the actualising tendency. This kind of client is frequently seen in counselling practices. He has developed his imbalance as a way of adapting to the dissonance between his experience of himself and the views others have of and for him. As we described in Chapter 1, he has lost touch and trust with his organismic valuing process and shapes his self-concept not through the dialogue between his self-experiences and the views of others but almost wholly by internalising the views of others as to who he is, as illustrated by Rachel who has only begun to question her chosen profession of primary school teaching in the final year of her training:

> I have suddenly realised that why I have been getting into more trouble on teaching practice is that I *don't* 'love children'. I was always told 'how good Rachel is with children'. Maybe that was a way of keeping me in the role of childminder to my four younger brothers and sisters. It was a nice definition to

accept for myself – it gave me an easy way to see myself and to be approved. Unfortunately, the delusion persisted and I've wasted these past four years. Constantly *having* to see yourself as 'a lover of children' is a hard pretence to keep up in the reality of schools. Also, you have no idea what you *really* would feel about children if you didn't *have to* love them.

Rachel's self-concept, in relation to the specific area of her love of children, has been distorted to reflect others' views more than her own self-experiences, but that distortion can spread throughout the self-concept, contaminating much of it. So, the person becomes generally vulnerable, incapable of trusting his own self-experiencing and self-judgement. Sometimes he cannot even trust his experiencing of his own emotions. His inner experience of sadness may have been unacceptable to parents who regarded that as 'soft' in a boy. If he experienced his sensing as anger and expressed that, he would still get into difficulty, but it would be an acceptable 'boy-type' of difficulty. Equally, in most western cultures, the girl's inner experience of anger can be redefined and expressed as sadness. Gradually, the person's locus of evaluation, mentioned earlier, becomes more externalised as they give up their own authority over themselves and accept the authority of others as their source for self-definition.

Rogers explored this direction of imbalance in the actualising process in great detail, but it is only part of the story as far as the creation of disturbance is concerned. Another direction of imbalance occurs when the person loses trust in his experience of social mediation. Instead of a dialogue taking place between the promptings of his actualising tendency and the cautions of his social mediation imperative, he comes to rely solely on his self-experiencing. As a result, his self-concept does not get a chance to develop in a socially articulated fashion – the dialogue that makes that possible is lost and his self-concept becomes grounded in his need to self-protect. Everything is centred around the 'I' in an effort at self-preservation. His process is 'I-centred': he only permits himself to understand his social world from that egocentric perspective, which is why Mearns (2006a) borrowed the psychological term *ego-syntonic* process to denote this pattern of being. This term merits detailed elaboration.

Ego-Syntonic Process

The developmental basis of ego-syntonic process is emotional abuse sometimes, though not necessarily, accompanied by other forms of abuse.

The person has survived a parenting in which love and valuing were unpredictable. Negative experiences would follow when positives might be expected – there was no way to rely upon the relationship. To survive this socially unreliable and damaging context the person needed to do three things:

1   Withdraw their emotional attachment
2   Find ways to control the relationship
3   Find ways to control themselves in relationships.

In a television documentary on the work of Bruno Bettelheim in his Orthogenic School in Chicago, a former patient, 'Sandy', now a successful Wall Street stockbroker, gives us a unique insight into how it feels to be in this situation as a young person. Sandy had been one of the most disturbed children the school had known, with severe suicidal and homicidal fantasies. He had described how he wanted to cut open the belly of his pregnant counsellor, Patti, and destroy her baby. Many years later, Sandy describes how it had felt to be him:

> The fellow who has a parent who is sometimes nice and sometimes horrible thinks that is the way the world is. Now, in my own case, that is how it was. At the time when I came to the school I think the difficulty was, among other things, that I was confronted by Patti [his counsellor], who was an exceptionally fine human being and a very affectionate and decent human being. I wasn't able to accept the affection, which caused even more anger because everyone likes to accept affection. But if you condition yourself to not accepting affection because, if by accepting it you only let yourself in for the next downfall, you put yourself in a position where you don't dare to hope that the affection is for real and you keep *testing* to find out if it is for real, and that's the process where, step by step, you find out whether it is. In a sense, maybe, that explains my own need to hurt those who had been kind, because I needed to find out if I hurt them, whether or not the affection would continue to come ... (Bettelheim, 1987)

In work with children's home staff, Sandy's statement induces a chill of understanding. Clearly, most people who exhibit ego-syntonic process are not so severely disturbed as Sandy had been, yet the social disability they carry into adult life can be chronic. The self-protective systems they developed to survive their emotional abuse become generalised to other relationships. (See Stern's notion of 'RIGs' – 'Representations of Interactions that have become Generalised' – Stern, 2003; Mearns and Cooper, 2005:

27–30.) The social consequences of the resulting process can vary hugely. In increasing severity for those around him the person may become:

popular but 'unreachable' → alone and lonely → controlling → cold → cruel → homicidal and suicidal

In its mild expression their ego-syntonic process leads the person to be *confused* and *scared* in relationships. They know that things go wrong for them and they come to expect things to go wrong. But they genuinely do not understand *why* they go wrong. They have done their best. They have even tried to think about what the other person wants and *be* that (within limits). But it always goes wrong. From the perspective of the other person, of course, the incongruence of these efforts and the lack of effective empathy are what are noticed.

In another expression of ego-syntonic process the person attracts relations but fails in relationships because, ultimately, they have to be so *controlling*. They need to define the reality and protect against its changing. They provide well on a material level and function adequately in more superficial relationships, but they need to be the 'star' in the relationship – the relationship is valued in so far as it places them at the centre and, of course, invokes no enduring demands upon them. Again, they are genuinely surprised when the other person ends the relationship because they had done their best.

In a more serious expression, the person is dangerous to themselves and others. They are so threatened by relationships that their self-protection manifests itself not in confusion or controlling, but in *detachment* and even violence. Their fear is so profound and the adjustment they have obtained so tenuous that detachment and even destruction (of self or other) may be the only existential protections they have left.

The purpose of this chapter is to outline the new person-centred theory, so we will not explore examples of counselling with the ego-syntonic client. However, the reader might look at the examples of work with the client 'Bobby' described in Mearns and Thorne (2000) and Mearns and Cooper (2005).

Recent developments in person-centred theory widen the client population to which the relevance of the approach is applicable. In the profession of counselling as a whole, not just within the person-centred approach, there is a tendency to narrow the boundaries of applicability to create comfort zones. It is easy for counselling to set its boundaries to work only with the so-called 'neurotic' population. Except with a particularly challenging client with *fragile process* (see later in this chapter), this population generally conforms to the structure and definition the counsellor chooses to apply to the work. Clients describing other forms of disturbance present new challenges to the therapeutic relationship and to the structuring of the work. For those who like to see counselling as a regular hour with a broadly cooperative client there may be resistance to this broader definition of the counselling arena. But that challenge must be raised because, at present, counselling is probably only thought to be relevant by ten per cent of the population. If we are to establish a wider relevance we need to attune our theory to a broader range of cultural belief systems and become much more flexible and creative in the way we define the therapeutic context. The classical psychodynamic obsession with structuring and boundaries that has been allowed to dominate definitions of professional propriety needs to be challenged on the grounds that it is restrictive of development and could eventually suffocate the profession.

Theoretical Propositions 1–4

By way of summarising the new theory to this point, we present four theoretical propositions in regard to the creation of disturbance. These are described in greater detail in Mearns and Thorne (2000: 181–4) and Mearns (2002).

Proposition 1: The actualising tendency is the sole motivational force. This view of the actualising tendency as the sole motivational force reflects Rogers' Proposition 4 in his original framing of the theory (Rogers, 1951: 487). There is no need to seek to change this proposition. As with any good theory, it reflects an elegant simplicity.

Proposition 2: The promptings of the actualising tendency inspire their own resistance within the social life space of the person. This resistance is termed 'social mediation'. This is a more established and emphatic framing of the 'pro social capacity' of the actualising tendency (Brodley, 1999). It places the person's experienced social world much more centrally within their processing. The person takes their social, relational context into consideration. As the actualising tendency prompts a response, part of that response is to inspire a counterbalancing vector representing the social rather than the purely individual concerns for growth. This is not the neurotic concern to please other people that Rogers challenged in

1963, it is a reasoned consideration for others and an appreciation of the importance others have in the continuing development of the person.

Proposition 3: A psychological homeostasis develops between the drive of the actualising tendency and the restraint of social mediation. The configuring and reconfiguring of this homeostasis is the 'actualising process'.   The *actualising process* is the key concept in this new theory and comes entirely from observations in clinical practice. The person is not governed by a single impetus such as the actualising tendency. The functioning of the human being is much more sophisticated than that. Metaphorically speaking, we could drive a car with only an accelerator, but we obtain a more sophisticated control when we add a brake. Just as, in physiological functioning, control is generally maintained by the secretion of hormones with opposite effects, so too, in psychological functioning, there is a system of dual control with delicate and precise balances established between the forces of the actualising tendency and social mediation. Moreover, these balances may vary considerably from time to time and across different areas of the person's life. It is fascinating to observe the actualising process at work – to see how people negotiate new balances appropriate to changing dimensions of their life. These adjustments are not merely accommodations to external pressures; they are constructive and sophisticated dialogues within the self and in relationship with others – dialogues that achieve growth for the person and facilitate growth in others. When the young adult develops radically changed balances in numerous areas of their life space in order to take on the challenges of parenthood, the actualising process and these internal and external dialogues are evident. It is just as striking to observe the actualising process in younger people. The period of adolescence and even earlier stages are characterised by the young person configuring and reconfiguring balances as they enter the struggle, not merely to survive life, but to add to its richness and diversity.

Proposition 4: 'Disorder' is caused when the person becomes chronically stuck within their own actualising process, such that the homeostatic balance cannot be reconfigured to respond to changing circumstances.   In this framing of person-centred theory it is the loss of fluidity that engenders *disorder* in the system. Fluidity is replaced by fixity, a term frequently used by Rogers: 'Individuals move … from fixity to changingness, from rigid structure to flow, from stasis to process' (1961: 131). The genesis of this fixity is described elsewhere by Mearns:

> The person may have developed self-protective systems enabling them to survive psychological stress and distress, threats to their existential being or their identity and any variety of challenges encountered in living. In normal systems the actualization process will allow them to move on – to reconfigure balances as the dangers diminish or increase and as their social circumstances change. However, where fixity remains, the person will find it difficult to move their living forward, particularly in the social milieu. We find this in many of our clients who are 'surviving their survival'. (2002: 24)

So, if we are to reflect upon our young adult engaging the challenges of parenthood, we may find that the actualisation process is stultified – there is no fluid reconfiguration of the balances. Earlier points of balance were hard won and are not given up easily. Re-balancing feels too much like giving up freedoms with no guaranteed or experienced counterbalance. Adjustments happen not proactively, but reactively in response to others. Anxiety grows as only the 'loss' dimension of change is experienced. The partner of a person in such a process will also be feeling anxiety.

Difficult Process

In the view of both the authors of this book, the most significant contribution to theory in recent years has been made by Margaret Warner in her elaboration of *difficult process*. Like any human being, the person with difficult process seeks to make sense, to create meaning, out of their social experiencing, but unlike others they have to do this while facing extremely inhibiting developmental circumstances. For example, in *fragile process* the person has suffered from 'empathic failure' (Warner, 2000a: 150) on the part of the parent figures in his life. In early development we rely on the empathy of our carers to help us to learn to process our experiencing. In empathy the carer conveys back to the child a reflection of his expression so that the child can gradually bring his experiencing and his expression into line and develop the sophisticated ability to work out what he feels, manage his feelings and relate with others effectively from his feeling world. But, in empathic failure, the feedback he gets may be non-existent, minimal or grossly distorted. If he bangs his knee and screams in pain, the response he might get from his parents could be variations of:

- 'Oh, that must have been sore for you' (and cuddles him)
- Parent ignores his distress

- 'Come on now – there's no need to scream as much as that'
- 'Now, now – big boys don't cry'.

The first response meets him empathically while the others fail to respond, respond only minimally and, in the last example, introduces a complex distortion that equates his hurt with weakness or lack of maturity.

The quality of a carer's empathy will vary on a daily basis. Sometimes they will be right there for the child and at other times they will be too taken up with their own survival. Variation like this is normal and is not damaging for the child in developmental terms. Indeed, such variation around a solid base helps the child to become even more sophisticated at processing their experience because there are times when they need to process the disjunction between their experiencing and the parent's feed-back, coming, perhaps, to the conclusion: 'Mother ignored my shouts ... but it still hurt'. However, when the child does not have the solid empathic base – when the norm is one of empathic failure – their process-ing becomes fragile. In adulthood, they feel acutely the deficits of this fragile processing. Margaret Warner describes the difficulties manifested by clients with such a style of processing:

> Clients who have a fragile style of processing tend to experience core issues at very low or high levels of intensity. They tend to have difficulty starting and stopping experiences that are personally significant or emotionally con-nected. In addition, they are likely to have difficulty taking in the point of view of another person while remaining in contact with such experiences. For example, a client may talk circumstantially for most of a therapy hour and only connect with an underlying feeling of rage at the very end. At this point he may feel unable to turn the rage off in a way which will allow him to return to work. He may then spend hours walking in the park trying to handle the intensity of the feeling. The client may be able to talk about feel-ings of rage with the therapist and very much want them understood and affirmed. Yet, therapist comments to explain the situation or disagree with the client will be felt as attempts by the therapist to annihilate his experience. (2000a: 150)

Margaret Warner also describes *dissociated process*. The first thing she notes is that every single client she has met who displays dissociated process had been traumatised by physical or sexual abuse before the age of seven. She goes on to describe the process:

At such early ages children have high levels of hypnotic suggestibility. Faced with overwhelming trauma and lacking the more complex ways of coping with experiences available to older children, our clients seem to have stumbled on dissociation as a solution. One client, for example, found that when she stared at dots on the wallpaper she could separate herself out from the terror and anguish of being raped by her father. Some clients describe experiencing themselves as out of their bodies and watching the events from the ceiling.

Understandably, dissociation under these circumstances is extremely reinforcing. Children go from an extreme of anguish to a lack of intense pain and an ability to put the whole thing out of their minds the next day. This capacity makes life seem tolerable and for some allows the illusion that they have a normal, happy family life. (2000a: 160)

Dissociated process can take many forms, with different parts of the person developing their own distinct features and the person switching from one to the other, sometimes consciously and deliberately and at other times in a fashion that is apparently out of control. It is interesting to compare dissociated process with the psychology of *configurations* (Mearns, 2002; Mearns and Thorne, 2000). Configurations are 'parts' of the self that have evolved to manifest different themes within the self (see later in this chapter). The same might be argued for dissociated 'parts' but these tend to be much more separate from each other, sometimes not even acknowledging each other's existence, and there is a greater degree of personification in dissociated parts – they can look like entirely different people. One interesting hypothesis is that dissociated process is a radical extension of configurations. In trying to cope with the trauma, different parts are formed to represent the themes and to create a holding, self-protective system. But, while that process can be effective in cases of less profound psychological conflicts, it is strained beyond its limits if applied to cope with high levels of trauma. Instead of the parts being able to contain and give expression to the conflict they are rent apart by it (Warner and Mearns, 2003).

In *difficult process*, of which the aforementioned ego-syntonic process may be another example, we see the results of the actualising process seeking to cope with challenging developmental circumstances and making the best job it can of helping the person to survive and also to develop (albeit within tight limits). The difficult process, in its inception, is not a 'disorder', a 'pathology', or an 'illness'. It is the person's efforts to survive, in the same way as the fever is not the illness but the body's attempt to fight it. This is a distinctive feature of the perspective of the person-centred approach. The approach is not aimed at 'symptom reduction' but at enabling the client to explore and understand their processes. Furthermore, the difficult process is not the whole of the person. It represents the person's historical efforts to survive challenging relational circumstances.

Clearly, the person will have had other relational experiences and these, too, will have had an impact. In our clinical experience there is generally another part, or parts, to the person that reflects something different from the difficult process. Often, this first manifests itself in counselling as a very small and dissonant voice. It is used to taking a back-seat in relation to the dominant thrust of the difficult process. One of the strengths of a relationally oriented approach like person-centred counselling is that this, initially small part, can be attracted to and engaged by the therapeutic relationship. In the context of this new and healthy relationship, it can present itself more frequently. As that voice grows in strength a fuller self-dialogue is established, the dissonance within the self intensifies and change becomes possible.

Self-dialogues

The concept of a 'dialogue within the self' has a common sense appeal in so far as we are all familiar with the notion of 'talking to ourself', but in recent years clinical observations by workers across a wide range of therapeutic approaches have shared the view that self-dialogues are common-place (Berne, 1961; Gergen, 1972, 1988, 1991; Brown, 1979; Bearhrs, 1982; Schwartz, 1987, 1997; Rowan, 1990; Hermans et al., 1992; Hermans and Kempen, 1993; Schwartz and Goulding, 1995; Hermans, 1996; Honos-Webb and Stiles, 1998; Rowan and Cooper, 1999; Hermans and Dimaggio, 2004). This area has become known as *self-pluralist* theory, where the person appears to symbolise their self as comprising different *parts*, *voices*, *sub-personalities*, *sub-selves* or, the word we have used, *configurations* (Mearns, 1999; Mearns and Thorne, 2000). We have defined this concept as follows:

A *configuration* is a hypothetical construct denoting a coherent pattern of feelings, thoughts and preferred behavioural responses symbolised or pre-symbolised by the person as reflective of a dimension of existence within the self. (Mearns and Thorne, 2000: 102)

A detailed analysis of this definition is given in the above reference (2000: 102–3), but it is important to know that what we are describing is not merely the fact that people have a variety of different inclinations, tendencies, or responses, but that a configuration is a developed 'self-within-a-self' that can contain a wide array of elements – a set of thoughts, feelings and behaviours that together represent an important dimension of the person's existence. Two or more configurations may be in *dialogue* with each other. That dialogue is often experienced as conflict, but the process is more constructive than that term suggests, with the different configurations promoting alternatives such that the person can listen to all the possibilities.

Within the person-centred approach there has been a wealth of work in self-pluralism (Müller, 1995; Gaylin, 1996; Keil, 1996; Elliott and Greenberg, 1997; Stiles, 1999; Stinckens, 2000; Stiles and Glick, 2002; Stinckens, Lietaer and Leijssen, 2002; Cooper, 2003; Cooper et al., 2004; Barrett-Lennard, 2005). While these observations present a powerful catalogue of evidence in support of the likely existence of different 'parts' to the self, we want to express a deeply felt caution. Although it is certainly the case that the concept of self-pluralism is relevant to many people, it is *not* meaningful to everyone. We developed configuration theory as a means of responding to clients who symbolised their self in a pluralist fashion. It is a leap of illogicality to presume that the theory should apply to everyone. It is not appropriately person-centred to make the presumption that our client will have configurations. Instead, we work with him as he presents himself. If he presents in a holistic fashion, we work with that whole. But if he presents what he experiences as his different parts, we work with all these parts of him.

The new theory helps us to meet the practical challenges of working with clients who symbolise themselves in terms of parts. Mary and Joe provide examples:

MARY: Most of the time I am a *little princess* – all sweetness and light. Butter wouldn't melt in my mouth. My *little princess* is friends with everyone and in general people treat her well. She developed in my childhood and she is still around. But I also have a hard edge – as hard as the *little princess* is soft. I call this part *vixen me*. I shiver when I think about her. She would scratch your eyes out – don't mess with her. She too arose in my childhood, for good reasons.

JOE: I have *strong me* and *weak me*. For years *strong me* hated *weak me* but that has changed during counselling. I understand now how *weak me* came about – it wasn't just that he was 'pathetic' – he was scared, deeply scared. *Strong me* helped me to survive but I need *weak me* too – he has parts of me that *strong me* doesn't.

Mary and Joe are familiar with their configurations and have even given them names that reflect their main themes. For other people there is less familiarity, less clarity, but still a sense of pluralism, as with Teri who, in surviving a hostage situation, had discovered another dimension of her self:

> TERI: At first I just cried. I felt that that was all I could do. Then something happened – I stopped crying and became cool, clear and determined. I started to work out strategy. I had read about the fact that more hostages survived when they made themselves 'known' to their captors. So I stopped snivelling and started to engage these people. I was amazed – this wasn't *me* speaking, but, in fact, it was. I wasn't 'acting' – I was being 'me', but a part of me that I didn't recognise.

We have documented work with clients who symbolise not only two parts to their self but many, as well as complex dynamics among the parts (see 'Alexander' in Mearns and Thorne, 2000: 120–6). Our first task was to describe a method of working with clients who symbolised their self in terms of parts. This stage took eight years, culminating in the first formal paper (Mearns, 1999). The difficulty was in retaining a consistent person-centred approach while relating with the different parts. Previously, the accepted wisdom within the approach was that we should 'work with the whole client'. We had to learn to distinguish that from 'working with the wholeness of the client', because many of our clients did not experience themselves as 'whole'. The system we developed, and which is described in Mearns and Thorne (2000: 127–43), closely resembles person-centred family therapy (O'Leary, 1999): all the parts are related, but some are currently in conflict, and we must offer a therapeutic relationship to *each* of them. The final task was to formulate theory that could describe the formation and existence of configurations. This process involved meshing together Rogers' own theory of the self-structure with the new evidence from our clinical observation. This has resulted in four further theoretical propositions.[2]

Theoretical Propositions 5–8

Proposition 5: Configurations may be established around introjections about self.   An introjection about self carries a message or judgement

---

[2]This is a conflation from the five propositions described in an earlier publication (Mearns, 2002: 19–21).

from others. One way to hold such an introjection is to house it within a 'configuration' whose sense reflects the introjection. This embodiment of the introjection gives it a more established and functional status, while also allowing for the possibility that other configurations may carry quite different narratives about the self. For example, our client, Lorraine, who introjects the imperative *I must be perfect/only if I am perfect am I accept-able* would not necessarily find that this dominated her whole existence. It might become a prominent part of her self, represented as *the part of me that needs to be perfect.* That part could give Lorraine a hard time over self-acceptance and might develop a sophisticated repertoire around avoiding testing situations. But it would not necessarily define her whole self. This is the adaptive beauty of configurations as psychological mech-anisms. They allow us to adapt to situations which could define us but they can restrict that definition to a part of the self (Mearns and Thorne, 2000: 108–113).

Proposition 6: Configurations may also be established around dissonant self-experiences.   Equally, the person needs to find ways to respond to self-experiences that are inconsistent with other dimensions of the self. These dissonant experiences may be encapsulated and embodied within configurations of self. Once again, the function is served of allowing the self to 'own' quite varied or even contradictory experiences. (Mearns, 1999; Mearns and Thorne, 2000). For example, our client Lorraine may have accumulated experiences of herself *not* being driven by the perfec-tion imperative, yet being acceptable to herself. Again, these might have become housed within a configuration represented by *the part of me that objects to having to be perfect.* Now Lorraine has a dialogical system in which to hold the dissonance between these imperatives. She is allowed to seek perfection and she is allowed to object to seeking perfection. She might well find that the different configurations attain prominence in dif-ferent relationships within her life – people often report on how they vary in different social contexts.

Rogers' theory in this area is consistent with the *unitary* emphasis of his time, and, indeed, with the 'consistency theories' of that era in social psy-chology (Festinger, 1957; Heider, 1958). From that unitary frame he could only refer to *denial* as the means of handling the dissonance, as in his 'Proposition XIII':

> Behavior may, in some instances, be brought about by organic experiences and needs which have not been symbolized. Such behavior may be

inconsistent with the structure of the self, but in such instances the behavior is not 'owned' by the individual. (Rogers, 1951: 509)

To Proposition XIII we might now want to add the following caveat:

In some cases the behaviour *may* be 'owned' but allocated to a part or *configuration* within the self. Such a configuration may well be inconsistent with other parts of the self and carry restricted access.

If we are not bound to thinking of the self as a unitary phenomenon but as comprising a range of configurations whose inconsistencies are tolerated by their boundaries and dynamics, we have a system which may now be able to describe human experience more comprehensively.

Proposition 7: Formative configurations assimilate other consistent elements.   A configuration is an *organizing principle* within the self. It can lend structure and function to individual thoughts, feelings and experiences. For example, Lorraine's configuration, developed initially to house her introjection about needing to be perfect, would collect further elements with the same message. Although the source of the initial introjection was no longer sustaining it, the configuration itself can accrue further elements. Hence Lorraine 'should be perfect' in all her adult ventures. Needless to say, in terms of this rather crippling imperative, Lorraine can only really collect failures. Of course, her other configuration, *the part of me that objects to having to be perfect* will also be adding elements, for example, the time when she walked out on her partner rather than continue to try to be the 'perfect wife', and the buzz of energy (as well as fear) she felt when she told her manager he should make his own coffee!

As both of these configurations expand their existence, each adding to its own veracity, the dissonance builds until it can be contained no longer. Such is the nature of the human development process contained within a dialogical framework and such is the impetus for change, sometimes monitored in counselling.

Proposition 8: Configurations inter-relate and reconfigure.   This is a more dynamic conception of sub-selves than in object relations theory (Fairbairn, 1952), which regards the 'objects' as remaining fairly static throughout life. In the present view, configurations are not permanently compartmentalised like 'psychic scabs'. Clients talk about parts changing and changing-in-relation to each other. Often the client will give a changed name to an evolving configuration. Our view is that such reconfiguring both assists developmental change within the self and also affords considerable sophistication in self-protective systems. The systems of self-protection may evolve with the changing of the person's social life-space. But, perhaps we never lose earlier self-protections: they simply evolve in a fashion that allows for less restriction, but retain a 'guarding' role.

There are other possible propositions that might be proffered in relation to configuration dynamics. For example, it is clear that some configurations carry a consistent *self-protective* narrative while others are more about *self-expression*. However, caution is needed before framing further propositions around these observations because going to that level of hypothetical specification could begin to erode the essential phenomenological nature of our work. It is perhaps sufficient to note the interplay among these different imperatives and leave the rest of the theorising to our investigations with each unique client – that is the essence of the scientific discipline of person-centred counselling.

Essentially, what is being described is a system for the development of the self that generates enormous latitude for adaptability. The self may develop a range of aspects, or configurations, which allows a wide repertoire of ways of meeting different social challenges. The person is not just a single 'self' but a multiple cast of players, each firmly attached and coherent so as to allow a congruence of expression. It may be this dimension of self-development that allows human beings to be expert 'actors'. The skilled actor will find an aspect of their self which may be entered in order to fit a role more fluently. What we are witnessing in this multiplicity of configurations within the self is creativity and expressiveness as well as an incredibly sophisticated adaptive system that can even allow the person to present opposite aspects of self congruently in different social contexts.

A Modern Person-Centred Conception of the Counselling Process

The new body of theory summarised in this chapter allows us to conclude with an updated conception of the counselling process from a person-centred perspective. This is illustrated in Figure 2.1.

Figure 2.1 depicts three possible areas where psychological work could be focused. The client might present his *problem* as being the fact that although he has plenty of short-term friendships, he never seems to have

Figure 2.1 *The counselling process*

a lasting relationship. A 'problem-centred' approach to counselling might seek to work with him at this level by considering various strategies he might adopt to improve the situation. However, most psychological therapies would probe more deeply than that and would be open to work with him on the *ego-syntonic process* that underpinned his problem in relationships. That work would also be open to engage the various *self-dialogues* which have come to characterise his processing. The person-centred approach would be one of a smaller group of therapies that would not define his ego-syntonic process or self-dialogues as the whole story but would be open to exploring his whole person, including the potentially powerful self-experiences that underpin his ego-syntonic process and the other fundamental aspects of his existence – the domain we term his *existential process*.

We use the word 'existential' as a simple adjective from 'existence' (not from 'existentialism') to denote something experienced by the person as of particular significance to them. Because this concept is entirely phenomenological, that is to say it describes a phenomenon experienced uniquely by each person, it is hugely difficult to describe and probably impossible to define, as definitions normally exist in Psychology. Also, providing individual examples can be misleading because each example is important only in the life of that person. The same example, to someone else, would not likely have the same existential significance. Yet, let us try to lay down some aspects of this existential process as we have termed it.

From our experience of our clients their existential process contains a rich mixture of self-experiences, self-assumptions, hopes, fears, fantasies, terrors, experiences in relation to others, assumptions about others and deeply held values. The elements and dynamics are experienced by the person as more fundamental to their existence than aspects of the self they normally present to the world and consequently they are closely guarded. To be judged by another on the basis of a self we are presenting is one thing, but to be judged for what we believe is our essence is particularly dangerous, indeed it may risk annihilation as the client, Sandra, describes:

> I had so much *hate* inside me. I could never show it in its raw state to any-one. It came out in lots of ways but I could not show it in the way it was to me. I could not show the bile, the vindictiveness, the 'foaming at the mouth' invective. I could not show it the way it was to me – I could not even show it to me the way it was to me. It was too destructive.

Paul describes material that appears quite different, yet, existentially, it carries the same potentially annihilating significance:

> I can't describe how I am to me in ways that will make sense to others. It goes around my head and body in dream-like waves, at times coming into the foreground and then receding. It is all ugly. It is all about how I am all ugly – how, at my core, I am rotten. I can feel the maggots crawling around inside me, eating me up. Perhaps they will eat the rot and help me. How could I show this to anyone else? How can I allow myself to see it?

It is not surprising that access to the existential process is closely guarded. In the case of Sandra and Paul the fear is of the potential destructiveness of the material, but the fear can also be about the danger of being destroyed by the other. This is well captured by Bernard whose presentational self was outgoing and powerful, fitting for his high position in the business world. But that was not how he was to himself:

> Sometimes the real me watches myself at work. It sees the smooth opera-tor, totally confident and blustering others with my confidence. It is as though it is a magnification of the opposite of who I really am. Underneath all I am is a crying little boy. I am curled up, rocking and sobbing. My face is puffed up with a lifetime of sobbing. My eyes are permanently closed – I can barely endure the pain of what it is to be me – I cannot open my eyes to see anyone else in case I see them seeing me.

Clients sometimes refer to this existential domain as 'the real me'. We need to follow that phenomenal sense of their self when we are working with a client. But we should not necessarily extend that to our more general psychological theorising. It does not mean that there is, in fact, a core to the onion or that material within the existential process is more important than dimensions of the presentational self, though that is how it can feel for some people.

There is considerable variation among people in the *access* they have to their existential process. For some people this domain is an old friend who is never totally known yet is always familiar. Their existential process is an enduring touchstone for them – they can readily weigh current experiencing against it to get a sense of value. At the other extreme is the person whose fear of their existential process has kept them a stranger to it except in dream-like glimpses. For this person to choose to locate the work at the level of their existential process is to potentially face their own terror.

Of course, crucial from a person-centred perspective, is that the location of the work is defined by the client. Yet, that definition is not made in isolation but out of the relationship the client experiences with the counsellor and the degree to which that relationship assuages the client's fear and in some cases, terror. For one client this will take them no further than the behavioural problem and that will be sufficient, for the present at least. For another, the relationship will be enough to take them into the pain of their fragile process or the terror of their dissociated process, and that will suffice. For some clients, perhaps through a combination of the progress they have previously made and the relational depth obtained with their counsellor, they are able to enter that most private arena where their formative self-experiences, doubts, fears, hopes and despair await exploration – an area that may as yet be unexpressed to any human being, including themselves. It is not the techniques of the counsellor that will help the client to develop that courage, but the humanity she offers. It is that humanity which the remainder of this book explores.

3

THE COUNSELLOR'S
USE OF THE SELF

A Stern Discipline

Being a counsellor is no task for the faint-hearted and it has sometimes been suggested that those who embrace the person-centred orientation are letting themselves in for a particularly rigorous discipline. There is certainly much to support this point of view. In contrast to many other approaches, the person-centred counsellor cannot seek refuge in her diagnostic skill or in the application of a clutch of therapeutic techniques. She must also avoid donning the mantle of the expert which can so easily bolster a sense of superiority. If she is to cultivate the kind of relationship where the client feels accepted as an equal and is increasingly prepared to risk becoming vulnerable and open to exploring difficult and painful terrain, she must resist the temptation of erecting barriers to the development of intimacy. Every new encounter presents a challenge to the counsellor's ability to offer herself as someone who is prepared to enter into relational depth and who is unafraid of a level of involvement where the client can face hidden pain and risk new ways of being.

This emphasis on involvement, intimacy and emotional risk runs counter to much in the prevailing culture. It is difficult to avoid the conclusion that for many in the helping professions the current climate, fostered by much recent legislation, encourages an attitude of caution and fearfulness which leads to a culpable under-involvement with those who are often in most need of assistance. The person-centred counsellor must somehow find the courage to oppose this tendency. Far from remaining 'objective' or even consciously aloof, she works on the assumption that it is precisely her ability to enter into her client's world and to offer a relationship in depth which will determine the effectiveness of the therapeutic endeavour. This is not to suggest that the person-centred counsellor has no need of a theoretical underpinning for her work. On the contrary, an understanding of both personality development and therapeutic process is of considerable importance. It does emphasise, however, that the initial concern for the counsellor is neither the acquisition of theoretical knowledge nor the development of therapeutic skills but the understanding and cherishing of her own being. The person-centred counsellor has a deep faith in the inner wisdom and potential of each client and she knows that her task is to offer a relationship where that wisdom and potential can be released and enhanced. Such faith will be groundless, however, if the counsellor cannot regard her own being with the same positive conviction. Nor can she offer the necessary relationship to her client unless she believes herself worthy of the same unconditional, affirming acceptance and the same empathic understanding that she wishes her client to experience. A person-centred therapist who is self-rejecting or self-punishing and who cannot exercise an understanding compassion towards her own being is in danger of perpetrating a charade that will be quickly sensed by most clients and certainly by those who are most gravely wounded.

The Counsellor's Attitude to Herself

The world is full of helpers whose activity is a desperate strategy to avoid confronting themselves. This self-evasion is sometimes mistaken for selflessness and can receive reinforcement from a misguided understanding of the Christian tradition where the concepts of selfishness and self-love have often become hopelessly confused. According to this misunderstanding one's own needs must always be subordinated to the needs of the other and it is considered unhealthy even to reflect unduly on one's own state of being. Once such a way of thinking is allied to a common distrust of introspection the scene is well set for the kind of helping that is permeated by a dogged sense of martyrdom, which further damages the self-respect of the person being helped. For the person-centred counsellor the ability to accept and affirm herself is, in fact, the cornerstone for her therapeutic practice, and in its absence the usefulness of the helping relationship will be grossly impaired. It is impossible to offer a client acceptance, empathy and genuineness at the deepest level if such responses are withheld from the self.

Self-acceptance let alone self-love is not easily attained and it needs tending once established. Essentially it requires a willingness to give oneself time, attention and care, not out of self-indulgence but from a sense of responsibility to clients in the service of the work of counselling. Often this will mean a preparedness to seek out, on a consistent basis, the support of a friend or colleague with whom it is possible to be open, vulnerable and confused. This may or may not be the same person who provides regular consultative support for the counselling work in progress. In the person-centred tradition, however, it is common for the work in supervision to include attention to the ongoing personal development of the counsellor. When the quality of the counsellor's being is such a fundamental factor in the creation of the therapeutic conditions this is perhaps not altogether surprising. The relationship the counsellor has with herself will, to a large extent, determine the quality of the work she is able to initiate with clients, and is therefore a natural subject for a supervisor's attention.

Listening to the Self

The cultivation of a cherishing and affirming relationship with the self is not accomplished overnight. Person-centred counsellors, like many of their clients, may have experienced judgemental and punitive relationships in the past that have left them with little self-esteem. They may also be burdened with deeply undermining guilt feelings. The self-awareness and self-knowledge that are crucial if self-deception is to be avoided may have to be won through the painful process of confronting condemnatory conditions of worth and establishing contact with the organismic valuing process whose promptings might have been intermittent at best and undetected at worst. It is precisely because of the potential pain involved that listening to the self is, for so many, a feared and resisted process. Be that as it may, for the person-centred counsellor in training there is no way of avoiding a task that will become a key activity in the disciplined life on which they are embarking. Listening to the self merits periods of undivided attentiveness and for the person-centred counsellor it is likely to become a daily undertaking. Not only is such regular listening crucial to the development and maintenance of self-awareness but it is also an essential element in ensuring the congruence or authenticity that will subsequently characterise the relationship with clients. Listening to the self in this way constitutes for the counsellor a disciplined monitoring of her inner world that will reduce the likelihood of being taken off guard by a client's revelations. It also helps establish the inner confidence of which self-knowledge is a primary ingredient and thereby lessens the fear of becoming entangled in the other's confusion or anguish. Such a diminishment of fear is a prerequisite for entering into the depth of relationship which the alleviation of existential despair demands.

For most counsellors in training, disciplined listening to the self is best undertaken in the presence, and with the skilled help, of another person. For many this is likely to be a therapist although a small group of fellow trainees can often provide an admirable environment of safety and attentiveness where parts of the self may dare to make themselves heard for the first time. Person-centred training never insists on trainees entering one-to-one therapy although many choose to do so. It is undoubtedly the case, however, that listening to the self is not always best served by establishing a formal counselling relationship. The group is often the preferred arena where risks can be taken and terrain explored which might remain hidden throughout a lengthy one-to-one therapeutic process. For others again the trusted friend may prove the ideal companion in the practice of listening to the self. There are also those for whom the practice of meditation or certain forms of contemplative prayer can be equally productive while yet others can listen to themselves with greatest acuity when they go on solitary walks or simply stand and stare at a scene of great natural beauty. Whatever the mode or context, however, it is almost certain that such opportunities will need to be deliberately or consciously sought out and planned for. The inner world is the counsellor's most precious resource and it would verge on the irresponsible to leave its exploration to chance given the frenetic environments in which most of us live.

There are those – and they may be the majority – who can benefit from a structured approach to listening to the self and the exploration which it inevitably engenders. They may adopt a method of their own devising. It is possible, for example, to design exercises to facilitate entry into deeper parts of the self. These may take the form of posing direct questions such as: What gives me most joy these days? When do I experience the most anxiety? What am I missing most? So simple a strategy can provide ample scope for lengthy periods of profitable reflection. The method known as 'focusing', developed by Eugene Gendlin, one of Rogers' earliest associates, is a more sophisticated elaboration of the same attempt to locate and articulate internal experiencing and we shall be revisiting Gendlin's work in Chapter 4. Some counsellors assiduously maintain a daily journal that focuses not on external events but on states of mind and the world of feelings. It may even be that it will fall to counsellors to reinstate the great art of letter-writing as they seek to explore inner experience and to share their findings with trusted friends or colleagues. In recent times, too, the writing of poetry has become for many counsellors a treasured mode of expressing complex or turbulent states of mind and it is perhaps significant that some highly experienced person-centred counsellors often find the language of poetry to be the ideal vehicle for conveying the outcome of the deepest listening to the self. In some ways, too, the discipline involved in fashioning a poem symbolises the dedicated commitment to the task of listening to the self that is required of every person-centred counsellor intent on becoming a fearless companion to those who suffer.

Self-Acceptance

Listening to the self is one thing but the resulting self-knowledge is another and may not always be easy to bear. Although such knowledge is infinitely preferable to the wilful ignorance which comes from the unexamined life it may well present the counsellor with a major challenge to her own self-acceptance. If the self is to be cherished and affirmed, then self-acceptance is the vital first stage along that path. What is more, the person-centred counsellor lacking self-acceptance runs the risk of living a contradiction that lies at the very centre of the therapeutic enterprise for she will be withholding from herself one of the attitudinal responses essential to the well-being of her clients. The self-acceptance of which we speak should not be confused with complacency nor should it be seen as a kind of weary resignation. The complacent or resigned person has ceased to listen to the self and has neither the will nor the energy to continue with the process of self-exploration which we have suggested is a life-long commitment for the person-centred counsellor. Self-acceptance, by contrast, has as its motivating force a desire to grow and a willingness to face the truth. Should the truth be painful, however, and particularly if it should cause or exacerbate feelings of guilt or deep unworthiness, then the quest for self-acceptance may prove arduous in the extreme. It is in such cases that the context in which the person-centred counsellor is living may be of critical importance.

Self-acceptance, especially if it is to be attained by those who have in the past been subject to countless adverse judgements, will almost certainly require the continuing presence of those who are themselves accepting and empathically attuned to the inner world of others. For the counsellor in training this is likely to be members of the training group itself, reinforced perhaps by tutors, a supervisor and a personal therapist. Loyal and trusted friends or relatives can also have a crucial role to play. These are the people who create a safe arena for self-exploration and then provide the support and acceptance when difficult or painful discoveries are made or guilt feelings come to the fore. They will also enable the person to discern the difference between those inappropriate guilt feelings which arise from having failed to live up to someone else's demands or expectations – that is, a falling short of the conditions of worth imposed by others – and those appropriate guilt feelings engendered by a betrayal of the self where there is a sense of having let oneself down and thus failed to fulfil the meaning of one's own existence. In the first case the guilt feelings need to be acknowledged, disowned and deprived of their force whereas appropriate guilt feelings can be the trigger for re-establishing contact with the organismic valuing process and can act as a powerful spur to growth and change. Ironically, person-centred counsellors are often skilled in distinguishing these differing guilt feelings in their clients and can display inordinate patience as the client disentangles the convoluted strands. When it comes to their own processes, however, they can quickly lose patience and sink into unhealthy self-recrimination. This is particularly liable to happen when the counsellor is living with a partner or relative who is dismissive of them or their work and spends much time passing adverse judgements or making cynical comments. For someone who is struggling to move towards self-acceptance it can be debilitating in the extreme to be confronted by criticism or even denigration on a daily basis. Sadly it is not uncommon for a person-centred counsellor to have to choose between the work to which they feel they are called and a relationship which, because of its invalidating impact upon them, prevents the progress towards the self-acceptance that is vital for their personal and professional well-being (see also Thorne 2002: 39).

If self-acceptance is a cornerstone of the person-centred counsellor's attitude to the self, it could be said that self-love constitutes an advanced flourishing of the personality which enables the counsellor to display an emotional fearlessness in the face of the most apparently intractable clients. Self-love is a cherishing and an affirming of the self which is quite the opposite to selfishness. It is based on a realistic assessment of the self with its qualities and shortcomings but it is permeated by a tender compassion which is transformative. The person experiences himself or herself as lovable and desirable with all their weaknesses and vulnerabilities and as a result can be utterly self-forgetful. For the self-loving person, the self is no longer a problem and it is possible to be fully present to the other without fear. The selfish person, on the other hand, is so preoccupied with self and its needs and desires that the other is neither acknowledged nor truly encountered. Without self-acceptance, the person-centred counsellor will gradually find her work impossible. With self-love she will experience the wonder of having found work that brings daily joy (see also Thorne 2002: 23).

The Development of Empathy

Self-acceptance is certainly strengthened when the counsellor experiences not only the understanding of others but the increasing range of her own empathic capacities. Empathy should not be confused with sympathy. Whereas sympathy arises from feeling compassionately moved by the experience of another, and to some extent sharing in it, empathy requires the much more complex and delicate process of stepping into another person's shoes and seeing the world through his or her eyes without, however, losing touch with one's own reality. Such a capacity is likely to be fostered by making the deliberate effort to move outside the confines of one's normal social environment or subgroup. The counsellor does well to encounter those of whom she has little knowledge or those by whom she feels threatened or intimidated. The benefits of this broadening of social experience go far beyond a simple increase in understanding of the actual people and groups she meets. In more general terms it tends to increase confidence and also humility, both of which facilitate the development of empathy.

Parochialism is the enemy of empathy but is as much a matter of attitude as of geography. Essentially it is the imagination which needs to be stimulated and enriched if the counsellor's empathic ability is to develop. It is in this respect that the discipline of psychology seems only rarely to provide the appropriate nourishment. On the contrary much psychological writing, in its attempt to convey the impression of objective scientific enquiry, oppresses the spirit by its laborious pedestrianism. Exceptions to this occur when attempts are made to explore subjective experience through the application of more humanistic paradigms and, fortunately, such attempts are beginning to grow with the increase in qualitative research projects and increasing emphasis on the experience of clients (e.g. Alexander, 1995; Sands, 2000; Bates, 2006). The person-centred counsellor is still more likely to find food for the imagination, however, in the works of novelists, poets and dramatists, and a good case could be made for requiring counsellors in training to make in-depth studies of some of the world's greatest creative writers. The counsellor who never reads a novel or never opens a book of poetry is neglecting an important resource for empathic development.

Learning to be Genuine

The counsellor's ability to be genuine in her therapeutic encounters will be related to the way she conducts herself generally in her social relationships. There is something not a little spine-chilling about the counsellor who has the apparent capacity to 'turn on' her genuineness at the moment when the therapeutic hour begins, as if congruence were some kind of behavioural technique which can be applied when required. The implications of genuineness in a therapeutic relationship are discussed at length in Chapter 6, but at this stage our concern is to look briefly at the 'way of being' which will characterise the counsellor's total existence and not simply her professional activity. This 'global' perspective is perhaps nowhere more relevant than in the consideration of what it means to be genuine in one's human interactions.

Learning to be genuine is usually a gradual process involving a dedicated and enduring commitment from the person-centred counsellor. She will delicately experiment with her genuine reactions to people and events and welcome feedback on the way others perceive her. Inevitably this 'testing' of herself is not restricted to the counselling context. Friends, colleagues and, most particularly, her loved ones might notice the difference as she gradually becomes more trusting of herself and consequently more able to be genuine even in difficult situations. Often the counsellor's evolution will be valued by those around her. For example, the counsellor who is a mother may begin to show her loving feelings more spontaneously towards her children; she may become more immediate in her intimate contact with her partner, and perhaps she will participate more actively and fully in family activities. However, there are likely to be other consequences of the counsellor's developing genuineness. She will probably become less guarded about her other not-so-loving feelings towards her children, more forthright in expressing difficulties with her partner and more determined in asserting her right to devote energy and time to interests outside the family.

All these outcomes of the counsellor's developing genuineness are changes, and change, whatever shape it takes, can upset the delicate balances and patterns within relationships. Such shifts can bring opportunities for the enhancement of relationships but like any change they carry some danger as well. For example, counsellors in training occasionally report a heightening of emotional, including sexual, expressiveness. It is easy to see how such an effect might be enhancing for the counsellor's relationship with her partner, but even such an apparently positive change might prove threatening and unwelcome in some cases. It is also the case that during training or one-to-one work the counsellor may discover aspects of her being (what we have come to call 'configurations') that have previously been dormant or perhaps suppressed for some years. This discovery is likely to be accompanied by the desire to give expression to the new configuration and this may result in behaviours that cause surprise or even disgust to those who believed that they knew the person well. The more self-awareness grows, the more likely it is that there will be fresh challenges to the task of being authentic in the world.

The 'Healthy Relationship' Between Counsellor and Client

All that has been said so far points to the central importance of the relationship that the counsellor has with herself. Can she be self-accepting and even self-loving? Can she be motivated enough to seek consciously for ways of extending her empathic abilities? Can she trust herself enough to give expression to her own self and to risk being open and genuine with her intimates? The answers the counsellor gives to questions of this nature (see Box 3.1) will to a large extent determine whether or not she is capable of offering a healthy relationship to her clients. Before proceeding to explore the nature of this healthy relationship it should be emphasised again, however, that person-centred counselling is only one form of helping, that there are many other forms not needing the kind of relationship with the self that has been described. Unempathic surgeons, for example, can do splendid work and it is well known that some of the world's greatest saints have brought untold blessings to others while remaining convinced of their own lack of worth. The healthy relationship which will now be explored concerns person-centred counsellors and their clients. It is not a template for all helping relationships, let alone for effective human relating in general. However, there is little doubt that the ability to relate to the self in the way that person-centred counsellors aspire to would dramatically alleviate the depression and anxiety that currently characterises our culture.

If the person-centred counsellor is 'at home' with her inner world and comfortable with her way of being it is likely that her work with clients will be marked by a number of factors that, taken in sum, point to a healthy therapeutic relationship as conceptualised in the person-centred tradition. Not all these factors will necessarily be present in every relationship, but they are likely to be discernible across the range of the counsellor's clientele and stem from the basic attitudes and beliefs that were outlined in the opening chapters.

Box 3.1   Self-Questioning of the Person-Centred Counsellor

1   Can I distinguish between self-acceptance, self-love and selfishness and commit myself to embrace the two former qualities?
2   Am I self-accepting and, if not, where are my sticking points?
3   Do I seek consciously to extend my empathic skills?
4   Can I be genuine enough to disclose my thoughts and feelings to my friends and intimates, especially when I am feeling angry or resentful, weak or unlovable?

The counsellor's concern to relate to her client on a basis of equality, and not to become trapped in the role of the diagnostic or treatment expert, means that she will do all she can to demystify the counselling process. She will be as open as possible about her way of working and will not seek to evade any direct questions that a client may pose as he struggles to decide whether or not to embark on a counselling relationship. She will be prepared, if called upon, to discuss with the client the underpinning rationale of person-centred counselling and she will likely stress the cooperative nature of the activity. She will indicate either explicitly or implicitly that she has no intention of taking responsibility *for* the client but that she will do her utmost to be responsible *to* him by committing herself to establishing a relationship in which he can explore his concerns in an environment of support and understanding. This openness about aims and intentions is the first and necessary sign of a healthy relationship and usually does much at the outset to 'dethrone' the counsellor and to establish a situation where the client recognises rapidly that he has to take his fair share of responsibility for his current predicament and for the changes that will be necessary if he is to move forward in his life.

It is important both at this early stage and as counselling proceeds that the counsellor monitors continually what she is prepared to offer to the client, and what lies outside the boundaries of her commitment. There will be no decreed limits about this and a counsellor's preparedness to offer of herself and of her energies may vary widely – between clients and with the same client – at different stages of the counselling process. What is crucial, however, if a relationship is to remain healthy, is that the counsellor is as clear as possible about what she is willing to deliver and that the client is appraised of this. Some counsellors fall unwittingly into the trap of offering the moon, and are then surprised or distressed at the client's increasing disappointment and resentment when the moon is not forthcoming. Where there is a lack of openness and a failure to spell out the extent of the commitment it is also possible for a client to fantasise in potentially damaging and often hurtful ways. The fantasies can differ dramatically. For one client there may be a permanent fear of being cast out at the end of the session, or before the next appointment, simply because the counsellor has not addressed the question of the duration of the counselling or of how it will eventually be terminated. For another there may be the growing fantasy that the counsellor has fallen in love with him and will never leave him. How otherwise could she treat him so kindly and offer him such sensitive understanding? It is only through a preparedness to be open and explicit about purpose and commitment that such fantasies can be confronted, and often it is only through continual reiteration by word and behaviour on the part of the counsellor that they can finally be dispelled.

The person-centred counsellor has nothing to gain by being anything other than transparent to her client. She does not profess to know what is 'good for' the client, and is not therefore concerned to exercise manipulatory skills, however well intentioned, in order to achieve 'good' outcomes. It is an indication of a healthy relationship when there is little preoccupation with 'progress' on the part of the counsellor because she knows that she is not the appropriate arbiter of this. Indeed, it is often amusing to discover that what may seem like a remarkable lack of progress to the counsellor may be seen quite differently by the client who, after all, has access to yardsticks for judgement of whose very existence the counsellor may be unaware (see Box 3.2). It is somewhat less amusing to acknowledge that counsellors who believe themselves to be highly successful would often have a rude shock if they consulted their clients, and if the latter felt courageous enough to speak the truth.

Box 3.2   Who Knows What Is 'Progress'?

The following is an extract from a taped counselling session where the counsellor has just expressed uncertainty and curiosity about what benefit the client has been drawing from their seven sessions thus far.

Client: What have I been getting out of it? Wow! … It has just kept me alive, that's all! I often go round and round in circles when I'm with you, and it seems like I'm getting nowhere, but all the time I'm *being me*: I'm being what I can't risk with anyone else – I'm being confused, distraught … crazy. I mean I know now that I'm not crazy … but I didn't know that before. It feels like the more I can just be these things with you, then the less frightened I am of them … the less frightened I am of me.

If the counsellor's lack of interest in manipulating her clients to 'good' ends is the mark of a healthy relationship, so too is her preparedness to *be* manipulated and even on occasions to be taken for a ride by an apparently scheming client. The person-centred counsellor, it will be recalled, has a basic trust in human nature and believes that there is in each one of us a desire for the truth and for constructive social intercourse. Such a belief does not mean that the counsellor is gullible and blind to human perversity, but it does imply that she is prepared to trust those who are manifestly untrustworthy so that they may gradually discover their own trustworthiness. In a strange way therefore the counsellor's willingness to allow herself to be deceived is again a mark of the relationship's health. The counsellor does not attempt to catch the client out, nor does she continually question the client's motives. She accepts that the client is doing his best, given his particular circumstances, to grow and to protect himself, and if this means that for the time being he has to manipulate and deceive her then she is prepared to stay with him through such deception rather than enjoy the dubious pleasure of unmasking him and preserving her own pride. By showing that she is not interested in playing power games or in scoring points the counsellor hopes that the client will gradually no longer have need to resort to deceit and manipulation in order to preserve his frail identity. Such behaviour will fall away once the client feels safe in a relationship where he is respected despite his initial inability to reciprocate such respect. It is sad to reflect that counsellors who are keen to manifest their cleverness and to expose manipulation on the part of their clients may well be the agents of further humiliation for people who already feel invalidated and ashamed.

A willingness to submit to manipulation if need be is but one sign of the counsellor's determination to stay with her client through thick and thin. A healthy relationship will not be undermined by the client's hostility or defensiveness nor by the counsellor's own feelings of dislike for the client. Instead, it will be characterised by a preparedness to 'fight' for the relationship in the sense of offering a solid commitment that can transcend difficulties of understanding and withstand the unpredictable vagaries of the client's moods and doubts. There will, of course, be the occasional relationship where the counsellor's feelings of dislike or even outright hostility for the client are of such intensity and duration that they have to be expressed if genuineness is to be preserved. Such expression, however, will again be a sign of the counsellor's commitment to the relationship and her willingness to face her own pain and the negativity engendered by the interaction with the client. The expression is not a defensive or aggressive response but an attempt to deepen the relationship. There is no sense in which a counsellor will give voice to her dislike in order to evade responsibility and commitment, or in the hope of getting rid of a tiresome and uncooperative client.

This preparedness to go to almost inordinate lengths to make manifest the commitment to the client is of crucial significance to those people whose life experience has taught them to expect rejection, fickleness and a lack of dependability in others. At the same time the counsellor must take care that her desire to indicate her commitment is not perceived by the client as an imposition or an unwelcome invasion. The tight-rope that sometimes has to be walked is often revealed when a particularly shy or self-rejecting client fails to appear for an appointment after a difficult previous session. Such people are prone to see themselves as 'unworthy' clients, as if their struggles in the counselling relationship are yet another sign of inadequacy to add to the long list of their previous failures. On the other hand it is possible that there is a reason for their absence which has nothing to do with such feelings of inadequacy. The counsellor is faced with a dilemma. Does she do nothing, thus possibly giving the message to the client that she does not really care whether he comes or not, or does she make contact and run the risk of being perceived as an interferer or a 'possessive' counsellor? If she is working in private practice does she simply send the client the bill for this missed appointment without comment? In practice it is likely that most person-centred counsellors will write to such a client in a way that attempts to convey the counsellor's continuing commitment while giving the client absolute freedom to make up his own mind what to do next. Letters of this kind are often difficult to compose and will clearly vary from one client to another. An example of such a 'tight-rope' note appears in Box 3.3. In some cases a client who receives such a letter may make no response in the short term and may seem to have disappeared without trace. Not infrequently, however, such a person will renew contact many months later and will express gratitude both for the counsellor's expression of commitment and for the 'permission' to opt out of counselling for a while.

Box 3.3   Commitment Without Imposition

Dear Michael, I was sorry not to see you for your appointment today and I do hope things are not too difficult. Do not hesitate, will you, to phone in to book another appointment if you would like that. It goes without saying that I shall be very pleased indeed to see you but shall quite understand if you wish to stop for the moment. With best wishes, Yours, Jean.

It is a popular misconception that a counselling process will invariably be of comparatively short duration. There are certainly many cases where five or six sessions will be sufficient to help the client along his road, and even times when one cathartic session may clear the air enough for the client to continue on his own. However, there are clients whose concerns are such that they desire contact over many months as they gradually reorient themselves and their living. In cases such as these the counsellor's willingness to 'fight' for the healthy relationship is a vital ingredient, lest the couple fall into a pattern of relating that is 'comfortable' rather than dynamic, or worse, a pattern which ensnares the client and reinforces his impotence. A sure indication of the counsellor's determination to 'fight for' the healthy relationship is her scrupulous attentiveness to the process to ensure that her commitment to her client does not result in a subtle abuse of power, landing the client in a compassionate 'prison' from which he feels unable to escape without wounding the kindly gaoler. Box 3.4 shows such attentiveness in action. In many ways the person-centred counsellor's firm commitment to her client and her equally strong desire that the client shall be free to find his own way forward are the two primary reference points for her way of being in this relationship. In different ways, and with varying degrees of emphasis, she will be attempting to say:

> I am willing to invest myself in this relationship with you and to let you see me as I am. At the same time I make this investment without strings attached. You are free to be you and to leave this relationship when you wish. I am committed to stay with you for as long as that commitment enhances your development, but when it ceases to do so I shall be equally committed to helping you to leave me.

Box 3.4   Commitment Not Entrapment

Counsellor: We have been working together for some six months now and I am aware that much has changed for you. I wonder how you are feeling about where we have got to.

Client: A long way to go, I reckon, but perhaps I can let go of your hand soon.

Counsellor: A few more weeks and then …

Client: That's how it feels at the moment.

Letting be, letting grow and letting go is not an altogether inadequate way to attempt to summarise the person-centred counsellor's complex and demanding task. It is in the service of this task that she strives to offer the 'healthy relationship' whose major characteristics are listed in Box 3.5.

Box 3.5   Characteristics of the 'Healthy' Therapeutic Relationship

1   The counsellor is open about her aims and intentions
2   The counsellor is responsible *to* her client and not *for* him
3   The counsellor does not manipulate her client but is prepared to be manipulated
4   The counsellor does not profess to know what is 'good' for the client
5   The counsellor is not oriented towards 'success'
6   The counsellor is clear about what she is willing to offer the client at every stage
7   The counsellor is committed to the client and will 'fight' for the relationship
8   The counsellor is prepared to invest herself in the relationship with no strings attached
9   The counsellor desires the client's freedom to be himself.

The Unique Self of the Counsellor

It is self-evident that person-centred counsellors, however much they may adhere to the same underlying principles in constructing their counselling relationships, will vary widely in temperament and in personal attributes. The authors of this book are no exception. One is a somewhat intellectual and literary Englishman, sometimes to be found sniffing incense in Anglo-Catholic churches with a furled umbrella on his arm, while the other is a no-nonsense Scotsman initially schooled in the hard sciences, whose idea of fun is braving the rapids to ensnare an unsuspecting trout. These two very contrasting personalities clearly bring different attributes and widely differing life experiences to their counselling relationships. As person-centred counsellors our concern is to ensure that our unique strengths – and vulnerabilities, for that matter – can be invested in our therapeutic work to the benefit of our clients. In short, we both wish to be ourselves in our work and are therefore anxious to make *all* our relevant attributes available to our counselling relationships, where this is appropriate. We do not wish to be confined to a narrow array of therapeutic responses as if acceptance, empathy and genuineness can only be communicated in certain stereotyped ways. Each counsellor has her own unique repertoire and the therapeutic enterprise will be much enriched if she is able to exploit such a repertoire to the full and to make appropriate use of her own particular talents.

A counsellor's special gifts may not always be apparent in the early years of practice. There is a sense in which the preoccupation with 'doing a good job' ensures a conscientious adherence to the 'norms' of the approach and a wholly appropriate emphasis on establishing the core conditions. The counsellor is likely to do her utmost to convey acceptance to her client and to track his inner world with all the empathic skill at her command. She will also be at pains not to put up a professional mask behind which she can take refuge when the going gets tough. It is unlikely, however, that as a fledgling counsellor she will be bold enough to take the kind of risks which are involved if a deeper level of her own personality is to be put at the service of her client. It is only when she feels a growing security in her own capacity to function as a 'good enough' counsellor that she is likely to discover and then to offer those attributes which constitute her own uniqueness.

In the case of one of us (Thorne), it was some years before it became possible to identify a particular quality of being and then to recognise this as being of fundamental importance in many therapeutic encounters (Thorne, 1985, 1991a, 2002). Today, however, this quality of tenderness, as he has come to describe it, is an important expression of particular gifts that spring from his unique personality and experience. The implications of these gifts for the counselling process have been explored elsewhere (e.g. Thorne, 2002: 72; 2006: 35–47), but for our present purposes it is relevant to focus on the experience of the counsellor himself as he came to trust parts of his own being that had not previously had much of an place in his counselling work. It makes sense for Brian Thorne to take up his own story.

Taking Risks with the Unique Self

For many years I had been aware that with certain clients I often felt an almost overwhelming sense of interrelatedness. Such clients varied widely in background and life experience and were often not people with whom I might have expected a natural affinity. My immediate reaction to such feelings was to distrust them and to suspect that some process of what my psycho-dynamic colleagues call projection or counter-transference was taking place. I should take note of this possibility, I told myself, and then proceed with the utmost caution.

One day, however, for I know not what reason, I decided to throw such caution to the winds. I suppose at some level I reminded myself that I was not a counsellor in the analytic tradition but someone who believed in the fundamental trustworthiness of human beings, and that this category included myself. I knew that I was an experienced and responsible counsellor and that I was committed to my client's well-being. My own congruence – the outcome of the discipline of my chosen therapeutic approach – was revealing to me a strong sense of being intimately involved at a profound level with someone with whom I apparently had little in common. I decided to trust that feeling, however mysterious or inexplicable, and to hold on to it rather than dismiss it or treat it with my usual circumspection. The result of that decision has been far-reaching, for I discovered that my trust in this sense of profound interrelatedness (and it usually happens quite unpredictably) gives access to a world which seems outside of space and time and where it is possible for both my client and me to relate without fear and with astonishing clarity of perception. I have attempted to give some sense of this experience as follows:

> My client seems more accurately in focus: he or she stands out in sharp relief from the surrounding decor. When he or she speaks, the words belong uniquely to him or her. Physical movements are a further confirmation of uniqueness. It seems as if for a space, however brief, two human beings are fully alive because they have given themselves and each other permission to risk being fully alive. At such a moment I have no hesitation in saying that my client and I are caught up in a stream of love. Within this stream there comes an effortless or intuitive understanding and what is astonishing is how complex this understanding can be. It sometimes seems that I receive my client whole and thereafter possess a knowledge of him or her which does not depend on biographical data. This understanding is intensely personal and invariably it affects the self-perception of the client and can lead to marked changes in attitude and behaviour. For me as a counsellor it is accompanied by a sense of joy which when I have checked it out has always been shared by the client. (Thorne, 2004: 10–11)

It is clear to me now that the decision to trust the feeling of interrelatedness was the first step towards a willingness on my part to acknowledge my spiritual experience of reality and to capitalise on the many hours spent in prayer and worship. It was as if previously I had refused to draw on this whole area of experience in the conduct of my therapeutic work. In my zeal not to proselytise it was as if I had deliberately deprived myself of some of my most precious resources in the task of relating to my clients. Once I had opened myself to myself, however, I was capable of entering into the communion of souls, or the membership one of another, which is a fundamental given of the spiritual life. I still remain convinced, of course, that it is iniquitous to use a counselling relationship for evangelising. I am no more likely now to talk of God or religion in my professional work than I was in earlier years. The difference is that I now attempt to be fully present to clients, supervisees and trainees and this means that I do not disown my eternal soul and leave it outside the door. Interestingly enough, it has also meant that I have been far less disembodied in my behaviour in the last twenty years than I used to be at the outset of my counselling career. My welcoming of my spiritual self has led to the liberation of using my whole self, including my physical being. When I am bold enough to accept my own uniqueness it seems that I am enabled to offer a tenderness that touches the soul while embracing (sometimes literally) the body. I have no embarrassment in writing these words, for I have come to believe that the person-centred counsellor has a particular obligation to be honest about all his or her attributes and to be prepared to acknowledge and explore their potential contribution to the counselling relationship. For my own part I know that if I had continued to deny the therapeutic significance of some of the deepest parts of my own being I might never have tumbled to the fact that I have a capacity to express tenderness both physically and spiritually. Perhaps it is in the offering of this gift that I give the highest expression to my unique self, and that is why it always feels a risky undertaking because vulnerability and strength are present in equal measure. Nowadays, however, I know that I usually have no option but to take the risk. What is more, the risk has sometimes proved costly in terms of professional misunderstanding and even calumny (Thorne, 1996; 2005: 191, 197).

The Changing Self of the Counsellor

Some twenty years ago Carl Rogers was asked to reflect on the experience of becoming old. He produced an article entitled 'Growing old', but before publication he modified the title to 'Growing old – or older and growing' (Rogers, 1980b). This anecdote enshrines an important precept for the person-centred counsellor, and indeed for anyone engaged in therapeutic relationships. The work on the self can never be complete and the counsellor is confronted by a lifetime's task if she is to remain faithful to her commitment. If this sounds unduly demanding it needs to be remembered that counselling is about change and development, and that an unchanging counsellor is well on the way to becoming a professional charlatan. What is more, the counsellor's obligation to keep on growing is, in fact, a glorious invitation to live life to the full. The person-centred counsellor is challenged not so much to face the horrors of the unknown (although some there may be) as to continue on a voyage of self-discovery knowing that many of the most delectable places are yet to be visited. It is the counsellor who dares to embrace life in this way who is ready to offer to her clients a depth of relationship where façades can gradually be discarded and authentic living becomes possible for the client for perhaps the first time.

The Experience of Relational Depth

At the end of Chapter 2, within the exploration of the more recent developments in person-centred theory, we suggested that in person-centred counselling we want to be able to work not only with the presenting problem but also with the client's processes and self-dialogues which might underly that problem and even, where that was meaningful to the client, to get behind such processes in order to meet the client within his *existential process*. We want to penetrate beyond what is sometimes called the *presentational* aspects of self (Mearns and Cooper, 2005) which the client will use in everyday interactions with other people. We human beings are skilful in putting on a 'face' to the world; indeed we can have many faces to fit different social contexts. These portrayals of ourself are real and important representations, yet they do not describe us in our entirety. Most especially, they do not describe what we feel and believe about ourself at the fundamental level where we do not have to *pretend* to people or to ourself. Those everyday portrayals are skilfully sculpted in order to present a face that both fits the social context and also to present ourself in a way that we want to be seen within that context. Much of the science of social psychology has been devoted to exploring the faces that we present in different social contexts and a study of the findings can only make us marvel at the skill of the human being. Arguably, one of the most important skills of childhood is learning how to present ourselves in different contexts. For the child who is not offered a broad base of acceptance but, rather, a narrow set of conditions of worth, this learning how variously to present themselves has distinct survival value.

The counselling relationship is unique in respect of the fact that it offers the person a context where they are not being judged, where they are not expected to *be* in any particular way. Furthermore, the relationship is distinctly loaded in their favour insofar as the counsellor is not asking them to give her reciprocal and equal personal attention. All of these conditions offer a context where the client might be able to show not only his presentational dimensions of self but more of his existential self. However, if we actually examine the reality of most counselling sessions, we find the client largely still hiding behind portrayals of self. Sometimes these self-portrayals are different from those he might show in other life contexts, but they are portrayals none the less, insofar as he is presenting an image that he believes is appropriate to the setting and will give a desired impression of him in the eyes of the counsellor and himself. Why does the client tend to continue in this presentational style? Some of it will be habitual – the social skills of portrayal and their use and adaptation to different social contexts have been such an important and ingrained dimension of our social existence that it is simply difficult for us to lay them aside and represent our self and our self-experiences just as we experience them. This is the main reason why participation in an encounter group experience can be so liberating. Often people begin their existence in an encounter group by also hiding behind portrayed aspects of their self – sometimes quite sophisticated portrayals based on earlier encounter group experience. But the longer the group continues, the more likely it is that other people will see through their portrayals and begin to challenge them.

In person-centred counselling we take this distinction between meeting presentational aspects of self and the more fundamental, existential self, extremely seriously. We are not satisfied with merely establishing a good *therapeutic alliance* with the client. The therapeutic alliance is well established in research as being a critical variable correlating with effectiveness in a wide range of therapeutic approaches (Lambert, 1992; Krupnick et al., 1996; Asay and Lambert, 1999; Hubble et al., 1999; Keijsers et al., 2000; Hovarth and Bedi, 2002; and Beutler et al., 2004). But we want a stronger relationship than that, because we want the client to be challenged and feel secure enough in the strength of the relationship being offered to enter territory that is new for him in human relating. We want him to dare to relate with the counsellor from his existential self. That is asking a lot of the client because he may have spent much of his life hiding what he believes to be dimensions of his self which, if expressed, would not be acceptable to others – indeed, might not be acceptable to himself.

We have come to describe what the person-centred counsellor offers in order to meet this challenge as *relational depth* which is described as follows:

> A state of profound contact and engagement between two people, in which each person is fully real with the other, and able to understand and value the other's experiences at a high level. (Mearns and Cooper, 2005: xii)

The same authors go further to describe the counsellor's experience of relational depth:

> A feeling of profound contact and engagement with the client, in which one simultaneously experiences high and consistent levels of empathy and acceptance towards that other, and relates to them in a highly transparent way. In this relationship, the client is experienced as acknowledging one's empathy, acceptance and congruence – either implicitly or explicitly – and is experienced as fully congruent in that moment. (Mearns and Cooper, 2005: 36)

In other words, the counsellor's part in the process of creating relational depth is to offer the core therapeutic conditions of empathy, unconditional positive regard and congruence, all in high degree, such that each enhances the experience of the other. In fact, it is somewhat misguided to seek to break up relational depth into sub-variables such as the core conditions. Relational depth is more than the sum of these parts. When a client experiences the power of the counsellor's empathy combined with a feeling of being completely accepted – no matter what he presents – and also realises that these offerings are completely congruent with the self of the counsellor and are not mere portrayals, then the power of that complex phenomenon is much more than any partial experience of the separate conditions.

Of course, offering relational depth does not necessarily mean that it will be received and responded to. The counsellor can only offer: the client must choose to respond or not. Sometimes it is a little more complicated than that because the client experiences the offering and stores that up for a possible future response. Also, the client's response will not necessarily mirror the counsellor's invitation. Only in some instances will the client consciously symbolise the relational power of the moment; more often the client's response will be to move to a more congruent mode of experiencing and expressing. The notion of the *mutuality* of the experience of relational depth is often misunderstood to imply that the counsellor and the client *experience the same thing.* But that is rare, because the counsellor and the client usually have different attention fields. For the counsellor the *figure,* the focus of her attention, is the relationship. But for the client the *figure* is his personal processing and the *ground* is the relationship. The relational depth is experienced by the client as opening doors that help him to drop self-protections and express himself more fully and congruently. This difference between the counsellor and client experiences is well illustrated in a study by McMillan and McLeod (2006).

Box 3.6 gives an insight into the experience of the client, Sally, of her counsellor's offering of relational depth through a powerful integration of the core conditions and the difference that made to her compared to earlier counselling experiences.

Box 3.6   'I Stopped Needing to Pretend'

I stopped needing to pretend. I had been in counselling three times before. They had all been good experiences and I thought that I had got a lot out of them. But this time was completely different. At first I didn't know how to take Mary [*the counsellor*]. She was more 'direct' than I was used to. My first thought was that she was a bit 'hard' on me. I was used to something softer. But, she could really 'meet' me more fully than anyone before. She could even meet me *through* my defences. Once she challenged me by asking if I was presenting what I was talking about in a particular way to her – in a way that would make her think well of me. It was an awful thing to say – but she said it really well – I felt it was coming from her understanding of me, not any 'judging' of me. I just answered, 'Yes', and looked her straight in the eye. I didn't even make my usual excuses. From that moment everything was different. I realised that I had two answers to every question – the 'pretend' one and the 'real' one. I began to give both of them. I was speaking to her in a way that was different to anything before. Even my tone of voice was different – it was less squeaky, more serious and, altogether, more 'fulsome'. I began to experience everything more fully. When I felt emotions, they were more powerful – again, more fulsome. I realised, with some horror, that I had almost never been 'real' in my life before. I had habitually 'put on a face' to the world.

With me not defending, we got to areas I had never been to before. I saw different feelings within me as well as the ones I was used to feeling. In relation to my mother's death I not only saw my sadness, but I felt my hate, and also my sorrow for her. An interesting thing was that my 'not defending' actually made me less scared. This is difficult to explain, but it is important. It wasn't just that she made it safe for me so that I didn't need to defend. It was that she challenged me as a truly caring human being and I responded. It was *me* responding and continuing to respond that made me less scared – there was no dependence on her. It's unusual.

Sally gives us an insight into the uniqueness of this experience for her. She points out the power of her counsellor's challenge and that she could respond to it because it was coming from her counsellor's understanding of her and valuing of her. But Sally also gives us another interesting insight towards the end of her statement when she tries to describe to us how it was her own 'not defending' that made her less scared more than anything the counsellor had actually done. This reminds us of the important person-centred work done on the client's *agency* (Bohart and Tallman, 1999; Bohart, 2004). We should not think of counselling being simply a matter of the counsellor offering relational depth, the client responding and that leading to an effective process. The crucial variable that will have an impact upon the client's changing is the client's *agency*, that is the degree of his ability to think, feel and act as an autonomous being who has the confidence to trust his own experiencing without neglecting the constraints of his social context. What we are trying to achieve is the stimulation and promotion of the client's agency. In the three chapters that follow, we will systematically look at the so-called *core conditions* of empathy, unconditional positive regard and congruence but we want to remember two things. First, breaking relational depth up into these constituent parts may help us to understand each of them in more detail but any one of them, without the others, would be relatively meaningless. The second thing we need to remember is that these conditions in themselves do not determine the client's ability to change. It is the client who will determine the extent of their impact. We can be sure, however, that the counsellor's ability to be fully herself and to live her life authentically and courageously will be a key factor in the mysterious alchemy of change and in the process whereby the client gradually learns to engage his own agency.

EMPATHY

One of the central dimensions of the therapeutic relationship is *empathy*. Brief definitions seldom capture the full meaning of processes, but as a prelude to the more complete description offered in this chapter, the following might suffice:

> Empathy is a continuing process whereby the counsellor lays aside her own way of experiencing and perceiving reality, preferring to sense and respond to the experiencing and perceptions of her client. This sensing may be intense and enduring with the counsellor actually experiencing her client's thoughts and feelings as powerfully as if they had originated in herself.

In the sequence reproduced in Box 4.1 the counsellor responds five times to the client, Bill. All these responses, including her touch on Bill's shoulder, are empathic responses in so far as they accurately reflect Bill's state of being in that moment.

| Box 4.1 | Empathising with Bill, a Disillusioned Teacher |

Bill: I guess I should have known that it wouldn't be that easy … to just do it 'as a job', I mean … like I thought I could just 'disengage' and save myself.

Counsellor: But you found that that didn't 'save' you – that it was just as bad or worse?

Bill: Yes, worse. I wouldn't have believed it could be worse. Like I thought that nothing could be worse than finding myself screaming at the kids and another time locking my door and crying by myself. But this is worse … like then at least I was alive.

Counsellor: And now you're not.

Bill: Now I'm a zombie … in fact sometimes I'm worse than a zombie.

Counsellor: … sometimes you're not even the *walking* dead?

Bill: Yes – now I often don't make it in [*to the school*] – like I think of going in and I nearly vomit – maybe I'm school phobic – imagine that! … the teacher's school phobic! What a laugh [*laughs*]!

Counsellor: Doesn't sound like you feel it's funny …

Bill: [*pause … starts to sob*].

Counsellor: [*gently puts her hand on his shoulder and says nothing*].

It is difficult to extract examples of empathy from tapes of counselling sessions because empathy is not a single response made by the counsellor to the client. Nor is empathy fully encapsulated even by a series of responses, as in Box 4.1. Rather than being a single response, or a series of responses, empathy is a *process*. It is a process of *being with* the client.

Although we share the same physical world we all experience it in different ways, because we look at it from different perspectives or *frames of reference*. In empathising with a client the counsellor leaves aside her own frame of reference and, for the time being, adopts the frame of reference of her client. She can then appreciate how the client experiences the events in his world; indeed she can even sense how he feels about events *as if* these feelings were her own. For example, near the end of Box 4.1 Bill is laughing, but the counsellor knows that that does not represent what he is feeling. She has been in his frame of reference for some time and she knows that his feelings about school and his place in it are thoroughly desperate. She is not only *thinking* about his feelings; it is likely that she too will be experiencing the same general 'tightness' or constricted throat that precedes his crying. She is experiencing Bill's feelings as if they were her own, but all the time the release of her empathic sensitivity is under her control: she does not 'get lost' in Bill's frame of reference, and can leave it whenever she wishes. This *as if* quality of empathy is a crucial aspect of the professionalism of the person-centred counsellor. She is able to work in this intense and feelingful way with her client and yet not become overwhelmed by those feelings. This control by the counsellor is crucial for the client: it offers him the security of knowing that although he may feel desperate and lost in his world, the counsellor will be someone who remains reliable and coherent, as well as sensitive.

Sometimes these particularly intense empathic experiences lead us to forget that in person-centred counselling empathy is going on most of the time and not just at profound moments. Right from the start of the relationship the counsellor endeavours to enter the client's frame of reference and walk alongside him in his world. When we are accompanying someone on a journey we are likely to comment on what we see, and the same happens on an empathic 'journey'; the counsellor comments on what she sees. These comments are commonly called *empathic responses*. The responses themselves are not empathy, but they are the products of sharing the client's journey which is empathy.

Historically this notion of empathy as a process rather than a response has been much misunderstood. Researchers found it much easier to work with the quantifiable empathic response rather than the empathic process (Truax and Carkhuff, 1967; Carkhuff, 1971). Research based on logical positivism must necessarily restrict and reduce human processes in order to examine them. Unfortunately, this narrow conception of empathy was not only used in research, but for many workers it became the basis for training in empathy. The result was that counsellors came to be trained in making empathic reflections on the false assumption that if they showed these behaviours, then empathy was taking place. In Box 4.2 the counsellor shows a reflection that looks empathic, but from this alone it is impossible to tell whether she is truly accompanying the client on his journey or simply responding with a stock reflection.

Box 4.2   The Simple Reflective Response

Client: Like I'm really flying in there – like flying through into that big black room. I'm not scared now ... I like the dark ...

Counsellor: So you're going into that dark place ... really fast ... and it feels different ... not scary now ... even pleasant ...

Client: Yeah ...

In Box 4.2 the counsellor's response shows that she has heard the client's words, but the response is not likely to communicate with certainty that she fully understands what he is experiencing. This response, alone, will not necessarily have an impact upon the client. But, if the client feels the counsellor's understanding consistently over an interactive sequence, he will feel involved in a *process* of empathy with his counsellor.

If research is to examine the *process* of empathy, then it must take into account not only the verbal response of the counsellor and how this is perceived by the client, but also the interaction sequence which has led up to that response and the shared understandings that have been built up in previous sessions. If research truly considers all this relevant behaviour and experience then it may begin to encompass the process nature of empathy and its power. Otherwise, it is an oversimple reductionist pastime that can only look at the 'communication skill' aspect of empathy.

In summary, then, empathy is not a 'technique' of responding to the client, but a way-of-being-in-relation to the client. Empathy often feels like being on the same train, or rollercoaster, as the client! The counsellor is joining and staying with, the client's journey, no matter how bumpy it is. Sometimes that journey feels smooth and at other times the traveller stops and starts, goes down blind alleys, gets stuck and feels confused. Such journeys contain the same qualities of immediacy and intensity whether they are in the playroom with a six-year-old, in the locked ward with a schizophrenic, or in the student counselling office with a student who cannot decide whether or not to leave university. Empathy is like a cine-film whereas empathic responses are still photographs of that moving process. In the beginning, however, examining the stills is one place to start; the trainee counsellor may well gain from exploring different examples of empathic responses.

An Empathy Scale

For such beginnings the notion of an *empathy scale* can be helpful. The empathy scale only focuses on the counsellor's empathic responses, but it is a useful way of appreciating that there can be different degrees of empathic accuracy. For the skilled counsellor who is familiar with her client's paths, it is relatively easy to stay fully in the empathic process, but for the trainee counsellor, finding the paths of her client involves considerable effort, some successes, some failures and some partial successes. The empathy scale communicates this notion of hitting, missing and partially hitting.

Truax and Carkhuff (1967) developed sophisticated eight-point scales of empathy. These were used not only in research but also in training as a means of rating the level of empathy the counsellor's response had exhibited on audio-taped interviews. Discussing these ratings, and the other possible responses the trainee counsellor might have made, could help to expand the trainee's repertoire of ways of communicating her empathy.

For our purposes a four-point empathy scale is sufficient to illustrate variety among empathic responses. On such a scale the different levels might represent the following:

Level 0: This is a response that shows no evidence of understanding of the client's expressed feelings. It may be a comment that is irrelevant to the client's feelings, or perhaps a judgemental response, advice-giving, hurtful or rejecting.

Level 1: This response shows a partial understanding of those feelings and responses that are very much on the surface for the client. Sometimes this level of empathy is called *subtractive* in the sense that the listener has lost something of the client's experience in the response she has given.

Level 2: In this response the listener is showing an understanding of the feelings and thoughts that the client has been expressing. This level is sometimes called *accurate empathy*.

Level 3: This response shows an understanding of the client beyond the level of the client's immediate awareness. As well as communicating comprehension of the surface feelings and responses of the client, the listener is showing an understanding that there are also *underlying* feelings. This is sometimes called *additive* empathy, but is more commonly referred to as a *depth reflection*.

These different levels are illustrated by the following example from counselling practice. The actual response the counsellor made was the one that is given at Level 3. However, as well as reproducing this response, we have constructed other possible responses that might indicate the different levels.

Example

In this extract the client is a mature student whose self-esteem has grown considerably upon discovering that she is both a popular and a highly competent student. However, she has become very unhappy with the pattern in her relationship with her husband. Through gritted teeth she says:

> He treats me like a baby – looking after me all the time, mollycoddling me all the time … *suffocating* me! He fails to realise that since I've come to university I am not such a baby any more … I'm independent … I'm strong.

Possible responses at each of the four levels might be:

Level 0:   *Men are all the same – you're better rid of them!*   As well as being an irrelevant and judgemental response that gives advice extremely early, this response does not seem to show an understanding of the client as a person. It is more the kind of response that a friend or acquaintance might give if they do not really want the client to go deeper into her feelings.

Level 1:   *God, that must be hard.*   This response seems to show a partial understanding of the client's feelings. At least the counsellor understands the seriousness and difficulty that the client is experiencing, though the quality of her feelings is not being reflected in this *subtractive* response.

Level 2:   *It's like he doesn't understand you … how you're changing … he still treats you like he used to, which may have been OK then, but not now … and you're damned angry at that.*   Here the counsellor's response is accurately reflecting back both the quality and the intensity of the client's feelings. This sensitive response has not only taken into account the client's words but has also encompassed the anger which was clearly evident by the client gritting her teeth as she spoke. The fact that the counsellor has pushed the client's response back to her in the counsellor's own words rather than hers is further confirmation of understanding.

Level 3:   *I see your anger that he doesn't understand that you're changing … that seems really really strong … but I also wonder … you look as though you're trembling … is that trembling just your anger or is there something else going on in you as well?*   In the actual counselling session from which this extract is taken, this response by the counsellor elicited a long silence from the client as it touched the edge of her awareness. Following this silence the client responded with what was to prove a very powerful discovery: 'yes … yes, I'm *scared* … I'm scared I'll lose him'. In this particular case the depth reflection proved important since it helped the client become aware that not only was she *angry* at her husband, but she was also extremely *scared* at the possibility of their breaking up. The client later traced this fear to the fact that while she was certainly becoming more and more independent, she was not all the way along that road yet.

Sometimes the counsellor's attempts at a Level 3 empathic response will fall on stony ground. For instance, in the above example the client might have reflected on the counsellor's statement and replied: 'No, I'm just damned angry at him!' This response would indicate one of two things: either the counsellor was correctly sensing something underlying the surface feelings but the client was not yet able to become aware of it or express it, or the counsellor was wrong. It does not really matter which of these is the case since the person-centred counsellor would be likely to drop it for the time being at least. Metaphorically, the person-centred counsellor wants to 'knock on the client's door' at a deeper level of his experiencing but she does not want to knock the door down.

As we mentioned earlier, looking at empathic responses can be illuminating since they take a very concrete form, but it does carry the danger that the trainee counsellor might assume that there are perfect responses which can suit any occasion. The response that the counsellor made at Level 3 in the above example very much fitted her relationship with that client. The client trusted and respected the counsellor, and was by no means overawed by her, but exactly the same response to exactly the same words of another client might not be empathic. In the example, the power of empathy was there because the counsellor sensed something else at the edge of the client's awareness: *that sensing was the empathy*. The words, that is to say, the empathic response, merely signposted the ongoing process of empathy. For trainee counsellors merely to rehearse responses like the one under consideration would be a totally meaningless activity, because they would have detached the words from the sensing. The words are not important – the same sensing that happened in the above example might have been communicated in a hundred different ways by the counsellor. For instance the counsellor might have leaned forward and held the client's hand in attentive silence. Such a non-verbal but powerful response might have helped the client to get in touch with the edge of her awareness.

The written word cannot adequately reproduce examples of empathy that involve the non-verbal, expressive behaviour of client and counsellor. The depth reflection relies greatly on the counsellor's sensitivity to the significance *for that client* of such expressive behaviour as a lowered head, a cracking voice, a clenched fist, a fixed gaze or a shiver. The client's whole communication consists of his words and his expressive behaviour. Sometimes these two aspects may even be giving different messages and the counsellor's depth reflection will likely reflect that difference; for example: 'You are *saying* that you are coping better now, but you also sound very tense ... is it really OK now?' This issue of the client's contradictory verbal and non-verbal behaviour is also explored in the section on *disguises and clues* in Chapter 7.

The counsellor's expressive behaviour is an important part of her empathic response, particularly in the case of depth reflections, for instance: the softness of her voice may be what reflects the quality of the client's experience more than the actual words the counsellor chooses, or perhaps it is the way the counsellor lowers her head, shows a faltering in her voice, clenches her fist, offers a fixed gaze, or shivers, which communicates the depth of her understanding.

While the depth reflection represents an impressive level of empathy, it is by no means the most frequent mode of response of the counsellor; responses at Levels 1 and 2 are much more common. At these levels the counsellor is showing a willingness to follow the consciousness of the client with varying degrees of success, while at Level 3 she is actually slightly ahead of that consciousness. Nevertheless, Levels 1 and 2 are the food and drink of counselling sessions. They enable the counsellor and client to monitor the closeness of their journey. Even a response at Level 1 may be enough to show the client that the counsellor is willing and also struggling to understand – often that willingness and struggle are appreciated as much as anything else.

Even where the counsellor expresses only a *partial* understanding of the client's experience, more often than not the client then goes on to clarify that experience both for the counsellor and incidentally for himself, for instance:

CLIENT: I feel I am in a real bind with it. Like I can't give up the job because it's too risky – I just don't know what will happen – it could be really desperate. And on the other hand I can't stay in the job because it's slowly and steadily destroying me – and that destruction is getting really critical.

COUNSELLOR: So it's a really difficult decision to make?

CLIENT: It's not just that it's a difficult decision to make ... [*pause*] ... it's an *impossible* decision to make – it's like I'm getting so desperate with fear that I can't move at all ... It's like this is the first time I've ever seen hope for myself and the first time that I've ever thought seriously about leaving the job ... And of course this is also the first time I've been so stuck in all my life.

In the above extract the counsellor has only shown a partial understanding of the intensity of the client's experience but, as often happens, the client then helped them both along and, in so doing, he realised the 'impossibility' he was experiencing.

Empathy and Locus of Evaluation

The person-centred counsellor is sensitive to her clients and their differences as well as to the influence of her own power. One important dimension of difference among clients is their *locus of evaluation* described in Chapter 1. The counsellor using her sensitivity will find that she communicates her empathy quite differently to a client with an *externalised* locus of evaluation compared to one whose locus is fairly *internalised*. The client with an externalised locus is extremely vulnerable to the evaluations others place upon him. He is in the thoroughly frightening position of not being able to trust his judgements of himself; in an extreme case he cannot even trust his judgements of his own feelings. This can be a terrifying situation and one in which he desperately grasps hold of even the possibility of an evaluation offered by another person. With this client, the counsellor's sensitivity would lead her to be wary of the potential invasiveness of her additive empathy. Most particularly she would not *name* any underlying feelings she might be experiencing in the client, for her client would have to accept these labels as truth – he would not have the reviewing and editing facility of the client whose locus of evaluation is more internalised. Box 4.3 gives an example of the way the counsellor's responses would take into account the client's locus of evaluation. Further exploration of the importance of being sensitive to the client's locus of evaluation is provided in Mearns (2003: 80–3), where a link is drawn to the danger of inducing *false memories* in such vulnerable clients.

Box 4.3 Empathy Sensitive to Locus of Evaluation	

The client, Adrienne, has a profoundly externalised locus of evaluation – it is difficult for her to make judgements even about her own experiencing. We present her statement with possible responses from incompetent and competent counsellors.

Adrienne:	I only have very hazy memories of what was, perhaps, 'abuse'. In fact, I don't even know that they *are* memories – maybe I'm just imagining them. I have feelings too, but they are all over the place as well. I feel a lot of sadness – well, I cry a lot, so I imagine I must have a lot of sadness. I get frustrated a lot … but I'm not sure whether my frustration is at others or at me.
Incompetent Counsellor:	How about anger? Is anger one of your feelings? [This person, who is trying to be a counsellor, has been on a course about 'adult survivors of childhood abuse'. She has learned that anger is often a repressed or suppressed emotion and that part of the process of healing is the client expressing that anger. Unfortunately, in the case of a client with an externalised locus of evaluation, this question is invasive and may lead the client to presume that she *must* be angry or *should* be angry. The client may even feel worse about herself because she is unable to access this presumed anger.]
Competent Counsellor:	Memories that may not be memories … crying that may be sadness … and frustration which may be at others or at yourself. What are you feeling *right now* … as you talk about this? [The person-centred counsellor is not directive about *what* the client is expressing but she may offer a *process direction* (Rennie, 1998) which, in this case, invites the client to come into the present and focus upon her feelings in the moment. In so doing, the counsellor is also inviting the client to exercise herself as her locus of evaluation.]

Why and How is Empathy Important in Counselling?

The fact that empathy correlates with effective counselling is well established in research down through the years (Barrett-Lennard, 1962; Lorr,

1965; Truax and Mitchell, 1971; Gurman, 1977; Patterson, 1984; Sachse, 1990; Lafferty, Beutler and Crago, 1991; Burns and Nolen-Hoeksema, 1991; Orlinsky, Grawe and Parks, 1994; Duncan and Moynihan, 1994). Such positive findings are consistent across countries (Tausch et al., 1970, 1972) and even in research studies examining other therapeutic approaches, for example cognitive therapy (Burns and Nolen-Hoeksema, 1991) and short term dynamic therapy (Vaillant, 1994). The significance extends not only to work with so-called neurotic clients but also to those with a schizophrenic diagnosis (Rogers, 1967). Indeed, in this last research, not only was a high level of accurate empathy related to a significant reduction in schizophrenic pathology, but those patients in relationships where empathy was very low showed a slight *increase* in their schizophrenic pathology (1967: 85–6). This suggests not only that with profoundly disturbed clients the presence of empathy is helpful, but that counsellors who fail to create the empathic process may actually be damaging. This evidence for the significance of empathy is supported by the fact that experienced practitioners across a range of counselling disciplines show similar attention to the empathic process (Fiedler, 1950; Raskin, 1974).

However, *why* empathy has such positive effects is more open to discussion. Certainly, empathy communicates the counsellor's understanding of the client and this fact alone might increase the client's self-esteem ('Gosh, I'm understandable!'). Perhaps, as we suggested in the opening chapter, it is the counsellor's willingness to *struggle* to understand the client that contributes to its effect ('I am important enough for this person to struggle to understand me'). In a few cases the importance of empathy may be that it dissolves alienation, for it is almost impossible to maintain an alienated position in the face of someone who is showing you profound understanding at a very personal level. It may represent a somewhat cynical point of view, but in some cases the importance of the counsellor's empathy may have to do with the fact that the client has seldom experienced such a gift from other helpers. ('Here's someone who's actually trying to understand me … someone who isn't just fitting me into her pet theories instead of really listening to me'). If the reasons why empathy is effective can be varied, so too can be the *process* by which it exerts its influence. Certainly one effect of empathy is that, by focusing on the client's surface and underlying feelings, his awareness of these is increased. Becoming aware of feelings that were earlier denied is the first step in taking responsibility for them and their implications. For instance, a woman might become aware of her underlying feelings of anger towards her husband, where formerly that anger had been denied and experienced only as 'irritation'. Another consequence of empathy which is well established in research is that it tends to encourage further and deeper exploration on the part of the client (Tausch et al., 1970; Bergin and Strupp, 1972; Kurtz and Grummon, 1972). In other words, when the counsellor shows that she understands the feelings and thoughts being expressed by the client, a natural step for the client seems to be to unfold ever-deepening levels of his *awareness*. Obviously the feeling of being understood will contribute to this, but much of the effect might also be understood in terms of the empathic process encouraging the client's 'self agency' (Bohart, 2004; Bohart and Tallman, 1999) as described at the end of Chapter 3. It is not counsellors who change clients – counsellors help clients to find their agency and initiate their own changing process. The counsellor's empathy is active in facilitating the client's agency. Empathy always asks a question of the client – it is never an answer to the client. Implicitly the counsellor's empathy asks the client to reflect on his experiencing and to come to his own judgements about his process. The person-centred counsellor shows her awareness of this awakening function of empathy even in the way she presents her words. Rather than encouraging closure by being definite and conclusive, for instance: 'so you feel angry about that', the counsellor may encourage further exploration by being more tentative and questioning: 'so ... you feel ... "angry" about that?' In delivering this as a tentative question the counsellor is not only checking her understanding but implicitly encouraging the client to move on by considering what else is present at the edge of his awareness. In so doing she is entering a particular area of expertise within empathy – *focusing*.

Focusing on the 'Edge of Awareness'

Already in this chapter we have referred to *focusing* and *the edge of awareness*. In using these terms we are recognising the striking contribution made by Eugene T. Gendlin to our understanding of the empathic process (Gendlin, 1981, 1984, 1996). Gendlin points out that what is important is not the feeling that the client is currently experiencing about an event, but the underlying feelings and responses of which the client is not yet quite aware. Already in our examples of *depth reflections* we have seen how significant underlying feelings can be. Sometimes such feelings are compatible with the current surface feeling and merely supplement it. However, on other occasions, the underlying feeling might be quite opposite to what is being experienced on the surface. For instance, a client may show superficial polite acquiescence towards an event while simultaneously, and not quite consciously, he is seething rebelliously underneath. At other times the underlying feeling is neither compatible with, nor opposite to, the surface feelings, but instead raises a whole new way of looking at the event. For example, what seemed on the surface to be a difficulty in making a practical decision turns out to be concealing an intense fear of loss. In all these examples recognition of the underlying feeling is important for progress.

Gendlin takes this further by pointing out that what underlies our surface feelings cannot always properly be described as a feeling in itself – sometimes it is less clear and less intense than a feeling and is better described as a *sensation*. It might be a sensation such as 'tightness', 'blackness', 'falling', 'a welling-up', 'stuckness', 'softness', or 'warmth'. Gendlin uses the term *felt sense* to talk about that edge of our awareness between the known and the unknown. The 'known' would be the client's surface feelings and other behavioural responses to the event, while the 'unknown' could include all sorts of deeper levels of feelings, associations with earlier events, or future aspirations. The known is readily available, but the unknown is not tapped simply by focusing on the known. Instead the appropriate focus is on the edge of awareness between the known and the unknown. Simply focusing on the known surface feelings may only be going over old ground, whereas focusing on the edge (the felt sense) can be the door to the unknown. In Box 4.3 the second counsellor invited the client to focus upon the edge of her present awareness rather than staying at the level of *rehearsed material*, as Rogers called it (Rogers, 1977).

In her empathic journey with the client, the counsellor may frequently be attending to what the client is saying and the feelings which accompany that, but being fully *with* the client will imply that the counsellor is attending to, and checking on, the client's felt sense of the issue as well. The easy movement from one to the other is illustrated in Box 4.4. In this box both the counsellor and the client try to find what Gendlin calls *handle-words* to fit the felt sense. First the counsellor tries 'tightness' to describe the sensation epitomised by the client's screwing up of his face and body. The client tries out this handle 'tightness' by repeating it for himself. Gendlin talks about the client *resonating* the handle-word with the underlying sensation. In our extract the client then improves the handle-word to a 'screwing up' and then further improves it to 'being wound up'. At this point the client has reached his felt sense, which then opens the door to the fear expressed by his metaphor of the clockwork toy. In a very short time the client has gone from the known – which was his excitement through his felt sense of being wound up – to the unknown which was his fear that all his activity might make no difference to his life.

Box 4.4   Attending to the Client's Felt Sense

Counsellor: You've made lots and lots of plans since we last met. I can see that you're excited by that ... but is that all you feel? Do you feel anything else when you consider your plans?

Client: [*pause*] No, I am just excited – and really looking forward to making a change [*pause*]. But [*long pause*] I do feel something else ... but it's not very clear ... it's a kind of [*screws up his face and his upper body*] ...

Counsellor: ... a kind of ... 'tightness'?

Client: Yes – a tightness – a screwing up ... like I'm being wound up like a children's wind-up toy – like I'm going to burst into action – frenetic action ... and then maybe stop like the toy, and everything will be the same as it was [*he shivers violently*]!

Sometimes handle-words take the form of *metaphors*, like the client's metaphor of the wind-up toy in Box 4.4. It is fascinating how metaphors often describe the quality and intensity of sensations more fully than single words or phrases. Even more amazing is the fact that metaphors can be culturally shared, for instance: *It feels as though the big boys have just stolen my new toy.* Almost universally, in western cultures at least, this metaphor communicates a sense of loss far overshadowed by violation.

The felt sense of an issue can be likened to its *flavour* in that, whether we are focusing on the whole issue or only on a tiny part of it, the felt sense is the same. This quality of the felt sense is illustrated in Box 4.5.

| Box 4.5 | The 'Flavour' of the Felt Sense |

In this extract Donald, the client, has for some time been getting blocked in talking about his relationship with his wife. The counsellor moves him from thinking about his relationship in wide general terms to focusing on just one aspect of it: his imminent holiday with his wife. Focusing on this one small concrete element enables Donald to see the *flavour* of his felt sense of the relationship with his wife.

Donald: I suppose Helen and I get on OK really. We have achieved quite a lot in our marriage – and the kids seem happy enough people. Maybe we can do more together now that the kids are up and away from home.

Counsellor: One thing you're going to do together is go on that holiday. I remember you said that this was going to be the first time that you have been on holiday together, alone, for more than twenty years. What do you feel when you reflect upon that holiday? ... Maybe take a few moments just to focus on that.

Donald: [*pause*] [*Donald sits rigidly up in his seat*] I feel ... scared ... terrified ... it's horrible – it's like I'm going to choke ... 'suffocate'.

Donald: [*some minutes later*] ... of course it's not just about the holiday – it's just that that throws our relationship into sharp focus. It's really that I have no idea what our relationship is going to be like. It's so long since we have just been with each other. I am so scared that I'm going to find it suffocating – that all the restrictions we've built up while having the kids will still be there even though they aren't ... that there will be nothing else left that's healthy.

In listening to her client the counsellor is trying to *echo* the client's felt sense so that he can hear it. The client can reflect on the counsellor's words and how far they seem to resonate with his felt sense. Often it helps if the client re-states the words for himself; indeed it is interesting how often a client will actually say the words again for himself as though he were sounding them out to see if they resonated with his felt sense. Perhaps they do, or perhaps he can improve them. When the right handle-words have been found, their resonance with the felt sense is usually experienced by the client as a release of tension. Indeed, often the client actually exhales deeply or expresses that relief in words. Gendlin also talks about *the body talking back*. This applies when there is a distinct lack of resonance between what the client is saying to himself and what his felt sense actually is. There was an illustration of this in Box 4.4 when the client paused, tried to contact his felt sense, but then said 'no – I am just excited'. These words clearly did not fit his felt sense, as was later evident. In saying this to himself it is likely that his body would have reacted to the lack of fit. Sometimes this is experienced as a sudden tension or just a powerful experience of wrongness. This *talking-back* has many striking parallels. For instance, a similar kind of phenomenon sometimes happens to people when they have very important decisions to make. Often it is only when people actually make a decision that they realise just how important the other choice is to them. For instance, when a couple finally decide that they will definitely separate, that is often the very time when one or both of them realise that deep down they really want to be together. Sometimes people also report a similar kind of phenomenon when they have come closest to taking their own life. It is only when they have been at the very point of choosing to end their life that they have the clarity of sensing that they do not want that.

While *focusing* is a distinct process in itself that has relevance in a wide range of human contexts, it is also a natural aspect of person-centred counselling. The counsellor implicitly invites her client to reflect on his current experiencing, often by very simple means. Even reflecting the client's own words in exactly the same form presents him with a mirror to himself and allows him to sense any underlying experiencing. Counsellors of other disciplines often miss the potency of this kind of reflection. On paper it can look like a simple parroting of the client's words. But, if it stems from the empathic sensitivity of the counsellor, it carries the power to help the client to get in touch with his own experiencing, at the edge of his awareness, as in the following example:

> CLIENT: … so … I just feel a bit depressed about it all … that's all.
> COUNSELLOR: … so … you just feel a bit depressed about it all … that's all.
> CLIENT: [*pause*] … shit … that's not right at all … I'm totally *devastated* about it.

In this example the counsellor has simply pushed the client's expression back to him, but she has done that because her sensitivity to his experiencing has told her that he is considerably understating the impact upon him (see Mearns, 2003: 84–7 for a fuller consideration of the counsellor's empathic reflections assisting the client's focusing).

Not Needing to Understand

A common misunderstanding in counselling is that it is important that the counsellor *understands* what the client is saying and that that is what empathy is about. In fact, the counsellor's understanding is not the aim of the endeavour – the aim is to create the conditions where the client comes to understand himself. Early in training, counsellors can be found interrupting the client's flow to check their own understanding. Generally their client politely affirms or corrects the counsellor's understanding and then tries to get back on to his track.

The counsellor's empathy will contribute more strongly towards the establishment of relational depth if she focuses upon trying to get close to her client's current *experiencing* more than simply understanding his words. It is more powerful for the client to feel that the counsellor is really close to him in this moment – that the counsellor is actually sensing how it feels to be him – than that the counsellor is understanding his narrative.

Consider the following two empathic responses:

RICHARD: I don't know where to go with this decision – I'm torn apart with it [*dips head and begins to cry*]. On the one hand I need to leave Robert. On the other hand I can't leave him. I need to leave him so that I can survive [*clenches and shakes fist*] – the weight of our relationship is too much for me to bear. But I can't leave him because it might kill him and I couldn't live with that [*shakes head and cries*]. What can I do? What on earth can I do? [*looks at counsellor*] What would *you* do?

COUNSELLOR A: Like it's a really difficult decision – to leave him or not – you can't win either way. And you wonder what I would do – is that right?

COUNSELLOR B: It is tearing you apart – I can feel that in you. You crave to be free – but at what consequences might that be – you shake your head and you cry – you feel it terribly. And you ask me to share the weight of it with you.

It is not the fact that response A is shorter than B and more subtractive. The key difference that is likely to be *felt* by Richard is that counsellor B is much closer to his felt experiencing. She *feels* his experiencing and is able to verbalise that rather than simply show an understanding of his words. This is what will contribute significantly towards the establishing of relational depth.

The person-centred approach has done more than most other orientations in exploring empathy in situations where understanding the client's communication is virtually impossible (Zinschitz, 2001). For example, in work with traumatised clients the trauma experience can be so powerful or so bizarre that the counsellor would struggle if she had to understand the client's words. In Box 4.6 we present an example from an earlier book (Mearns and Thorne, 2000: 129–30).

Box 4.6   Listening to the Expressing

Tony was in pain. He had been sitting on the floor in a corner of the group room all morning, crying. This was new for Tony – crying was new. More characteristic for Tony was *either* extreme gregariousness *or* complete silence. Tony was twenty-three years of age and a 'veteran' of two tours in Vietnam. He had not spoken about his experiences in war. Tony's therapist, Bill, was sitting on the floor beside him, very close but not touching. For an hour nothing had been said between them and the communication had been intense. Now Tony spoke for the first time:

Tony: I can't, I can't, I can't, I can't, I can't …
Bill: No, … you can't.
Tony: No-one can.
Bill: [*silence*]
Tony: [*Thumping his fist on the floor and screaming*] I need to kill myself.
Bill: [*silence*]
Tony: I need to go … I must go … I must go away from me.
Bill: [*silence*]
Tony: I don't know how to do it.
Bill: It's hard, Tony … It's hard … there's no way …
Tony: No way … no way … how do people do it?
Bill: God knows Tony.
Tony: Can you warm me Bill?
Bill: [*puts his arm round Tony*]

Much later Bill comments on this meeting:

It's an example of how you can be *with* someone and have conversation without having any idea what it's about. Yet all the time you can *feel* them – and be with them feeling. It was weeks later that I found out the 'content' of this meeting. Tony was *being* the part of him which had done some bad stuff. In war people can do bad stuff that they can't live with later. Tony was *feeling* that part – he wanted to get rid of it – to kill it or for it to go away – to 'exorcise' it might be a good metaphor. But, of course, there was no way to do it – that's what we were in.

In Box 4.6, if Bill had felt he needed to understand Tony's words he would not have got far. Yet he could still be with Bill in a powerfully empathic way without understanding but by listening to his experiencing. In another case, reproduced as chapter 6 of Mearns and Cooper (2005), the counsellor is challenged to empathise with the traumatised client, Rick, during the first 26 sessions throughout which Rick is completely silent.

In the field of client-centred Pre-Therapy, the worker, who could be a counsellor, nurse or key-worker, is challenged to relate to people with severe communication difficulties, for example, those with profound learning difficulties or acute psychoses (Prouty, 1994; Pörtner, 2000; Lambers, 2003; Prouty, Van Werde and Pörtner, 2002; Van Werde, 2003a and b; Kreitemeyer and Prouty, 2003). Garry Prouty, the originator of Pre-Therapy, links the process firmly with empathy:

> The practice of Pre-Therapy is applied empathic contact … Pre-Therapy is a 'pointing at the concrete' … It is an extraordinarily literal and concrete form of empathic response. (Prouty, 2001: 158)

The system of Pre-Therapy teaches the worker how to respond initially in a very concrete empathic way to the specific behaviours the client is showing, or to the context in which they are meeting. Here the worker is seeking to help the client make closer contact with his experiencing and also to establish some psychological *contact* between the worker and the client in order that communication meaningful to the client's experiencing can continue and be developed. In his description of Pre-Therapy, Van Werde gives examples of different kinds of *reflection* that seek to establish contact, for example, *Situational Reflections* about elements of the context in which they are meeting; *Facial Reflections*, 'you smile'/'you look angry'; *Body Reflections*, 'you are rocking in your chair'; *Word-for-Word Reflections*, where the client's words are repeated; or *Reiterative Reflections*, which repeat reflections that were previously successful in order to strengthen the contact further (Van Werde, 2003b: 122). These may seem to represent very small, concrete steps but the work is with people whose emotional life has largely been neglected. In client-centred Pre-Therapy we have a system of communication that can be applied within the whole supportive context – the hospital ward, care home or familial home.

One of the interesting features of Pre-Therapy reflections is that counsellors tend to use them, naturally, when their client becomes communicatively cut-off. Without any background in Pre-Therapy, the counsellor will become more concrete with their client when the client becomes stuck: 'You are screwing up your face John'/'Mary, you are sitting up rigidly in your seat'/'You are staring out the window, William'. In following her client into the concrete the person-centred counsellor is using her sensitivity in trying to find new ground on which to meet him empathically. Empathy is all about releasing our sensitivity in relation to the other.

Releasing our Empathic Sensitivity

Are empathic counsellors born or made? There are a variety of assumptions about the basis of our empathic ability. Some people assume that we are either born with it or not. If this assumption were true then much of counsellor training would be superfluous – all that would be needed would be a way of selecting those who 'had it'. An opposite assumption is that empathic ability is wholly learned. This puts the emphasis much more on training than selection, since it becomes possible to 'train' any person to be empathic.

The writers take a stance which is only slightly different from this second position; we see empathy as the counsellor's own *intellectual and emotional sensitivity focused on the client*. This sensitivity has been developed through many years of observing and relating with people in life's varied contexts. Even the three-year-old has already developed sufficient sensitivity to judge her parent's mood and reaction to small misdemeanours. By the time adulthood is reached this sensitivity to others has been built upon literally millions of interpersonal encounters. Each one of us has this immense reservoir of sensitivity that, potentially, we can focus upon our client. Hence the object becomes one of *releasing this sensitivity*. The effect of training should be to help the counsellor to release her sensitivity more often, more fully, and with more variety, as she requires. We regard this gradual release of sensitivity as a developmental process in the counsellor – a process that can be facilitated by trainers, supervisors and counselling experience, but one that is essentially under the control of the counsellor. In the early stages of this development the issue for the counsellor may be her *willingness* to take the step of empathising. It is much easier – and *safer* – to stay within one's own frame of reference and pronounce upon the client's situation. Insofar as that procedure conforms precisely to the medical model the client may even expect and accept that level of un-involvement from the counsellor. But the potential person-centred counsellor is likely to be dissatisfied with such superficial contact, and more and more she will take risks with releasing her empathic sensitivity.

Research through the years has consistently supported the finding that experienced counsellors offer a higher degree of empathy to their clients than less experienced counsellors (Fiedler, 1949; Barrett-Lennard, 1962; Mullen and Abeles, 1972). But as well as experience being a variable so too is the degree of *integration* of the counsellor. At one extreme, a lack of personal development in the counsellor could result in weaker empathic understanding, but even feelings of discomfort and a lack of confidence in relationships reduce the counsellor's empathic understanding (Bergin and Jasper, 1969; Bergin and Solomon, 1970; Selfridge and van der Kolk, 1976). This last finding is particularly interesting because it reminds us that empathy is not necessarily a static quality that we exhibit regardless of circumstances. The counsellor's ability to draw upon her sensitivity, and have confidence in it, is dependent on the relationship the counsellor has with the client and also on how centred she is as a person. The counsellor *empties herself* in order to *receive* the client's experiencing, and it follows that whatever disturbs the stillness of the counsellor is likely to interfere with the release of her empathic sensitivity. Such factors are usually called *blocks to empathy*, a few of which are discussed in the following pages.

Blocks to Empathy

The Problem with Theory

Perhaps the most surprising block to the counsellor's empathy can be her own theories about human behaviour (see also Mearns, 1997a: 129–32). Any theory that she uses to predict individual human behaviour is a potential menace lying in wait to distract the counsellor from focusing her own highly developed sensitivity on the individual world of her client. Sometimes these theories have some basis in research and might be termed *psychological theories*, for instance:

- Depressed people can't think well.
- Less intelligent people will be less able to verbalise their problems.
- The client's anger or affection towards me will likely be signs of his transference.

Other theories have no basis in research, but may be held just as strongly; often these *personal theories* might take the form of prejudices:

- Rich people don't have *real* problems.
- Facing squarely up to difficulties is the best way to progress.
- Women are likely to be more vulnerable than men.

Both psychological theories and personal theories are useless for predicting the behaviour of an *individual* client. Even theories grounded in psychological research only reflect trends or averages in human behaviour: they cannot, with any reliability, tell us how a particular client will feel or behave. Rather than be seduced by theories it is more productive to empathise with our client in order to discover his individual and unique responses. Perhaps this is one of the reasons why some psychologists find the person-centred approach so difficult. They have to lay aside so many of their riches, their theories of human behaviour, before they can fully experience the individuality of their client.

But we all have theories about human behaviour, and to some degree we will have an emotional investment in their fulfilment. We shall not only expect them to be correct, but at an emotional level we may *need* them to be correct. For this reason a major emphasis in person-centred training is on the uncovering and challenging of personal theories. However, even when personal theories have become explicit, as Box 4.7 illustrates, they might still be a 'block' to the counsellor's understanding of an individual client.

Box 4.7   Personal Theories Can Get in the Way

A counsellor reports on her work with an earlier client:

I remember working with a client who was recently separated from her partner. I kept waiting and expecting to see some element of sadness or loss or depression – but none came. I kept thinking that I saw hints of such emotions, but she denied these. So then I began to think that she must be blocking all these things, and I tried to help her to find ways through these blocks. I think she got pretty fed up with that. It was only after some weeks of distinctly inaccurate empathy that I realised that what was getting in the way was my personal theory on what recently separated people felt: that they would feel sad/lost/depressed. It had been extremely difficult for me to see this lively cheery woman who wanted a little bit of assistance with restructuring a new set of elements in her life.

One particular kind of personal theory can be so disruptive of empathy that it deserves separate mention. This theory might be stated thus: 'If I have been in the same kind of situation as my client, then my client will probably experience it in a similar way to myself.' Having had such *common experiences* can often ease communication and make it easier to establish early trust between client and counsellor. To the extent that the experiences actually are similar, then empathy might also be assisted: the counsellor might make intelligent guesses as to what the client might be experiencing. However, the counsellor should also be aware that common experiences can sometimes prove a hindrance to counselling by actually making empathy more difficult. The danger is that the counsellor will begin to identify with the client's position. This might be called *false empathy* because it can look like empathy but in fact it is not. It is where the counsellor puts herself in the client's position and wrongly assumes that what *she* would feel in that position is what the client is in fact feeling.[3]

It is evident, then, that both psychological and personal theories can get in the way of the releasing of our empathic sensitivity. The counsellor's development will help her to become aware of the theories she holds and how they influence her perception of clients. Sometimes person-centred counsellors take this point as an argument that they should know as little as possible about the client and his life before they meet him – that any knowledge might become a block to their empathy. We believe that this is an unsophisticated position to adopt. A larger challenge to the counsellor is to allow such knowledge to stimulate their *imagination* about their client, so that they are prepared to encounter a wider range of experiences from him. The counsellor does not allow the information to define the client to her but, on the contrary, to expand the possibilities she is ready to entertain. One domain where the relevance of this attitude is evident is in empathy across cultural diversity. Lago (2006) rightly points out that her particular emphasis on empathy puts the person-centred counsellor in a strong position to meet her client from a different ethnic background. However, this can become a shortcut for some person-centred practitioners who then argue that it is not necessary for them to learn about the range of ethnic backgrounds of their clientele, or, worse, that they will

---

[3] At a sophisticated level of functioning the counsellor can make powerful therapeutic use of many of her personal self-experiences as 'existential touchstones' through which to make closer contact with her client (see Chapter 6). The difference is that she knows that such a self-experience is *not* her client's experience but simply a means of putting her (the counsellor) into a feeling state that will be more fully receptive of her client.

learn about their client's background from the client himself. This may seem to represent a logical argument but clients would certainly feel the burden of it. The result has been considerable writing to expose this person-centred deficit, not only in respect of ethnic diversity (Inayat, 2005; Khurane, 2006; Lago and Haugh, 2006) but also in work with the gay, lesbian, bisexual and transgender community, particularly well exposed in the 'Pink' series (Davies and Neal 1996, 2000; Neal and Davies, 2000). It seems clear to us that the person-centred counsellor should be craving knowledge about the diversity of her clientele. Indeed, this is a central thrust of the person-centred counsellor's ongoing developmental agenda – to broaden her awareness of humanity (Mearns, 2006b; Mearns and Cooper, 2005). For example, a study of the Islamic concept of the self (Inayat, 2005) introduces the counsellor to rich concepts such as *qalb* (the spiritual heart), *nafs* (the ego), *ruh* (the soul) and *fitra* (the divine potential) from a theology that is steeped in the notions of continuing personal development and responsibility to others. Certainly, such study would not tell the counsellor about her next Muslim client and, like any faith, there are variations too numerous to compute, but it would widen the counsellor's imagination and open her sensitivity to the potential differentness of her client's experiencing. Her client would also be pleased not to have to explain his faith concepts to yet another uninformed helper.

The Needs and Fears of the Counsellor

By far the most pervasive and troublesome blocks to the counsellor's empathy are *her own needs and fears* in the therapeutic relationship. 'Troubled people can't empathise' is a saying that is often applied to clients but sometimes it describes the counsellor as well. For instance, the counsellor's empathy might be blocked by such things as a mind temporarily preoccupied with other emergencies, by embarrassment, or perhaps even by a fear of the client's pain. Strong feelings of sympathy or antipathy towards the client can be blocks, making it difficult to stay in the troubled present of the client. Sometimes inexperienced counsellors are blocked by their need to see the client as 'improving in every session', or perhaps by a more generalised 'need to be helpful'. The main symptoms of this last dis-ease are that every session will have to end on a positive note; pain will never quite be faced; and empathic journeys will only follow safe and increasingly ineffective routes.

Where the counsellor has strong needs to be *liked* or *needed* by her client, stuckness is also likely to occur, as the fullness of the counsellor's empathic experience may be lost in competition with such forceful needs. In some such cases the counsellor is so linked through need with her client that she cannot be open to him changing because that changing might fundamentally affect herself. Every counselling approach recognises this dilemma as one of *over-involvement* (see Chapter 8). It is much more difficult to listen to someone whose change will affect oneself. One special case of this is in the counsellor's relationship with her partner. Often there is the implicit assumption that someone who spends her time listening to strangers should be particularly effective listening to her partner. But of course that is not so easy, because we are somewhat 'involved' with our partner. As we open ourself to listen to our partner's changing we may be hearing about our own life being about to change! Trainee counsellors sometimes give themselves a hard time with that kind of expectation.

Releasing one's empathic sensitivity is an act of giving. The counsellor is giving herself as a mirror to her client. In one of the last articles before his death, Carl Rogers (1986) reminded us of the importance of clarity in this mirror. He quotes from an earlier article by Sylvia Slack, who commented thus on a counselling session with him:

> It was like Dr Rogers was a magical mirror. The process involved my sending rays toward that mirror. I looked into the mirror to get a glimpse of the reality that I am. If I had sensed the mirror was affected by the rays being received, the reflection would have seemed distorted and not to be trusted. (Slack, 1985: 41)

When the counsellor is troubled – and therefore vulnerable – she does not so readily offer empathy and if she does it is likely to be distorted with her own turmoil. When one is vulnerable a normal response is to become *self-protective* – not to open oneself through empathy, but to withdraw and keep the client at a distance. As counsellors develop through training, experience and supervision, it is to be hoped that they become sufficiently *self-accepting* so that they have less need to be self-protective with clients. Part of the process of training and continued development as a person-centred counsellor is becoming aware of the personal factors that are likely to be blocks to skills such as empathy. Indeed, *personal development* is regarded as the fundamental dimension of training (Mearns, 1997a) and in Chapter 3 of this book we explored in some depth the key issue of the counsellor's self-acceptance.

Concentrating as we have on the notion of blocks to the release of our empathic sensitivity is a rather negative way of looking at the counsellor's development. We might equally well have described that development in terms of 'blocks overcome', for, as the counsellor grows in confidence and competence, she becomes able to release her empathic sensitivity in a wider variety of ways. She can trust, and therefore use, more and more of herself in relationship with her client. As this development progresses the three basic interpersonal dimensions of empathy, congruence and unconditional positive regard become more integrated until they are as they should be – inseparable.

Empathising with Different Parts of the Client

While the counsellor may be seeking this integration of her faculties, some of her clients may be showing distinct separation of different *parts* of their self. This notion of *self-pluralism* has been described in Chapter 2 and one of the encouraging features of the growing psychology of self-pluralism is that workers from a range of disciplines and orientations appear to be observing the same kind of phenomenon, albeit describing their observations in their various languages (Cooper et al., 2004).

The person-centred version of this psychology has coined the term *configurations* of the self and is detailed in Mearns and Thorne (2000: chapter 6) and the person-centred theory of therapy with configurations is laid out in chapter 7 of the same book. In this latter exploration there is a particular challenge for the person-centred counsellor in regard to her empathy. For example, how does she empathise with her client when different parts of the client are pushing in opposite directions and may even be in mortal combat? Consider the client, Arlene:

ARLENE: One part of me says that the only way I can be at peace is to kill myself. The other part is a snivelling coward screaming for mercy in a high-pitched little girl's voice. The more she screams the more I want to kill her – the more angry I get at her. I want to cut her throat and watch her bleed to death. I want to watch her beg, then smile and kill her.

Working with Arlene is a serious business, for her conflict is powerful and it may be dangerous to herself. One of the chilling possibilities in some suicides is that one part of the self is seeking to kill another. The fact that 50 per cent of those interviewed the day after a failed suicide attempt are thankful that they failed (O'Connor, Sheehy and O'Connor, 2000) makes us wonder just how prevalent is this dynamic. In this territory we would find a divergence among person-centred practitioners. With a client like Arlene, some would stay close to the principle of non-directivity and work with whatever part or parts presented themselves, in the trust that Arlene would come through to save and, indeed, enhance herself. Others, like the present authors, are not so trusting of the inevitability of that process. We would strive to make empathic contact with *both* these parts of Arlene in the, equally contestable, hope that if we can establish some sort of dialogue with all the parts, Arlene would make her decision from a more complete knowledge of herself. So, the person-centred discipline we espouse in working with parts of the self is to seek to empathise with *all* the parts, as is illustrated in the continuation of the dialogue with Arlene:

> DAVE: You really want to *destroy* her – but it's stronger than that – you want to see her suffering – you want her to know she is dying … and … you want her to *beg*.
>
> ARLENE: By God – she's got to beg. The bitch has got to beg. She got me fucked time and time again. She's got to beg … and then find that she is still going to bleed to death.
>
> DAVE: She must have done really bad stuff to you.
>
> ARLENE: Oh yes, oh yes.

It is important to note that, although Arlene's characterisation of these different parts of her self is strong, she is not dissociating. The parts are not so separate and personified, and there is no information blockage between them as there would be in dissociated process (Ross, 1999; Warner, 2000). She is simply, but powerfully, manifesting a conflict within her.

The worst thing the counsellor can do in this situation is to become frightened and immobilised by the power of this conflict or try to close it down. Arlene is expressing dangerous things, but she is doing that in the context of her relationship with the counsellor. That offers more hope than if she were isolated and not having the dialogue.

In the dialogue thus far, the counsellor is seeking to empathise with that part of Arlene who wants to destroy the other part. That dialogue led to the later disclosure that Arlene had had a pattern of getting into relationships where she would, eventually, be abused. However, the other part of Arlene has not yet had a voice in the session and it is important that she does. The responsibility of the person-centred counsellor is to the *whole* of the client, not just to the loudest voice. So, at a later point in the session, we find the following exchange:

DAVE: Arlene, we've heard a lot about your resentment about that part of you that got you into so much trouble – no, 'resentment' is not right – your *hate* of that part. Yet, she is part of you. I wonder where she was coming from?

ARLENE: The fucking bitch was a whore – she *is* a whore.

DAVE: She is still there – still here – still part of you, but … by God you hate her … you *really* hate her …

ARLENE: SILENCE

DAVE: SILENCE

ARLENE: She is crying.

DAVE: SILENCE

ARLENE: She only did what she could only do.

The reader will sense that there is so much more to this. But Arlene has taken us far enough to make our point. The person-centred discipline, as espoused by the present authors, is to seek to empathise with the *whole* of our client. Sometimes, where our client symbolises their 'self' in terms of different parts, this requires a discipline of seeking empathic contact with the different parts. This can mean the kind of negotiation exemplified in the work with Arlene. But it is more than mere 'negotiation' – it is the humanity of the counsellor reaching out, not just to one part, but to the whole of the humanity of her client.

5

UNCONDITIONAL POSITIVE REGARD

If it was difficult to restrict the process of empathy to specific behavioural responses, unconditional positive regard is just as elusive since it is an *attitude* of the counsellor. However, it is possible to define this attitude in fairly straightforward language:

> Unconditional positive regard is the label given to the fundamental attitude of the person-centred counsellor towards her client. The counsellor who holds this attitude deeply values the humanity of her client and is not deflected in that valuing by any particular client behaviours. The attitude manifests itself in the counsellor's consistent acceptance of and enduring warmth towards her client.

The distinctiveness of this attitude in the person-centred approach lies in its consistency. The person-centred counsellor is able to manifest the attitude with the whole range of clients regardless of how they behave. It is easy to value the client who works hard and shows a lasting respect for the helper but the attitude is more challenged where the client is repeatedly self-defeating, sees himself as worthless, actively manipulates other people to their detriment, or masks his vulnerability with direct aggression towards the helper. This attitude of acceptance towards the client is not only consistent from client to client but endures throughout the person-centred counsellor's relationship with any one client. The client feels that the counsellor values him consistently throughout their relationship, despite the fact that he may not value himself and even if the counsellor does not like or approve of all the client's behaviour. It is possible to accept the client as a person of worth while still not liking some of the things he does. Often this basic acceptance will be severely tested by clients whose outward behaviour may at times be very unpleasant. Box 5.1 gives an example of one such client who was difficult to appreciate, but whose behaviour became understandable once the counsellor was able to make the step of acceptance.

Box 5.1   A Nothing Person Who Is Scared to Love

Mary was a teacher who came to the counsellor on the recommendation of a friend. Throughout the first interview she remained cold, somewhat aloof and not particularly enthusiastic about what counselling could offer her. She talked with relish about her hatred of schoolchildren:

> I hate the little —s. They come in every day laughing at you. When you shout at them they snigger and go quiet for no more than a minute. To try to teach them French is pointless: all I try to do is teach them the rudiments of polite behaviour, albeit in French. Probably the only pleasure I get is making them squirm. Some of them are so cocky you shouldn't take them on, but you can do a good job on some of the little ones. I take great delight in making them cry.

Most people would be offended at the brutality of this teacher's attitude towards young children. A normal reaction would be to dismiss her attitude as unacceptable and endeavour to get her to rethink the morality of continuing in the profession. However, making such judgements is not the job of the counsellor, for these would merely close communication rather than deepen it. Accepting that this violent behaviour does not represent the whole of the human being helps the counsellor to stay interested, concerned and even warm towards her. In the third counselling session we discover something that helps to make sense of this teacher's outward violence towards others when she says:

> I get so sad sometimes ... so very sad. I never can show that to anyone. I just cry alone in my flat. I can be so horrible with people ... it's just that I'm scared of them ... I suppose I'm scared they'll see me ... me as I really am ... a nothing person who is scared to love.

There are many words used to describe this attitude. Already we have referred to *unconditional positive regard* and *acceptance*. Another term that was once widely used is *non-possessive warmth*, and *respect* has on occasions been a preferred label, although it does not in itself describe many of the essential features of the dimension: it is possible for instance to respect someone quite coldly and conditionally. A word Carl Rogers used to represent this dimension was *prizing*. In his American context this was a good choice since it communicated a greater intensity of feeling than most of the other terms. Similarly, David Cain (1987) uses the word *affirming* to emphasise the function this attitude serves for the client – it 'affirms' his value. One word that is *not* an appropriate label for this dimension is *liking*. This difference is important for trainees to whom the thought of liking every client who comes through the door does not make sense. As is described elsewhere (Mearns, 2003: 3–5), 'liking' in our culture is a highly conditional matter. We generally attribute our liking to someone who shows similar or complementary values to our own. Our liking is thus conditional on that similarity or complementarity. However, *valuing* the client as a person of worth is not conditional – it is equally possible to feel that deep valuing of the humanity of a person who displays a pattern of values quite different from our own. Box 5.2 reproduces an anonymised quotation from a person-centred counsellor as she describes this difference between liking and valuing in relation to her client who is a prominent politician.

Box 5.2   I Don't Like Him But I Care for Him Deeply

When I hear him on the radio or see him on television I have two reactions, side by side. I grimace, shake my head and scowl at his right-wing policies and statements. I feel he is thoroughly heartless – completely unconcerned with the pain the poor are in. But, at the same time, I often find that I have a smile. I know him pretty well. I know that, while he sounds absolutely confident, he will have been pacing up and down with nervous anxiety before the interview. I also know he has a heart – it may be in a different place from mine – but he has one. He really *believes* his bullshit ('bullshit' to *me*, that is). He genuinely believes that people will be helped, in the long run, by being left to their own devices and not mollycoddled (his word). He is sincere and as well as that, he has integrity – he says what he believes and he is consistent in his beliefs. Although I would never vote for him I think he is trustworthy – a quality that would challenge many in my own party. I don't like him, but I care for him deeply.

While the difference between *liking* and *valuing* is important for counsellors, the distinction is generally lost on clients who tend to use the word 'liking' rather than our more esoteric alternatives.

Why is Unconditional Positive Regard Important?

The client who has been reared under oppressive *conditions of worth* (see Chapter 1) will have learned that he has value only insofar as he behaves in accordance with the expectations of significant others. Unconditional positive regard on the part of the counsellor towards her client is important because it directly sabotages such conditions of worth: the counsellor values her client irrespective of the client's conforming to 'conditions'. Lietaer (1984) uses the term *counterconditioning* to describe the process set in motion by a counsellor's unconditional positive regard: the conditioned link between meeting conditions of worth and being valued is broken by continually treating the client as valuable in his own right, regardless of whether he meets the conditions of worth set out for him in his life.

In sabotaging conditions of worth, unconditional positive regard breaks into the client's negative, self-defeating cycle (see Figure 5.1). The client who is lacking self-acceptance behaves in a way which reflects that attitude: he does not expect people to value him, so in relation to others he is particularly *self-protective*. He may appear weak, inappropriately aggressive, unemotional, or perhaps he tends to withdraw from intense social contact. Behaviours such as these are scarcely welcoming for other people, and may indeed drive them away, a fact that offers further evidence to the client that he is unloved and unlovable. Unconditional positive regard breaks into this cycle as the counsellor refuses to be deflected by the client's self-protective behaviour and instead offers the client consistent acceptance of his intrinsic worth.

This different behaviour of the counsellor has effects on the client's behaviour in the relationship. Since there is now no need for the client to be self-protective in relationship with the counsellor he begins to feel safe enough to disclose more about himself and explore his experiences more deeply.

As well as having influence through contradicting conditions of worth and helping the client to feel less need to protect himself, the counsellor's unconditional positive regard has a much more direct impact upon the client's valuing of himself. In a sense the client becomes *contaminated* by

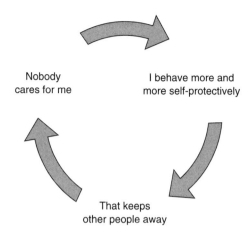

Nobody
cares for me

I behave more and
more self-protectively

That keeps
other people away

Figure 5.1   *Self-defeating cycle*

the counsellor's accepting attitude and little by little he begins to experience the same attitude towards himself. It is only when the client begins, however tentatively, to value himself in this way that real movement can take place, and in the case of so many clients this first self-valuing is the direct outcome of sensing the counsellor's valuing of them and accepting that such an attitude is possible. The research review by Watson and Steckley (2001) evidences the important therapeutic functions served by unconditional positive regard. That her attitude of unconditional positive regard can eventually have such a dramatic effect is something which the person-centred counsellor should remember early in the therapeutic encounter when the client may come armoured with sophisticated self-protective mechanisms that have been serving the purpose of keeping other people away.

Some Self-Protective Clients

Sometimes it is hard work for the counsellor not to be put off by the developed self-protections of her client. For instance, Mary, Roger and James are clients who had evolved their individual ways of protecting themselves from human contact by preventing intimacy in relationships.

Mary was 45-years-old and did not look after herself. Her hair was unwashed, her clothes were old and a mixture of black and grey. Her face was drawn and relatively expressionless despite the intensity of feeling that underlay her appearance. She also smelled. She sobbed during most of the first two sessions and ended both with the sentence 'I don't know why you would want to bother with the likes of me'.

Roger, 35-years-old, was a successful businessman who came reluctantly to counselling with his wife. In the first session he spoke about his wife being the cause of their problem because 'she doesn't know her place'. In Roger's opinion new friends of his wife were 'filling her head with a lot of fancy ideas'. Roger's solution to their problem was that 'if she would just return to being a proper wife then everything would be OK'. Speaking about his work, Roger talked with relish about a small competitor whom he had recently put out of business through granting a loan that he knew could not be repaid in the allotted time: 'It was less costly to take a loss on his loan, then buy up the bankrupt business for a song, rather than to buy him out as a going concern.' Roger thought that his former competitor was a 'wimp' for attempting suicide after the affair.

James was 18-years-old and difficult to work with because he was alienated, suspicious and angry. The following extract occurred 30 minutes into the first counselling interview. Much of the preceding time had been taken up with James taunting the counsellor: asking her if she had any training, why she was 'so very old', and laughing at the clothes she wore. The counsellor had not found the 30 minutes easy by any means, but had been intent upon outlasting James' barrage. As time went by, James escalated his attack until he climaxed it with:

JAMES: Okay – you tell me how I should get a job ... go on ... tell me ... 'advise' me – that's your job after all ... go on ... earn your money, you charlatan!
COUNSELLOR: [*after a long pause*] It feels like you're trying to push me more and more ... like you really want to fight or something like that.
JAMES: Yes. You're right I want to fight – you're just like all the rest ... a do-gooder who's only in it for herself. I bet you like to think of yourself as 'a good person who helps people'. Well I think you are a ———. I think you're no good – go on earn your money, you bitch.
COUNSELLOR: [*after a long silence*] I do feel hurt ... I feel sad as well [*silence*]. What do you feel? ... do you feel hurt as well? [*Long silence*]

As it later transpired, these three clients had four things in common:

- They were all deeply sad
- They all felt intensely unloved
- They did not love themselves
- They were all highly vulnerable.

The behaviour of these clients looked quite different because their vulnerability showed itself through different self-protective patterns. Mary withdrew into her deeply hurt 'child', while Roger projected unfeeling arrogance and superiority. James used anger, suspicion, alienation and outright aggression as his way of keeping people away. Their self-protections repelled other people because, as shields to the outer world, they hid who they really were as people. Unconditional positive regard involves not being deflected by such self-protective shields but waiting, continuing to value the worth of the person and thereby *earning the right* to be allowed behind the shield.

Personal Languages

The particular way in which an individual protects his vulnerability is just one aspect of his *personal language* – his characteristic ways of expressing the various facets of his self. If the counsellor was working with a client from a different culture and with a different language she would be particularly patient, tolerant and concerned to discover the meaning of his language. She would be wary of forming early judgements because she would know that those judgements might simply be based on her lack of understanding of his language and culture. For the counsellor who is trying to develop her attitude of unconditional positive regard it can be helpful to make the same kind of assumption about *all* her clients. She might start by assuming that each new client has his own personal language that he will use to express himself. The counsellor's task, principally through empathy, is to uncover and understand that language. This is a useful approach for the beginning counsellor because it helps her to stay focused on her client rather than be deflected by any of his behaviours. Instead of becoming judgemental about his behaviour the counsellor is concentrating on the question *what does this behaviour mean for this client?* Here are a few examples of aspects of personal languages with their individual meanings for the clients concerned:

- Jim's jokes usually mean that he is tense
- Polly's tears often mean that she is angry
- Robert's anger often means that he is sad
- Sally's effervescence usually means that she needs to be admired
- *That* smile from Peter means that he is hurting
- Jane's 'crying for the world' is her being in touch with her 'soft' part, which she values enormously
- A tender word from Gus is a strong message of love
- Brian's precision with words reflects his genuine desire not to hurt others through miscommunication
- Dave's brusque directness reflects his fear of manipulation
- Donald's repeated lateness probably means that he is uneasy with what is happening
- Doug's repeated lateness probably means that he likes to feel that he is in control
- Charlie's repeated lateness means that he is sloppy about timekeeping.

As the counsellor gradually learns the personal language of her client his behaviour becomes more intelligible and the person behind the behaviour becomes progressively easier to see and to accept. In a similar vein the psychoanalytically trained Bruno Bettelheim referred to the task of working with severely disturbed children as one of 'discovering and understanding the logic upon which the child's behaviour is based' (Bettelheim, 1987).

But What Do I Do When I Just *Don't* Accept My Client?

Later in this chapter we shall go into more detail on the personal work that the counsellor can do to foster her attitude of unconditional positive regard, but an early concern that inexperienced practitioners might have is what practical steps they can take when faced with their non-acceptance of a client. Usually this problem arises earlier rather than later in a counselling relationship; it may be that the counsellor instantly dislikes the client, or that as early as in the first or second session feels herself withdrawing a little from the relationship. When the counsellor senses such withdrawal she might recall what we have been saying about systems of self-protection – that they are designed to create this kind of response – to keep other people away. Even this awareness can help the counsellor to bracket her judgement and stay open and curious for a while longer.

Another practical step she can take is to pay much more attention to *empathising* with the client. This effort might not come easily when her instincts are to withdraw and she may have to reinforce her efforts by repeatedly reminding herself of the fact that 'I don't know this person yet'. This conscious move into empathy can have two beneficial consequences: first, it shifts the counsellor's attention from herself to her client and, second, the empathic process itself can help to disclose new facets and depths to the client that may bring the counsellor's early judgement into question (as in Box 5.1).

The next step the counsellor can take is to attend to herself in supervision. With the help of her supervisor she might address the question: 'What do I *not* know about this client?' This can be a useful question because it not only opens up new areas for possible exploration, but it reminds the counsellor of the limited evidence upon which her early judgement is based. Attending to this question might be supplemented by the exercise: *focusing on the therapeutic relationship* described in Box 5.3.

Box 5.3   Focusing on the Therapeutic Relationship

Adapting the discipline of a *focusing* exercise (Gendlin, 1981), the counsellor can attend to her *felt-sense* of her relationship with her client. Each question is taken in turn, with enough space given to allow reflection beyond the level of superficial responses, so that previously unsymbolised reactions may emerge.

- When I consider my client, what sensation do I experience – *Is that all?*

What are his beautiful bits? (focusing on each in turn)

  o What do I experience when I focus on this? – *Is that all?*

What are his ugly bits? (focusing on each in turn)

  o What do I experience when I focus on this? – *Is that all?*

- What does he most need from me?
- What do I most want to give him?
- Who am I in our relationship?

Hopefully, explorations such as that described in Box 5.3 will help the counsellor to find a key in herself to the source of her judgement.

Underlying these practical steps that the counsellor can take is the acknowledgement that the counsellor's dislike is indeed *hers* and therefore her responsibility. It is not sufficient for the person-centred practitioner repeatedly to project responsibility for her feelings on to her client.

We started this section by assuming that most cases of non-acceptance would occur early in the counselling contact, but there are, of course, instances where difficulties arise later in the therapeutic relationship. If the counsellor does not attend to these difficulties they can lead to her gradual withdrawal from the relationship and a consequent *stuckness* in the therapeutic process. Once again the counsellor may attend to these problems in supervision, but she may also openly explore such difficulties with the client so that they can both be involved in their resolution. This procedure not only contributes to the development of their relationship, but may uncover important therapeutic material for the client. Examples of the counsellor being open about difficulties such as these are given in Chapters 6 and 8 and in the exploration of the *unspoken relationship* between counsellor and client (Mearns, 2003: 64–73).

Can the Client Accept My Acceptance?

Most often the client is relieved to find that his counsellor seems to value him. Clients may even voice their relief at the end of a first session and comment on how good it feels to be attended to in this way. However, sometimes a client has had such a history of rejection that he also expects to be rejected by the counsellor. In some cases the client seems to be so ready for rejection that he also actually encourages it: 'I can't see what you see in me – I'm really no good, you know!' A danger for the inexperienced counsellor is that she is drawn into the client's self-fulfilling expectations and becomes increasingly judgemental towards her client. One counsellor reflected upon this during supervision on her work with the client, Andrew:

> I realise that as time has gone on I have come to dread appointments with Andrew. He is just so negative that it has drawn me into also becoming negative with him. In recent times I have been increasingly stern with him and have made far too many suggestions as to how he might change his life. I bet I've become more and more cold with him too. For his part I think this has let him retreat more and more into his 'rejected little boy'.

If a client has a long history of not being accepted, he may initially distrust the counsellor's acceptance. His life may have been a catalogue of people offering different forms of love and then withdrawing the offer, so why should he trust it this time? Such a client may reserve judgement on the counsellor's acceptance, and in some cases the client may even present the counsellor with a series of *tests* of her acceptance – if the counsellor negotiates these hurdles then the client may be prepared to trust (see 'Sandy' in Chapter 2). Box 5.4 reproduces the reflections of one client who had had difficulty in trusting the counsellor's acceptance.

Box 5.4   Acceptance Can Be Difficult to Accept

Near the end of their time together, or as a regular feature of their work, a counsellor and client may devote some time to reviewing their counselling process (see Chapters 6 and 9). The following extract is taken from one such session, where the client is reflecting on the ways in which she had tried to dismiss the counsellor's acceptance.

> At first I had a lot of difficulty with the fact that you thought I was OK as a person – that you even seemed to like me. That was so strange for me that I didn't believe it at first – nobody had ever liked me – including me! When I realised that you weren't pretending – that you really *did* like me – I began to think that *I* was the one who had been pretending – I must have been pretending to be OK as a person, otherwise you couldn't possibly like me. The next explanation I came up with was that if I really showed you all my horrible bits then you couldn't possibly like me – so I proceeded to show you me as I saw myself – the lowest of the low. It was only when I found that even this didn't put you off that I realised that *I could be all of me* with you and that wouldn't be destructive to either of us.

A particularly difficult situation for any counsellor occurs when the client does not accept the counsellor's unconditional positive regard on the same basis as it is offered, but misinterprets the counsellor's warmth as offering the possibility of an intimate relationship beyond the counselling setting. One of the many issues involved for the counsellor in such a situation is to communicate her limits, while at the same time continuing to show her acceptance of the client. An over-reaction by the inexperienced counsellor might be to withdraw some of her acceptance lest it continue to be misinterpreted. If she did this she might find that she was unwittingly repeating a pattern of rejection that had often occurred in the client's life. It is not easy to be clear about limits while at the same time also communicating valuing. There can be no stereotyped way of handling such a delicate situation, but Box 5.5 reproduces one such example.

Box 5.5   Accepting the Client Who Loves You

This extract is taken from near the end of a fairly lengthy counselling contract. The counsellor had tentatively raised the issue of it ending since it seemed to her that the work had been substantially done and the contract might well be ended with provision made for the possibility of future reviews. During most of the session they had been discussing this possibility, although all the time it felt as though the client was coming to something special. A fairly long monologue from her ended with:

Client: … so I realised that what I've been feeling really for the first time in my life, is how much I love someone. I guess it's pretty inconvenient that that someone happens to be you … but it's true. I realise that that's why I've been hanging on – I've dreaded the thought of ending. I don't really *need* you anymore, but it's difficult …

Counsellor: … difficult to let me go?

Client: Yes – I know it's the right thing to do … but it's difficult …

Counsellor: I feel that at this moment you are trusting me with something precious … something very tender and delicate … an important gift …

Client: … it feels like all of that to me too.

Counsellor: Scared I might damage it?

Client: No … not really … I don't think I would have given it to you if I had feared that. [*Silence*.]

Counsellor: What are you thinking?

Client: I'm thinking that it's OK for us to end now.

Focus on Warmth

Simply *feeling* accepting towards the client is not enough – that acceptance has to be *communicated*. For one counsellor a genuine, spontaneous smile will be a means of communicating, while others will show their warmth by using words or physical contact. Each counsellor will likely have her own particular *repertoire* – her own characteristic ways of showing warmth. One aspect of developing as a person-centred counsellor is the expansion of one's repertoire so that warmth can be shown in different ways with different clients. This is part of what we describe as the counsellor 'expanding the person she can offer in the counselling room' (see Chapter 6). If the counsellor is to be able to offer a meeting at relational depth to every client who comes to her door she will need to develop a broad repertoire. For some clients verbal messages of warmth are not trusted, or perhaps are not trusted as much as, for instance, touching, but on the other hand there are clients for whom touching might represent an assault. Box 5.6 lists a number of ways in which counsellors communicate their warmth. This list is by no means complete but it can be useful to help the counsellor to reflect upon her own repertoire and its gradual development.

Box 5.6   Ways of Communicating Warmth

Each individual counsellor will have her own repertoire of ways of communicating warmth. It is interesting to reflect on how easy or difficult it might be to express our warmth through each of the following:

- going to the door to meet the client
- shaking hands with the client
- using the client's first name
- smiling
- using a warm tone of voice
- holding eye contact
- genuinely laughing as the client recounts a funny incident
- using words to show warmth
- showing genuine interest in the client
- physically moving towards the client
- touching the client's arm
- touching the client's shoulder
- holding hands
- hugging the client.

Warmth helps to develop trust within the counselling relationship. Too little warmth will slow the development of trust and the process of counselling. There will also be some cases where too great a show of warmth, however genuinely felt by the counsellor, may be difficult for particular clients. These cases will be rare and confined to clients who are particularly suspicious of warmth from other people. In such instances it would be a mistake for the counsellor to stop showing warmth for that would simply repeat the cycle of rejection mentioned earlier. Instead, the counsellor should continue to show warmth but perhaps could use other, less powerful, methods from her repertoire. However, the person-centred counsellor would not just do that – she would be open about what she was doing – for the object is not simply to obtain an easy communication with her client but to use their relating to uncover therapeutic dimensions. Box 5.7 illustrates the counsellor *showing her working* in this way. Further examples arise in Chapter 6 when we consider the counsellor's use of her self more fully.

Box 5.7   A Tear Too Far

Sandra and her client, Simon, are quite different in their comfort with human warmth. For Sandra, warmth comes easily and can be expressed fully. For Simon, warmth is difficult – historically, it was not to be trusted, so he is uncomfortable with effusive expressions. This time Sandra has reacted to Simon's struggling – she has felt every ounce of his effort and his 'small steps' towards reaching out to others in his world. When he eventually ends and looks her in the eye she finds herself giving him a beaming smile – but not only a smile – for there is also a tear in her eyes. This is a powerful show of warmth – too powerful for Simon at this time. Sandra talks about it:

'Sorry Simon – I kind of blew you away there – It's hard enough for you without me doing that. I'll try to be more respectful of you. But, also I *felt* it – I *felt* how much you had been trying.'

Box 5.7 illustrates the delicate balance where the counsellor respects the client's ways of being – his comforts and discomforts – but is also willing and able to work with the differences between the two of them. Fundamental to this is the person-centred counsellor's willingness to comment on her own experience and behaviour – openly to *show her working* (see Chapter 6), rather than powerfully hiding behind her own mystery.

Touching is a natural and literal reaching out of one human being towards another, but many workers in some cultures find it enormously difficult to show their warmth through touch. The problem with touch is circular: when there is not much touching in a culture it begins to be feared, mistrusted and little used. Yet, when touching occurs in counselling it is usually experienced as perfectly natural and not at all discontinuous with the flow of communication between those involved.

For some counsellors the use of touch comes easily, while for others it is slow to develop. The difficulty centres on *trusting one's touching*; knowing when touching is our genuine felt response to our client rather than an imposition of our own need. As the counsellor explores her own use of touch, she might uncover instances where her touching is *imposing*, and she will learn to recognise those signs. An example of imposing touching might be found in the helper whose hugging of her client is not an expression of her warmth and willingness to stay with her client's feelings, but instead is saying something like 'there there now – stop this crying … because I can't stand it!'

Since the first edition of this book nineteen years ago we need to acknowledge that the counselling culture has changed more in relation to touching than to any other dimension of counsellor behaviour. There is certainly a rational and evidenced fear that some counsellors abuse their power through touching. But the fear of that possibility has resulted in some counselling agencies withdrawing physical contact of any kind. Other professions, further down the road of institutionalisation (Mearns, 1997b), note a similar re-positioning with respect to physical contact. The primary school teacher who, in 1988, might have sat the hurting pupil on her lap and given her a cuddle, would be advised by her union and her management to maintain strict non-contact in 2007. The social worker who regarded seriously the position of having a child 'in care' might have offered an appropriate parental 'holding' in 1988, but would maintain her 'professional distance' in 2007. In fact this imaginary 2007 worker may not be making an entirely safe choice in obeying protocols that prohibit physical contact with children in her care. It is not beyond the bounds of conjecture that, just as those who used physical contact to abuse twenty years ago, the present worker may be faced with litigation twenty years hence. The litigant could reasonably accuse the worker and her agency of causing lasting psychological damage and not remediating earlier damage by failing to offer appropriate physical contact. The accusation would be difficult to rebut because there is a wealth of psychological research establishing the importance of physical contact in the development of the person (Lambers, 2002).

As two men in a profession where clients are often vulnerable and men are more often the abusers, we feel this dilemma painfully. Both of us have struggled in our own ways with the issue, and we have also offered each other enormous support. There is no easy answer to the dilemma – indeed our personal distress over this matter is best expressed by the conclusion, 'there is no answer in a sick society'. Yet, we continue to believe that person-centred counselling is an endeavour which is grounded in our humanity and if we are to withdraw dimensions of our humanity from the work we would be offering a charade to our clients and to ourselves. So we will not restrain our gentle touch on the hand or shoulder – a touch that arises spontaneously out of our sense of being *in contact* with the other human being. Nor will we restrain our sincere offer of a hug when we genuinely want to offer that and when our client wants to receive it. We *will* be respectful of our client in these instances and we will take care to appreciate his experiencing. But we refuse to withdraw our humanity from our work and an essential part of our humanity is that we are embodied. The danger in our writing these words is that others will take them as licence for their own abusiveness. There is no way out of this dilemma. It may eventually silence us as writers or finish us as practitioners but at least we shall have retained our integrity.

Focus on Conditionality

Early in this chapter we asserted that most liking in everyday life is *conditional*. Implicit in any relationship is a whole set of conditions that could complete the sentences: 'I would like you more if you ... ', and 'I would not like you so much if you ... ' Even in very close relationships much of the liking of one person for the other would still be conditional on the other 'not changing too much' or 'continuing to love me' or any number of other conditions. Counselling is *not* everyday life and unconditional positive regard is not the same as our conditional liking. The challenge for the person-centred counsellor is to enhance her own security, stability and self-acceptance so that she has less need to meet others in the kind of self-protective fashion that engenders conditionality. A great deal of the emphasis in person-centred training is focused on this dimension of the counsellor's self-acceptance, and we have repeatedly returned to this issue throughout this book.

A first step for the counsellor would be to become aware of the different kinds of situations in which she is likely to find difficulty with conditionality. Box 5.8 reproduces 26 situations that have been used in voluntary sector training with couple counsellors to help them to explore the conditionality of their liking (Mearns, 1985).

Box 5.8   How Conditional Is My Liking?

In an exercise to explore conditionality, couple counsellors were faced with this list of 26 situations and asked to reflect on how easy or difficult it might be for them to accept such clients:

- A husband who questions your competence as a counsellor
- A husband who says, 'My wife promised to obey me and that is what she must do; there is nothing further to discuss'
- A feminist who has come to dislike men in general, including her husband
- A woman who says: 'I want to leave him because he's boring and I've found someone younger'
- A client who swears continuously
- A client who talks non-stop, but never about his feelings
- A drug pusher who works the primary schools ('elementary schools', in the USA)
- A miner who talks about 'breaking heads' on the picket line
- A heroin addict
- An Evangelical Christian who always seems to be trying to convert you
- A father who has battered his baby
- A client who discloses that he is gay
- A couple who tell you: 'You haven't helped us a bit, and if nothing happens in this session we may as well stop'
- A woman who feels that the husband should make all the important decisions in a relationship
- A husband who lets his wife do all the talking and gives you the look that says 'What right do you have to pry into my life?'
- A couple who repeatedly accuse you of not telling them the solution to their problem
- A policeman who talks about 'breaking heads' on the picket line
- A young man who has mugged an old woman
- A client who tells you that she is lesbian
- A client who never seems to change
- A woman who accepts that being beaten regularly is a normal part of married life
- A husband who regularly batters his wife
- A client who complains about his life but doesn't seem to be trying to change
- A mother who has battered her baby
- A client who tells you that he is in love with you
- A client who tells you that she is in love with you.

An exploration such as the exercise in Box 5.8 can begin the process of clarifying the counsellor's values, because it is when values are contravened or threatened that the counsellor is more likely to become conditional in her valuing of the client. Awareness of her values and the effect these are likely to have on her acceptance, can in itself give the counsellor some measure of control. Furthermore, awareness of values also gives the counsellor the opportunity to question the basis of such values and explore them further. Sometimes the counsellor might find that the value has very little basis in her actual experience but is something she has introjected from parents and serves no important function for her in the present. However, at other times the counsellor will find that the value that is being challenged has a firm foundation in her own psychology. It may, for instance, be rooted in her own needs and fears. Accepting the client unconditionally might thus be particularly difficult and even threatening for the counsellor.

Supervision as well as training in the person-centred approach involves giving continuing attention to the counsellor's personal development and is concerned with uncovering and understanding needs and fears in the counsellor that might channel her into conditionality. Box 5.9 illustrates a trainee counsellor's discovery of personal needs that had inhibited her work. In this case the needs were related to her valuing of the person-centred approach: the counsellor discovered that her acceptance of clients was to some extent conditional upon them following person-centred values.

Box 5.9   Can the Person-Centred Approach Accept Its Opposite?

In the following extract a trainee counsellor speaks with her supervisor on her development over the past year and in particular on two significant hurdles that she has negotiated:

Critical issues for me this year have been first to realise how unaccepting I had been towards clients who only seemed to want to talk about their thoughts rather than explore their feelings. Of course, I was so convinced by the importance of feelings that I thought that every client had to go there right away – it was just one of the things that the person-centred approach would take so much for granted, that I kept pushing my clients down that road and was decidedly unaccepting of their resistance. The other hurdle, although it was related, was more difficult to overcome: I found it very difficult to accept one client who seemed intent on moving in a direction which clearly seemed to be opposite to that of growth … It's like all my work with clients was at some fundamental level conditional upon them moving in the direction of growth … conditional upon them confirming the person-centred hypothesis. I had great difficulty with this one client who seemed intent on going back to her husband for regular beatings.

I could be open to her thoughts about leaving him but every time she talked about going back I would 'get her to reflect on it more deeply'. The poor woman soon realised that she could only give me that part of herself that was wanting to leave her husband; meanwhile the other part, which wanted to return to the marriage, remained unexamined, mysterious and even more compelling. It was through that client that I realised that the person-centred approach was even more challenging than I had ever thought, because to be really person-centred you actually have to value the client who may be moving in a direction opposite to growth – opposite to everything you value.

Sometimes the counsellor's needs and fears are related to the institutional setting in which she is working. Institutions, appropriately, are institution-centred rather than person-centred, and their clients are seldom accepted unconditionally. Hence, the counsellor in an institution might actually be open to criticism if she is *not* conditional. For instance, the school counsellor may be criticised by colleagues for valuing the disruptive pupil, or the clinical psychologist might find difficulty with psychiatric staff who see her acceptance of a 'manipulative' patient as 'naive'. Such pressures as these would be rightly feared by the person-centred counsellor, because loss of credibility in the eyes of colleagues is a severe sanction. It would not be surprising if the counsellor gradually became more conditional with her clients, and in that way reflected the conditionality of her institution. There is no easy answer to this problem of institutional working. The counsellor might respond by moaning about the fact that her institution is not person-centred. The psychological significance of moaning is that it helps us to reduce the dissonance we feel between what we want to do and what we are expected to do. By that means, moaning actually helps us to *obey* the external demands and go against our conscience (Milgram, 2004). A more challenging response is to value the institution for what it has to be – 'institution-centred' – and to work within its politics without abrogating our principles. This important area of applying person-centred principles within the politics of institutions is explored elsewhere (Mearns, 2006b; Mearns and Thorne, 2000: chapter 2).

Unconditional Positive Regard Is Not About 'Being Nice'

Unconditional positive regard is sometimes misconstrued as being 'nice' to the client, but that is not what it is about – it is about deeply valuing the client while making no contingent demands upon him. 'Being nice' is a socialised mask – it is a face to project to the world in order to cover up what we really feel or in order to pre-empt any counter judgement from them. Being nice does not help the client to see and trust our unconditionality. Being nice does not give our client an experience of human warmth – indeed, because it is often used as a disguise to other responses, it can leave the client feeling decidedly cold. Being nice has more to do with relational superficiality than relational depth.

One of the early tasks in person-centred training is to challenge the 'nice' trainee to find, in their responding to others, what is genuine and what is not. Sometimes people are genuinely nice – it is not a matter of them putting on the appearance of being nice – it is simply who they are, in most contexts. However, the fact that their 'niceness' is congruent does not lessen the difficulties they will find. Some clients will revel in the warm, secure, environment offered and will be shocked when this nice counsellor makes relational challenges. Other clients will have a hard time in believing the nice counsellor – they have seen enough people 'being nice'.

There follows three statements from a person-centred counsellor to her client – statements that many would judge to be 'not nice'. Yet each of them, in the specific relationship in which they arose, were deeply valuing of the client:

- I feel pissed off with you!
- I feel you've just dumped me again!
- So – is that it – am I just expected to wrap things up and go away?

When reading specific counsellor statements like these it is important *not* to transpose them to other contexts and imagine ourselves using them with our own clients. Whatever the nature of the statements, this rarely works, because the specific statements are born of a particular relationship and cannot meaningfully be literally transposed. What *can* be transposed, however, is the counsellor's communicated *intent* behind the statements. These previous three statements were all from a counsellor's work with the client, John. The counsellor's *intent* behind all of them was twofold:

1 To make *contact* with John – to encounter him at a level that was deeper than John's normal pattern of keeping the other at distance.
2 To show John that she (the counsellor) *really cared* for him, and for their work together – a realisation that was difficult for John.

John's counsellor picks up the commentary in her own words:

John is a really slippery character – he goes a little way in relationships, then he gets frightened and pulls back. But his is a sophisticated pattern because he can usually get the other person to become frustrated, irritated and angry, so that they pull away from him. I also get frustrated, irritated and angry, but I don't pull away. When I said to him, 'I feel pissed off with you'; 'I feel you've just dumped me again'; 'So – is that it – am I just expected to wrap things up and go away?', I was expressing my positive regard for him and I was not being conditional. He knows that I am not saying to him, 'Don't do these things!' What I am saying is, 'John, I know you have to do these things – and this is how another human being feels in relation to you'. What I am saying to him is: 'You matter to me'; 'Me relating with you matters to me'; 'I will fight for our relationship'; 'Yes, you can close off and retreat – I accept that you do that – I know you do that – and I know you know I know you do that'; 'But as well as accepting that in you I am not also going to go along with it – I am not going to diminish what I am offering because you need to withdraw!'

My irritated, 'I feel pissed off with you' is the initial, shorthand version of all of this. Probably, at least part of John will know that it stands for all this – if not, I will tell him.

Students of a strictly non-directive approach to client-centred therapy (Bozarth, 2001; Brodley and Schneider, 2001) may feel a divergence here in the more relational approach described in this book. In non-directive client-centred therapy there is a tendency to proscribe certain counsellor behaviours that might be seen to offer direction to the client:

Unconditional positive regard is also communicated by the *absence* of communications that display challenge, confrontation, interventions, criticisms, unsolicited guidance or directive reassurance or support. Whether it is intended or not, all of these omitted types of communication, if expressed, are likely to be perceived as the therapist's expression of conditional approval or explicit disapproval. (Brodley and Schneider, 2001: 157)

We would not disagree with the *intention* behind this advice – to avoid developing a relationship where the client cedes their personal power to the counsellor. We are all of the view that fundamental to the approach is that the client stays at the centre in regard to his locus of evaluation. The difference is that we would not seek to achieve this by either prescribing or proscribing specific counsellor behaviours. Ironically, the issue of directivity in the client-centred/person-centred approach has been tackled in a purely counsellor-centred fashion. The behaviours in Brodley and Schneider's quote are proscribed because they are 'likely to be perceived' as conditionality. In fact, this places little trust in clients' abilities to relate with the counsellor yet retain their sense of self. Historically, the directivity debate has ranged between these two extremes – proscribing specific counsellor behaviours against trusting the client's integrity. Our view is that it is not particularly person-centred to hold to *either* of these extremes, for both make singular assumptions about the nature of the client. In one view the client is readily influenced – in the other they can be trusted to retain their self integrity. A more client-centred/person-centred position is to recognise that clients vary widely and our aim is to recognise and respond to their individuality. So, with a client whose locus of evaluation is profoundly externalised, the counsellor would take great care to avoid behaviours that are likely to direct. In fact, this challenge is considerable because a person this vulnerable is so in need of the other's evaluations – even to judge his own feelings – that he will distil direction from the smallest of clues:

COUNSELLOR: Why did you make that decision?
CLIENT: Because that was the decision you thought was better for me.
COUNSELLOR: What made you think that?
CLIENT: You smiled more when I talked about making that decision than the other one.

In working with this client our behaviour would likely look very similar to that of the non-directive client-centred therapist, though we might also want to build in frequent reviews to check what the client is taking from our communication. An example of this work is given in Chapter 6 and in a case described in Mearns (2003: 80–3), where there were numerous reviews in each session, so vulnerable to influence was the client.

On the other hand, with a different client – one who had more command in relation to his locus of evaluation – it would not be particularly client-centred/person-centred to ignore his differentness. If we are seeking to establish a relationship with this client we need to trust him to be able to be his own person in relation to us. Such was the case in the work with the client John, who, after describing a new job offer in glowing terms asked his counsellor if he should take it. The counsellor's response was clearly 'directive':

COUNSELLOR: Of course you should take it – it sounds great.

JOHN: [*Pause*] Yes – when I put it *that* way, it does, doesn't it? Now let's see how it sounds when I put it another way …

John's counsellor knew that he had a well enough internalised locus of evaluation to go through his own decision-making process. Her straightforward, affirmative response would not be directive for John – instead he would use it as a 'mirror' to reflect back his own construction.

In the relational emphasis to person-centred counselling, the practitioner will find herself relating in many different ways across the range of her clients. To prescribe or proscribe particular behaviours across that range would deny the uniqueness of her clients and the uniqueness of the relationship she will craft with each. It also offers a challenge to her. If, rather than displaying a consistent set of behaviours with all her clients, she desires to meet each in different ways, she will need to cultivate both a breadth and depth of being. This is what our next chapter is about – helping the counsellor to broaden and deepen what she can offer in the counselling room – helping her to become more fully *congruent*.

6

CONGRUENCE

Towards the end of that period of his life devoted to developing person-centred therapy, Rogers wrote:

> I believe it is the *realness* of the therapist in the relationship which is the most important element. It is when the therapist is natural and spontaneous that he seems to be most effective. Probably this is a 'trained humanness' as one of our therapists suggests, but in the moment it is the natural reaction of *this* person. Thus our sharply different therapists achieve good results in quite different ways. For one, an impatient, no-nonsense, let's put-the-cards-on-the-table approach is most effective, because in such an approach he is most openly being himself. For another it may be a much more gentle, and more obviously warm approach, because this is the way *this* therapist is. Our experience has deeply reinforced and extended my own view that the person who is able *openly* to be himself at that moment, as he is at the deepest levels he is able to be, is the effective therapist. Perhaps nothing else is of any importance. (Rogers, 1973: 186)

If Rogers' assertion is right, we are faced with an exciting but frightening challenge. It is exciting to think that it is the unique humanity of the other, offered in encounter, that can be most healing. But it could also confront us with the frightening possibility that we may not have the courage to meet that challenge.

Box 6.1   Can I Dare To Be Me?

In response to my client, can I dare to:

Feel the feelings that are within me?
Hold my client when I feel he needs to be held?
Show my anger when that is strongly felt?
Admit my distraction when challenged about it?
Admit my confusion when that persists?
Voice my irritation when that grows?
Put words to my affection when that is there?
Shout when something is seething inside me?
Be spontaneous even though I do not know where that will lead?
Be forceful as well as gentle?
Be gentle as well as forceful?
Use my sensuous self in relation to my client?
Step out from behind my 'professional facade'?

Can I dare to be *me* in response to my client?

Congruence poses challenging questions like those in Box 6.1, but its challenge only exists because helpers generally support a norm of incongruence. Indeed, we are often dismayed at the level of incongruence we find in mental health provision. Can it make sense to work with clients and patients who struggle with their incongruence by offering them our own incongruent relating? The fact that this question is not seriously asked in mental health provision needs to be addressed from a sociological and social psychological perspective. Incongruent relating is so thoroughly ingrained within our culture that it has become viewed as the healthy and even sophisticated reality. As human beings we use our considerable skills to cultivate our incongruence such that we are protected from being truly seen by the other. As is described elsewhere, we create '*lace curtains* and *safety screens*' (Mearns, 1996; 1997a) to hide from others and, in collusion with others, we develop restrictive norms to ensure that in our relating we minimise the possibility of meeting each other freely (Mearns, 2003: 67–8). If we were able to free ourselves enough from our cultural norms of incongruence we might be able to question our stance – we might even be able to consider our culture in terms of its *collective pathology of incongruence*. This critical review of incongruence in social relating is, of course, only one account. Equally, we could, from a social psychology perspective, marvel at the sophistication of the human being who is able to present different faces across a range of social settings. That diversification has enormous survival value for a social being. It enables her to present an appearance that she judges will best fit her purposes in different contexts. Thus, the child rapidly learns the value of incongruence in relating. For example, if Jill finds that her *anger* is consistently disapproved of, she can transpose it into a *sadness* that is comforted instead. If Jack finds that his *sadness* does not fit with his carer's image of what it is to be male, then he can always transpose it into a more fitting *anger*. If Jack and Jill later get together as partners, there might be some work for a couples counsellor at an early stage in their relationship.

If we did not have the ability to be incongruent it would be difficult to maintain our present sophisticated social structures. For example, we rely on each other being able to lay aside our present concerns to play the different roles we fill in social systems. That confidence in each other's ability to be incongruent allows us to engage those systems with at least a sense of security. If we could not predict that – despite what is going on inside her – our dentist will still fulfil her professional role, we would scarcely be letting her put a drill into our mouth!

We defined empathy as a *process*, unconditional positive regard as an *attitude* and now we define congruence as a *state of being* of the counsellor in relation to her client:

> Congruence is the state of being of the counsellor when her outward responses to her client consistently match her inner experiencing of her client.

The counsellor is *congruent* when she is openly being what she *is* in response to her client – when the way she is behaving is reflective of what she is experiencing inside – when her response to her client is what she experiences and is not a pretence or a defence. On the other hand when she *pretends* to be 'clever' or 'competent' or 'caring' she is being false in relation to her client – her outward behaviour is not congruent with what is going on inside her. Moustakas talks about the importance of his congruence in psychotherapeutic work with children:

> I saw that I must stop playing the role of the professional therapist and allow my potentials, talents and skills, my total experience as a human being to blend naturally into the relationship with the child and whenever humanly possible to meet him as a whole person. (Moustakas, 1959: 201)

Congruence is not a complicated concept, yet it is the most challenging one for the person-centred counsellor in her early development. The difficulty is in learning to challenge the sophisticated systems of incongruence that we have developed as part of the socialisation described above. It seems easy to suggest that the new counsellor could simply express her responses as she experiences them rather than withholding them or dressing them up in some incongruent fashion. But it is really difficult for the trainee counsellor to defy her socialisation and it takes time spent in the new learning context of the training environment where those around her share in the task of creating a congruent community that the re-learning can occur. In that environment she can learn about her incongruence and how her congruence can be expressed. She can learn that most of the person she is can be freely offered to her clients and is healthy for both her and them. She can also learn about those parts that are difficult for her – parts that are so tied up with her needs or fears that they intrude into and distort the psychological space for the client. Gradually, she can learn to trust and use the wider range of who she is as a person, and smile and be patient with the parts that are still in the process of being acknowledged and reclaimed.

Like unconditional positive regard, congruence has several names in common usage, one of which is *genuineness*. This can be confusing to new students since in everyday language the word genuineness implies some conscious control, that is to say a person can *choose* whether to be genuine or not. However, as we shall see later in this chapter, incongruence on the part of the counsellor is not necessarily a deliberate withholding. On the contrary, it can arise from the counsellor's complete lack of self-awareness in regard to her feelings towards the client. Another word sometimes used is *transparency*, a term made famous by Sid Jourard (1971) in his book, *The Transparent Self*. However, Germain Lietaer (2001), in what is otherwise an insightful paper, confuses students by restricting the word *congruence* to the counsellor's accurate awareness of her experiencing and adopts the word *transparency* for the communication of her experiencing. Other alternative terms are *realness* and *authenticity*. These have the advantage of describing how the client often experiences this dimension: '*She* [the counsellor] *behaves like a real person – she seems really authentic in the way she relates to me.*' One disadvantage of these terms, however, is that they beg the question of what is *authentic* or *real*: is the counsellor ceasing to be *real* when she is behaving defensively and hiding her responses? The word *congruent* has the advantage of emphasising that what is being described is the contiguity between the counsellor's underlying experiencing and her outward behaviour. However, even this most used term can occasionally cause difficulty to the new student who confuses it with the notion of 'congruence between two people'. The student might take the statement: '*the counsellor was perfectly congruent with the client*' to mean '*the counsellor was perfectly in tune with the client*', hence early confusion between congruence and empathy can arise.

Whether we use genuineness, transparency, realness, authenticity or our preferred term, congruence, it is useful to highlight its two different facets:

1   the counsellor's awareness of her experiencing
2   the counsellor's communication of her experiencing.

To be congruent in response to her client the counsellor needs both to be self-aware (1) and willing to express herself (2). These are quite different capabilities and counsellors in training find both to be demanding in different ways. We shall return to this distinction later in the chapter when we look at different forms of *incongruence*.

Why is Congruence Important?

Like empathy and unconditional positive regard, congruence makes it easier for the client to *trust* the counsellor and the counselling process. If the client accepts the counsellor as congruent then he will know that the response he gets from her can be accepted as open and honest. He knows that the counsellor is not concerned with manipulating him and consequently he can feel more free in their relationship. In the person-centred approach congruence dissolves the mysteriousness of the counsellor. Mystery evokes the illusion of power; transparency dissolves it. As was mentioned in Chapter 5, in person-centred counsellor training the counsellor (and also the trainer) is consistently challenged to 'show your working' to the client (or the trainee). Just as the teacher would encourage pupils attempting an arithmetic problem not just to give their answer, but to *show their working* – show the steps towards their answer – so too the person-centred counsellor would be encouraged not just to give a powerful response to their client, but to show all the detail that led to that reponse. This is illustrated in Box 6.2.

Box 6.2   Show Your Working!

The discipline of the person-centred counsellor *showing her working*, rather than simply coming out with unsupported, powerful and sometimes mysterious statements is illustrated by the alternative A and B responses to the client, Paul, who is talking about leaving his partner:

Client: There is really no point in me staying with George. We've had our time together. We're finished. It's just too much hassle – I don't need it – time to move on to pastures new.

Response A: Historically, you would have left a partner in this situation, but maybe not now?

Response B: Historically, you would have left a partner in this situation, but maybe not now? I mean – I hear you keeping saying that it's finished – that it's time for you to move on. And, yet, I'm not convinced. I don't know what it is – maybe it's that once or twice I've seen you less strident – more 'cracking-up' when you consider leaving him. Why do I get a sense that it's different this time? Is it just me? Just me *wanting* it to be different for you? That could be part of it – I certainly want things to be better for you.

The difference between A and B is that B includes all that is *behind* the initial response. It shows all the aspects that contribute to it, including elements that may have more to do with the counsellor than the client. This fuller congruent response reduces the mystery to the client, but it also gives him much more to go on. This is not to say that the more cryptic response A is always inappropriate. In some relationships its very brevity could help the client to focus – but the counsellor would still want, later, to describe where the response had come from in them.

'Showing your working' demystifies the counsellor's utterances and reduces their possibly unhelpful impact on the client. Furthermore, it shows the humanity that is behind the counsellor's words, a central concern in person-centred therapeutic relationships. Showing your working is not difficult, yet it is striking how often person-centred counsellors in relation to their clients (and trainers in relation to their trainees) fail to do so. Of course, in showing our working, we render ourself transparent; perhaps it is difficult to be deprived of the trappings of mystery and power, and to be exposed in all our vulnerability.

Trust clearly can exist in relationships where the counsellor is mysterious and hidden, but it is very much the kind of trust one would have in a being who is regarded as superior. In the person-centred approach the aim is to establish a more egalitarian relationship where the counsellor *earns* trust rather than *commands* it through mystery or superiority. The trust which the congruent counsellor earns is that of a person who is willing to be fully present as a real human being and who is not hiding behind any kind of façade.

A second, but related, way in which congruence can be important occurs through the counsellor's willingness to be open about *weaknesses*. She is open to being confused, powerless, mistaken, and even at times apologetic, when these are parts of her congruent response to her client. This openness about apparent weaknesses can introduce whole new possibilities for self-acceptance in the client who spends his life in fear of weaknesses in himself. As one client commented:

> It blew my mind when she [*the counsellor*] admitted that she hadn't been really understanding me – I mean she was serious, and apologetic, and yet still solid. If I had been her, that kind of thing would just have destroyed me. That was the moment when I first realised that it was *possible* for someone to have imperfections but still be OK.

A third reason for the importance of counsellor congruence relates to the very goal of counselling where, implicitly at least, *the client is endeavouring to become more congruent himself.* The client seeks to become more able to represent his feelings and responses in a straightforward, accurate way rather than hiding or disguising them. While 'modelling' is not a direct aim of person-centred counselling, it would be quite inappropriate for the counsellor to portray something *opposite* to the desired therapeutic outcome: it would indeed be both impertinent and perverse for a counsellor to expect to further her client's congruence by being incongruent herself.

While the enhancement of trust, openness about failings and the modelling of congruent relating are important effects of congruence, they are adjuncts to the main therapeutic process that congruence fosters – a process unique to this way of working. The counsellor's congruence *creates an interactive sequence where the phenomenal realities of the client and the counsellor can be compared.* Observed discrepancies between the two phenomenal realities can indicate important therapeutic material for the client – *or* new self-learning for the counsellor – and sometimes both. This issue is so central to relational person-centred therapy that it needs careful elaboration. First, the term *phenomenal reality* may be unfamiliar. Essentially, it means *reality as the individual experiences it* – which may be different from how someone else experiences it. Consider the phenomenal realities of both client and counsellor as these unfold in the following interactive sequence. The client, Jim, had missed three sessions running, for various given reasons. After the third missed session his counsellor had written to him to say that she would like to see him again, if he would welcome that. We take up the dialogue early in the following meeting.

COUNSELLOR: I wasn't sure if different things had just got in the way of you coming these past three times or whether you weren't sure that you wanted to come.

JIM: I just didn't think it was any use.

COUNSELLOR: That it wasn't getting anywhere ... or something else?

JIM: It was nice that you wrote. That was nice of you.

COUNSELLOR: I was concerned. I didn't know what was going on for you. I wanted to respect you if you wanted to stop – but I also wanted to say, 'Hey Jim' if you didn't.

JIM: So, you feel sorry for me?

COUNSELLOR: No, I don't feel 'sorry' for you, Jim. Far from it. I feel a bit 'sad' for you – you've talked about how 'lost' you feel – I feel a sadness about that. But I don't feel 'sorry' for you.

JIM: You don't feel I'm 'pathetic'.

COUNSELLOR: Far from it Jim – I don't feel that, and I've never felt that.

JIM: But I was 'pathetic' the last time we met – I was crying all the time – I was a blubbing idiot.

COUNSELLOR: That's not how I felt – it's not how I feel. I feel now, as I did then – that you are so so lonely – that you have always been so lonely. It takes my breath away to see you struggling as hard as you do. I don't know if I would have that strength – the strength to survive feeling so alone – and to keep trying.

JIM: [*looks at counsellor*] That's how you feel about me?

COUNSELLOR: Yes.

JIM: I didn't come back because I was sure you would think I was 'pathetic'.

COUNSELLOR: You were sure that's how I would feel. Like, you had no doubts. Do you believe me when I say that that's the *opposite* of what I feel?

JIM: It's difficult ... it's difficult to believe it ... but it's difficult *not* to believe you.

For our purpose of exploring congruence, we can leave Jim and his counsellor at this point. But the reader can see how they have opened a potentially important therapeutic area: Jim's expectation that the emotionality he was showing would be seen as 'pathetic'. Had the dialogue not been maintained to this point, with the counsellor being as clear as she could about what she actually felt, Jim might have continued to maintain his illusion. This was how he had been seen in childhood by both his father and his mother; his showing of his loneliness, his sadness, was 'pathetic'. He internalised that self-judgement which further alienated him from his own experiencing. In this congruent sequence, which actually begins with the counsellor's letter, Jim finds that his *phenomenal reality* – that his sadness would be regarded as pathetic – contrasts sharply with his counsellor's phenomenal reality of the same events. It is still difficult for him to accept the difference – all human beings struggle to hold on to their concept of reality – but, as he says in his last phase, 'it's difficult *not* to believe you.' This illustrates how important it is for the counsellor to be utterly believable, to be completely and fully congruent. She needs to show what is going on in her experiencing in as much detail and with as much accuracy as she can because she is in the privileged position of giving her client an alternative perspective on reality.

In the above example, the important therapeutic process was that Jim and his counsellor could compare their phenomenal realities and work with the difference. The same applies even when the counsellor's experience of the client is not so positive. Consider the following extract of dialogue between Robert and his counsellor. Robert has been talking about his most recent in a long line of rejections by potential partners.

ROBERT: So – there I go again – I tried yet again and yet again it didn't work out. I don't know why I bother – it never works out – it never will work out for me …

COUNSELLOR: Robert – STOP! Stop right there – you're driving me crazy. Robert, you're a darling – but sometimes you drive me crazy! I want to shake you and say, 'Quit quitting on yourself.' 'Stop playing this same record.' If I were a young man whom you were interested in, I *too* would run a mile. Oooh! I feel frustrated. You have so much that you could offer in relationships – and get from relationships. But how can it happen? How can it *ever* happen? How can you ever *let it* happen?

ROBERT: Finished?

COUNSELLOR: Yep.

ROBERT: Finished with me?

COUNSELLOR: Not by a long way, Robert.

ROBERT: I suppose I do do that, don't I?

COUNSELLOR: Carry on, Robert.
ROBERT: [*smiles*] Yes, I do 'carry on' a bit, don't I!
COUNSELLOR: [*smiles, and winks at him*]

Throughout this book, we caution the reader against imagining counsellor responses transposed into work with their own clients. Interactive sequences like that between Robert and his counsellor are unique to their relationship and to who they both are as people. However, once again the *intent* behind the counsellor's response can be transposed to other work. Her intent is to be as clear as possible about her experiencing in relation to Robert. That is what she can offer him – the reality of a reasonable person – so that he can use that to examine his own, different, phenomenal reality. Also, she is not scared to offer him a critical perspective on himself. He might not like it – at first at least – but she would then work with whatever was his response. In this case Robert is slightly edgy with his 'Finished?', and, partly in humour but also perhaps partly seriously, he needs to check with 'Finished with me?' His counsellor's response to that is a strong one, 'Not by a long way, Robert', and the two of them find a common humour for the rest of the sequence.

It is interesting to note the counsellor's language in this sequence. She uses phrases like: 'You're driving me crazy' and other frank expressions. She does *not* dress them up in more indirect and less critical language. She does not attempt a sentence like: 'Robert – when you behave like that I feel a growing sense of irritation – it is *my* irritation' – ... etc, etc, She does not use 'counsellor-speak' because she has too much respect for her client, for herself, and for their potential to sort out their communication.

The most common early mistake made by person-centred counsellors in regard to their congruence is that they censor responses such as that of Robert's counsellor because they see it as 'negative'. It does not take long for this censoring process to build up a collection of unexpressed reactions towards the client and for an initial and potentially useful 'irritation' to grow into a growing frustration, giving rise to lasting resentment and even anger. By this stage the counsellor's experiences in relation to the client have more to do with her than with him. They would have become part of the *unspoken relationship* (Mearns, 2003: 64–73) between them. Indeed, at some level, the client would likely be experiencing things in relation to his counsellor's unspoken but perceivable judgements of him. Sometimes counsellors compound their incremental emotional abuse of their client in this process by determining, finally, to 'be congruent' with him. Usually this means venting their own pent up wrath – it has nothing to do with therapeutic congruence. An alternative intervention by the counsellor, if she had let communication deteriorate in this way, would be to start with an appropriate apology and then to describe in detail her own process ('showing her working') while expressing no inferences or judgements about her client's process. At the very least, this might help the client unravel what were his responsibilities and what were his counsellor's.

Earlier in this section we made passing mention of the fact that, in the normal course of congruent relating, it may be the counsellor, more than the client, who does the learning. This is what happens in the following sequence between Troy and his counsellor. Troy has been speaking at length of his grief at the loss of his mother after a long illness, ending with:

TROY: I feel lost without her. I never expected to feel that.
COUNSELLOR: I really feel for you in that, Troy – it really hit you – only when she was gone – how much she really meant to you.
TROY: [*long silence*]
COUNSELLOR: [*pause*] I think I missed you there, Troy. I think that was *me*, not you.

A lot is happening in this short sequence. The counsellor thought that she was responding congruently and empathically. But, in Troy's silence, she senses that her statement has been about her and not about Troy. Furthermore, she is able to re-find her congruence in expressing that sensing.

Counsellors get it wrong sometimes, indeed, quite often. That is not something about which we should feel overly disturbed. As well as enriching the quality of presence we can offer to our clients, our own humanity will sometimes become confused with that of our client. In training and also in our later development we will become aware of the vulnerabilities in ourself and how these tend to encroach on our work as counsellors. That allows us to sense them as they are surfacing, smile gently at ourself, and lay them aside for the moment. That is an ability that person-centred counsellors develop. Another skill is to *notice* these personal processes when they do interfere, as in this instance with Troy. Once noticed, the counsellor needs to re-take possession of the material before it can begin to contaminate her client's experiencing. Troy's silence may be indicative of his strength in noticing that his counsellor's response did not fit him, but a client with a profoundly externalised locus of evaluation might well be forced to integrate her counsellor's experience as his own.

Resonance

Peter F. Schmid offers the useful concept of *resonance* to help us to clarify the nature of the counsellor's experiencing in relationship with her client:

> Through self-awareness in therapy the therapist becomes conscious of their experiencing, i.e. the immediate present flow of experiences. What they experience is *resonance* to both the client's world and/or for their own world. Resonance … means the echo in the therapist triggered by the relationship with the client. (Schmid and Mearns, 2006: 181)

Three forms of resonance are identified: *self-resonance*; *empathic resonance* and *personal resonance*.

Self-Resonance

Self-resonance is the reverberation of one's own thoughts, fears, desires, doubts, feelings, etc. It may have been triggered off by the client's description of his experiencing, but it is entirely our own. It was self-resonance that Troy's counsellor was experiencing and initially confused it with Troy's experiencing. Another example is provided by Schmid, where the client is talking about her partner:

> CL: Shall I love him or hate him? I don't know, I am confused …
> TH: [*thinking of his own partner*] Good question! You never know. (Schmid and Mearns, 2006: 183)

As was mentioned in relation to Troy's counsellor, in her development the counsellor will want to discover her vulnerabilities in relation to self-resonance.

Empathic Resonance

Much of the reverberation the counsellor will experience in relation to her client will be empathic – the counsellor will be picking up the sensing of the client and reflecting that back to him. It is worth distinguishing two forms of empathic resonance in order to describe the richness of the counsellor's responding.

First, there is *concordant* empathic resonance, where the counsellor is depicting as accurately as possible the expressed experiencing of the client. This is what is described in Chapter 4 as *accurate empathy*. Continuing the example from Schmid:

> Cl: Shall I love or hate him? I don't know, I am confused …
> Th: [*primarily sensing the client's confusion*] There are mixed feelings in you. You experience affection, you experience dislike and these are in you at one and the same time. (Schmid and Mearns, 2006: 183)

Second, there is *complementary* empathic resonance, which means that the client's symbolisation is complemented, the counsellor adds something else to the client's current expression, but what is added is also the result of empathy. The addition might reflect a dimension of the client's experiencing at the edge of their awareness. Complementary empathic resonance is what was described in Chapter 4 as *additive empathy* or a *depth reflection*, for example:

> Cl: Shall I love or hate him? I don't know, I am confused …
> Th: [*sensing primarily that the client gradually has been growing tired of the person he talks about*] … or even forget about him? (Schmid and Mearns, 2006: 183)

Personal Resonance

While self-resonance springs from the counsellor and empathic resonance from the client, personal resonance comes from the relationship between them. In personal resonance the counsellor includes her own responses, as a reasonable person, to the client's experiencing. It is what we were describing in the previous section as the counsellor lending her phenomenal reality to the client. Continuing the example:

> Cl: Shall I love or hate him? I don't know, I am confused …
> Th: [*personally touched by the client's bewilderment*] … which makes me aware how much I truly hope you come to the right decision this time. (Schmid and Mearns, 2006: 185)

This is different from only referring to the client's experiences (empathic resonance) and also different from telling one's own story (self-resonance) in response to the story of the client. In personal resonance the counsellor shows her side of the relationship with her client. Personal resonance is an integral expression of the quality of presence offered by the counsellor and is powerful in encouraging the client to move into relational depth.

It is certainly personal resonance that Lietaer is depicting in his paper on congruence as he describes work with patients who had been diagnosed with schizophrenia:

> With this very withdrawn group of patients, the 'classical' type of intervention – reflection of feelings – fell short: there was often very little to reflect. In their attempts at establishing contact, the client-centred therapists learned to use an alternative source of help, their own here-and-now feelings. (Lietaer, 2001: 46)

He goes on to cite Gendlin:

> When the client offers no self-expression, the therapist's momentary experiencing is not empty. At every moment there occur a great many feelings and events in the therapist. Most of these concern the client and the present moment. The therapist need not wait passively till the client expresses something intimate or therapeutically relevant. Instead, he can draw on his own momentary experiencing and find there an ever-present reservoir from which he can draw, and with which he can initiate, deepen, and carry on therapeutic interaction even with an unmotivated, silent, or externalized person. (Gendlin, 1967: 121)

These accounts of Lietaer and Gendlin are similar to the experience of one of the present authors (Mearns) in working with a hospitalised patient, Rick, whose traumatisation in war had rendered him mute:

> I began our first meeting by *talking*. In working with a mute patient it is important not to expect them to speak or to reciprocate communication in any way. At the same time, we are always looking for a 'window' for their speech or other communication. My speaking in that first session is to represent who I am and what I am about. That is quite a challenge in the circumstance where we are getting absolutely nothing back from the other person. I must describe 'who I am' and it must be real … So, my 'who I am' speech has to show Rick that I am going to be a real person with him, rather than a representative of the military. I have to present myself exactly as I see myself, warts and all, with all my doubts, fears and, particularly, including how I feel *here and now*. My communication must be excruciatingly congruent because this patient will have a nose for the slightest incongruence. (Mearns and Cooper, 2005: 100–1)

This is an interesting example, because it bridges the gap between personal resonance and *willingness to be known* (Barrett-Lennard, 1962).

Most of the time, the last thing a client wants to know about is the counsellor and her life – but there are exceptions, particularly where the counsellor is trying to make a fragile contact, as in the above examples.

Metacommunication

Metacommunication is communication about our communication – it is talking about what is happening to each of us and between us (Kiesler, 1982, 1996; Rennie, 1998; van Kessel and Lietaer, 1998). Metacommunication can be structured by inserting formal review times in the counselling process or by the use of exercises that encourage both client and counsellor to reflect upon their process and their experience of the other (Mearns, 2003: 69–73). Equally, metacommunication can be informal, simply part of the dialogue within the counselling session, with the counsellor (and also the client) giving their own experience of the events between them and inviting the reflections of the other, as in the following statements and questions by counsellors and clients:

- How has this session been for you?
- I've been feeling that you're getting fed-up with me.
- When I said that – I really meant it – I wonder if you heard it that way?
- I don't believe you – you say that – but a little voice in my head says it's not true.
- I worry about how much you are getting out of this.
- We've had a nice time today, but we haven't spoken about what happened last week.
- You are being very nice to me ... but I still think you are a witch!

Metacommunication is important because it helps the two persons to become aware of more elements of their relationship. In any human relationship there is the spoken and the unspoken, with the latter usually larger and more psychologically significant (Mearns, 2003: 68–73). The best informal medium for metacommunication is the congruence of the counsellor (and the frankness of the client!). Often the inspiration for such congruence leading to metacommunication is the personal resonance of the counsellor. Perhaps the counsellor feels a growing discomfort in her communication with the client – it feels that something important is not being said. She is reverberating with the discomfort and it does not go away. Perhaps it leads to her own realisation of what she has not been saying, or perhaps it feels like the client is holding back. In either event a congruent response is called for. A mistake counsellors sometimes make is to try to work it out too much in advance. While that feels safer, it puts the counsellor too far ahead of the client and can sound too powerful. If it is expressed earlier, when it is still emerging, though still strong, there can be a more equal exchange, as in the following sequence between the counsellor, Rachel, and the client, Sylvia:

> RACHEL: It may be nothing, but I've been feeling uncomfortable in our session today … like … I wonder if there's something between us. Are you feeling anything like that?
>
> SYLVIA: NO!
>
> [*SILENCE*]
>
> RACHEL: You say 'NO', but you say it pretty strongly, Sylvia …
>
> SYLVIA: [*lowers her eyes, fidgets, looks uncomfortable*]
>
> RACHEL: Want to leave it … or go with it?
>
> SYLVIA: [*pause*] Someone I met during the week said that I should stop seeing you – that it would do me no good.

Needless to say, there was a lot more to this now opened dialogue between Sylvia and Rachel. There is nothing magical or mystical in Rachel's sensing of something being unsaid. She was using sensitivity that she, like any person, has developed from her experience of hundreds of thousands of human interactions. She was also employing her professional discipline in raising the question in as facilitative a fashion as she could. Moreover, she was skilled enough to know that this was personal resonance and not self-resonance. A parallel, self-resonance, example might be the inexperienced counsellor harbouring fears that her client was not expressing doubts about her (the counsellor) and actually inviting that expression from a client who, up to then, had felt no such thing.

The discipline of congruent metacommunication is critical in work with clients whose *locus of evaluation* is profoundly externalised. With such vulnerable clients, counsellors sometimes believe that congruence is contraindicated. Nothing could be further from the truth. The client whose locus of evaluation is profoundly externalised has enormous difficulty in knowing the difference between him and the other person, so it is essential that the counsellor does not contribute to that confusion through her own lack of clarity. Also, it is important for both the counsellor and client to keep track of the inferences the client is taking from their relationship, so metacommunication plays a much larger role. An example of this work is given in Mearns (2003: 80–3), with the client, June. June was so vulnerable in relation to her locus of evaluation that she would take 'direction' from the counsellor where none was offered. She *needed* to take direction and she had become skilled in detecting a different tone, a pause, a change in eye contact and numerous other verbal and non-verbal cues that she regarded as clues to what the counsellor would want her to believe, to do, or even to feel. On average, there were ten occasions in each session when the counsellor found himself pausing to check what June was inferring from his behaviour and openly matching that against his actual experiencing. The work was painstaking, but June was highly motivated to become able to monitor and manage her own experiencing.

In contradistinction to June, whose locus of evaluation was profoundly externalised, Brian Thorne writes of his work with a client, Emma, who has become increasingly at ease with her counsellor and dares to address what is happening between them in a quite startling and intimate fashion:

Emma: [*fighting back tears without much success*] You love me don't you? [*These words were spoken in little more than a whisper and with an intonation of incredulity.*]

Brian: Yes, I do – that is if love is measured by the depth of desire for someone's good. I so much long for your well-being and happiness that there are moments when I think I shall burst. [*I knew that in speaking these words I had laid all my cards on the table and I felt immensely vulnerable.*]

Emma: I think I knew that but I couldn't really believe it. You're not *in* love with me, are you?

Brian: No, Emma, I'm not in love with you, but I do feel pretty passionate about you. [*The silence which followed this last exchange seemed to go on for a long time. Indeed, I have no idea how long it lasted but it seemed to be outside of time and space. When she next spoke Emma seemed to be returning from far away and yet to my eyes she was more sharply delineated, and it was as if I had known her since the beginning of time.*]

Emma: I thought for a moment just now that you were my father. He never knew me as a woman.

(Thorne, 2002: 73–4)

In this instance the preparedness of both counsellor and client to address their unspoken relationship resulted in a major step forward in the client's management of her unresolved grief at the death of her father in early adolescence.

Incongruence

Most cases of incongruence are not as glaring as the examples that follow. In supervision, incongruence may be identified after examining the whole taped interview or even a series of interviews: only then is the gradual change in the counsellor observable. For instance, it may be that the counsellor is slowly becoming less spontaneous and more guarded. No single piece of the interview stands out as incongruent but gradually the counsellor is detaching herself from the relationship. This creeping incongruence is difficult for the counsellor to notice without help through supervision and analysis of recordings of her work. Occasionally, incongruence is more glaring; for instance, there is the 'double-message' where the counsellor is trying to hide her true response – her words may say one thing, but her non-verbal expression says another. Such a case would be the counsellor who says: 'I think it would be good for us to meet again as soon as possible', while simultaneously looking bored! Other common examples include the counsellor's warmth which is so effusive that it takes on an air of unreality, or that irritatingly regular 'mm-hmm' which pretends that the counsellor is listening when, in fact, she may not be.

Counsellors will have developed numerous ways of being incongruent because incongruence is so ingrained in our culture, as we described earlier. One of the reasons why person-centred training places more emphasis on group work than individual therapy for personal development is that it is more difficult to sustain incongruent forms of relating in groups, at least in groups where there is a norm of true encounter (Mearns, 1997a).

Examples 1 and 2 report two glaringly incongruent responses reproduced verbatim from tape-recordings of sessions.

Example 1

CLIENT: I don't think you like me.
COUNSELLOR: Of course I like you.
[*Silence*]

In this example the counsellor was perfectly aware of the fact that she did not like the client, but she lied. It is never easy for a client to challenge the counsellor, and that was certainly true in this particular case. It had been a tremendous opportunity for the counsellor to respond to the fact that her client was willing to invest so much in the relationship that he could even look at its difficulties. Unfortunately the counsellor could not take that opportunity by providing a congruent response and a comprehensive follow-up to that response.

Example 2

CLIENT: You seem angry with me today.
COUNSELLOR: No, I'm not angry … it's just that I've had a lot on my plate today.
[*Silence*]

The reader will have guessed that the counsellor *was* angry. However, in this particular case her incongruence was due to a lack of awareness of that anger within her. In this case there was no lasting damage from her incongruence, only temporary confusion in the client who was, of course, quite clear that the counsellor was angry. In between sessions the counsellor realised her incongruence and made a point of raising that fact, explaining it fully and apologising, not for her anger, but for her incongruence.

These examples illustrate two quite distinct forms of incongruence which can occur at points A and B in Figure 6.1.

Incongruence A is where the counsellor is *unaware* of aspects of her experiencing in response to her client and hence cannot give expression to them. Example 2 exemplifies this form of incongruence. Incongruence B is where the counsellor is aware of her experiencing but *chooses* not to give expression (e.g., Example 1). Another example might help to clarify the difference between A and B. In incongruence A, the counsellor might have mounting feelings of irritation or impatience, but because she is not aware of these she cannot respond to them. Although the counsellor does not notice her own incongruence, her client might sense that something is wrong as he perceives changes in the counsellor's non-verbal behaviour. He may feel the counsellor's tension or perceive her tone of voice becoming more cold and detached. He may notice the counsellor avoiding eye contact or sense the loss of quality in the interest she is showing. In incongruence B the same result can arise, but for a quite different reason. Here the counsellor would be aware of her mounting feelings of irritation or impatience, but she may resist giving expression to these feelings even though they are persistent and relevant responses to the client. Again, her

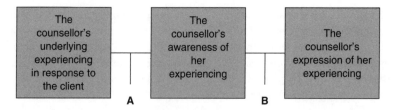

Figure 6.1   *Two forms of incongruence*

client may be sensing the discontinuity between the counsellor's experience and expression. The client does not know what the counsellor is doing but his own sensitivity leads him to be suspicious. This difference between incongruence A and B was shrewdly alluded to by one client who, after repeated incongruence on the part of his counsellor, faced her with the question: '*Who are you trying to fool, ma'am: me or you?*' If she was trying to fool *him* then it was incongruence B, but if she was fooling *herself* it was incongruence A!

In exploring reasons for counsellor incongruence it is again important to distinguish types A and B. Incongruence A can be related to the counsellor's lack of self-awareness, or it may be that she has personal difficulties in the area to which the client is attending. For instance, a counsellor who fears anger might find that her incongruence increases as that issue is approached by her client. Alternatively the incongruence may mirror the position of the counsellor in the relationship. For example, she may be unaware of her growing alienation or detachment in relation to the client. All these factors would lead to a deterioration in the quality of the counsellor's presence and consequent incongruence.

The bases for incongruence B, where the counsellor is consciously withholding, can be similar or quite different. Perhaps the counsellor is able to give expression to 'nice' feelings, but not to 'bad' feelings, and in a few cases the exact opposite may be the case. Alternatively, the counsellor may be too tired, emotionally or professionally, to be fully present and so she prefers to go through the motions of a helping interview rather than actually get involved in it. At other times the counsellor may be protecting some image of herself in the client's eyes; for instance endeavouring to have the client see her as *expert, powerful,* or *coherent and stable.* Protecting such myths about the power of the counsellor might help to engage the faith-healing dimension of helping but does not have much to do with being congruent. In some cases incongruence B, like A, may be related to other emotions within the counsellor; for instance *fear*. One of the present authors writes about this elsewhere:

> I am aware that my incongruence B has a lot to do with *fear*. When I protect my client from my authentic response I am in fact protecting *me* from the possible consequences of my feelings. It is nice and easy to say 'that would be too difficult for my client to take right now' or 'perhaps I'll work that out a bit more in my head and then talk it out with her – it might be too confusing the way it is just now'. These are nice reasons for not responding to my client, but they can just as easily be rationalisations. Underlying them can be things like 'she might be horrified at me saying that'/'he might stop liking me if I said that'/'I don't know what would happen next if I said that'. Such fears inhibit congruence. For that matter, fear can also inhibit empathy and unconditional positive regard. (Mearns, 1986: 8)

Guidelines for Congruence

Our definition of congruence at the start of this chapter looked clear and simple. It suggested that for congruence to be present the counsellor's outward responses to her client should consistently match her inner experiencing in relation to the client. For a more complete understanding we have to explore in detail the kind of counsellor experiencing that is implied, because plainly not all the counsellor's sensations are appropriate to the counselling contract. The counsellor cannot simply express whatever she is feeling in the moment on the grounds that she is 'being congruent'. If she were to do this the counselling session would become more focused upon her than on the client. It is necessary to lay down three guidelines that would generally govern the counsellor's therapeutic congruence.

First, when we talk about congruence we are referring to the counsellor's *response* to the client's experiencing. The counsellor may have lots of feelings and sensations flowing within her but it is only those which are in response to her client that are appropriate for expression. In this regard it is important to note that congruence is not the same as 'willingness to be known', already discussed in this chapter. When the counsellor is being congruent she is giving her genuinely felt response to the client's experience at that time. Only rarely would this response disclose elements of the counsellor's life, and even then the focus of attention would remain on the client rather than the counsellor. For instance, the counsellor might say:

I remember when I lost a close loved one – I also felt that kind of 'desolation' which you've described, but you are saying something more … you are saying that as well as feeling desolation, you are feeling … a kind of … annihilation?

In this example there is a mixture of self-resonance and empathic resonance. The counsellor is reverberating with her own sense of desolation (self-resonance) which happened to be similar to the client's experiencing, but she is also sensing the client's feeling that is akin to 'annihilation' (empathic resonance). Her response clearly labels the self-resonance and does not seek to continue to focus upon it, moving instead to the empathic resonance. The element of self-resonance has no therapeutic significance – it is simply a passing gift – a willingness to be known.

A second guideline for a congruent response is that it must be one that is *relevant* to the concerns of the client. Sometimes the response the counsellor has towards the client's experience is only really relevant to the counsellor herself. For instance, the client talking about his marriage might lead the counsellor to think about the marriage of another client; or the client talking about his stress might lead the counsellor to reflect upon the phenomenon of stress in general. Although these experiences of the counsellor are in response to the issues that the client has brought, the counsellor would not normally interrupt the client's flow to express them, because it is unlikely that they will be relevant to the client's present experiencing.

In general, the counsellor's self-resonance would not be relevant to the concerns of the client and would not be voiced by the counsellor, whereas the empathic resonance and personal resonance are highly relevant. The exceptions might be the kind of passing 'willingness to be known' exemplified above but even here the self-resonance is merely mentioned, it is not made a focus for the work. Another exception is where the self-resonance is so persistent or striking that it needs attention because it is in danger of disturbing the counsellor's presence. This takes us to the third criterion for congruence.

In a counselling session the counsellor may experience a catalogue of responses to her client. Even if she were only to respond to those relevant to the concerns of the client, the counsellor might still dominate the session. Hence, a third guideline becomes necessary: that the experiencing the counsellor responds to tends to be *persistent* or particularly *striking*. The counsellor would not do anything about a mild feeling of irritation that drifted in and then out of her awareness, or a brief flash of annoyance in relation to one particular thing that the client said. But if that irritation or annoyance persisted or recurred, or was so striking that it was important to the relationship between counsellor and client, then it would require attention. Most such examples fall into the categories of empathic resonance or personal resonance, but, exceptionally, the persistent or striking response is self-resonance. Consider the account in Box 6.3 of a counsellor in some distress.

Box 6.3   When Self-Resonance Spills Over

Generally, the counsellor's self-resonance is not relevant to the client or their work together. But, occasionally, it is felt so strikingly or persistently that the counsellor voices it in her attempt to stay 'present' in the relationship. The counsellor, Rani, gives such an example:

> My refugee client, Tariq, was talking about his experience of torture. My own personal experience of being tortured generally helps me to stay close to such a client – I can stay close when many other counsellors would be in terror. But this time it got *too* close to my own experience and I lost control. As he described the detail of his torture I felt my own. I felt every cut of the knife. I came out in a cold sweat and I started shaking. His voice drifted into the background and the sadistic smiles of my own torturers came face-to-face with me. For a while Tariq didn't notice me and he carried on. Then he slowly ground to a silence and just looked at me. I forced myself to speak. I had to tell him about me – not the detail of my story – but what I was experiencing there and then:

Rani: Tariq, I'm shaking with fear. I need to say it because it is so powerful that I'm fading away from you. I too have been tortured – a long time ago. For years it has not affected me, in fact, it sometimes helps. But just now it flooded me. I was taken over by my fear – the enormity of my fear. I'm hoping that by saying it, it will subside. I can feel it subsiding as I speak. I'm sorry that I couldn't stay with you.

Tariq: I understand.

Rani: I suspect that you do.

In Box 6.3 the counsellor discloses her self-resonance as part of her professionalism. She is not seeking to use the session to talk further about her own experiences but she needs to take time to voice them in order to help her to come back from them. To do otherwise would be an act of deception; her client is aware that she is distressed, so he should be made aware of the reasons for it. When handled congruently, even a powerful disruption such as this can add to the depth of the relationship, as in the present example.

In summary, then, it is necessary to qualify our working definition of congruence lest it is presumed that the counsellor should give expression to every fleeting sensation that she experiences during the counselling session. When we talk about being 'congruent', apart from exceptional circumstances as in Box 6.3, we are referring to the counsellor giving expression to *responses* she has that are *relevant* to her client and that are relatively *persistent* or *striking.* These guidelines may appear to rule out a lot of what is conscious for the counsellor, but in fact they include most of the important material. This issue of guidelines for congruent responding is explored more fully in Mearns and Schmid (2006).

Even then these are only 'guidelines' for the less experienced practitioner who might otherwise struggle with the question of the appropriateness of her reactions to the client. As she gains experience and understanding of herself she will become fluent in her congruence and able to trust her instantaneous judgement of appropriateness. At this stage in her development the counsellor is able to be fully present and use herself in the therapeutic relationship. Her easy congruence, combined with an empathy that can track the client's experiencing accurately as well as dipping to the very edge of his awareness, and an unconditional valuing of his worth as a human being, together offer a powerful humanity.

How Can the Counsellor Develop her Congruence?

Trainee counsellors come to the person-centred approach with at least the rudiments of the attitude of unconditional positive regard and early in training it is common to pay particular attention towards helping the trainee to release her empathic sensitivity, but the therapeutic condition that is usually slowest to develop is congruence. Anything that has considerable power carries a proportionate threat of danger; the person-centred counsellor investing her *self* in the therapeutic process is full of power and danger and the trainee is wise to be cautious.

Essentially, the danger implicit in congruence is that the counsellor's *self-resonance* disturbs the process, that her own needs and fears become too intimately tied to her awareness of her client and hence confuse her congruent responses. 'But I was only being congruent!'is a weak excuse for the counsellor who has imposed her own needs and fears on to her client. The freedom offered by congruence carries particular responsibilities for the counsellor's continuing self-development because it is only through such development that her own needs and fears can become less imposing in the therapeutic arena (see Box 6.4).

Box 6.4   Congruence Does Not Mean Imposing One's Own Needs and Fears

In Chapter 4 we explored how the counsellor's personal needs and fears could contaminate her empathy. Similarly, they can have a disturbing impact upon the counsellor's congruence. The following two statements are from supervision sessions with counsellors in the process of discovering the ways in which their own needs and fears impose themselves in their counselling.

A   I wanted to just go over to her [*the client*] and give her a big squeeze – but I realised that that was my need to say 'there, there now, don't cry – I'll look after you – you poor little girl'. Squeezes can sometimes be 'giving' but sometimes they are 'taking away'. In this case it would have been keeping her as the little girl whom I can handle – and taking away the woman whom I find more difficult.

B   I feel so *angry* towards him – it is strong, it is persistent, and yet it is just not appropriate for the simple reason that it has absolutely nothing to do with him – it is my own horror of being partner to a man like him who treats his wife like furniture. I can't see his loving, his softness, or his fear, while I am blocked by my own fear.

The counsellors in Box 6.4 were aware of the influence in these examples of their own needs and fears. Learning in the person-centred approach involves the counsellor discovering and exploring those aspects of such needs and fears that impose themselves in the counselling setting. As this work progresses the counsellor becomes more trusting of herself; learning to be congruent is inseparably linked with learning to trust oneself. If the counsellor is to use herself, including her congruent reactions, in the counselling relationship, then she must trust that self and those reactions. Usually she will not know where her reactions are leading nor even, in the moment, from where they are coming, but she will have learned to recognise the difference between a reaction that is probably empathic and one that is likely to stem more from her own needs or fears. In learning to trust herself she will have found that even her spontaneous reactions do not seek to destroy, and more often than not that they prove to be helpful to the client.

This kind of discovery cannot be made by the counsellor simply reflecting on herself even with the help of the most able supervisor. It can only be achieved through the counsellor 'experimenting' with herself in real helping contexts, including counselling. New counsellors may feel uncomfortable with this idea of the counsellor experimenting, but in fact if the counsellor is to develop and change as a helper, then experimenting, in the sense of using different aspects of herself, is inevitably involved. Box 6.5 reproduces a counsellor's report of one example of experimentation. In this box the counsellor uses the phrase '*I forced myself to let it happen*'. This is a perfect way to describe the idea of experimentation with one's congruence. The counsellor had gradually grown to trust herself more, including her touching, but an important step in the process was to begin to let that happen in practice. Paradoxically, it often takes some deliberate intent to '*let it happen*'.

Box 6.5   A Touching Experiment

This extract is taken from a trainee counsellor's 'personal profile' which is a journal focused on the personal development aspect of counselling training.

Yesterday Ben [a client] was shaking and strained in his grief and I really wanted to reach out to him and put my hand on his. So often in the past I would have got lost in thought about how appropriate that may be, but this time I just forced myself to let it happen. As soon as I touched him it was as though some of my warmth went over to him and his tension released – he gasped and exploded in sobbing.

Such experiments are important steps in the counsellor's fostering of her congruence. In the example from Box 6.5 the counsellor has gained further confirmation that her congruent response was to be trusted. She has found one more aspect of her being that she can potentially trust with clients. In the process of fostering her congruence the counsellor will uncover more dimensions of herself that she can use constructively in counselling. These discoveries are exciting because the developing counsellor moves from a position where she invests very little of herself, often looking somewhat stiff and stereotyped, to one where she becomes progressively more free until it seems that almost every part of her being might be used in her work.

This is the essential challenge for the person-centred counsellor in her development. As was mentioned at the conclusion of Chapter 3, the ultimate aim is that the counsellor will be able to offer an encounter at relational depth not just to some clients but to *every* client who comes to her door. This is not achieved in initial training. Early training succeeds if it helps the counsellor to *initiate* the self-development attitude. Most of the work happens later – in the counsellor's continued professional development. There are two large parts to this self-development curriculum: expanding her experience of humanity and broadening the self she can offer in the counselling room.

Expanding our Experience of Humanity

Here the aim is to become experienced and comfortable with an ever broadening range of humanity. This also involves the kind of 'experimentation with self' just mentioned and the broadening of social experience discussed in Chapter 3. The counsellor, with the aid of her supervisor and sometimes a continuing professional development support group or an *intervision* support,[4] will identify different people and groups who might initially represent 'challenges' for her if she met them as clients. Sometimes this has to do with fear or prejudice that has not been sufficiently challenged by her previous experience. The trainee counsellor, Debbie, tells us about one of her challenges:

> Eventually I realised that if I was going to work professionally as a counsellor, I had better find out something about the other half of humanity. So I started to work with men!

---

[4]In Holland, Belgium and recently in France the term 'supervision' is being replaced, for experienced practitioners, by 'intervision'. Intervision can either be between two experienced practioners or in a small group.

Debbie's lightness and even humour in relating her challenge carries an important message. If we can approach the self-development agenda in a positive, expansive spirit, this will make it easier for us to take on challenges. The person-centred supervisor, for whom this continuing self-development agenda is her prime concern in work with her supervisee (Lambers, 2000, 2006), can be a considerable resource in helping the developing counsellor to adopt an expansive rather than defensive perspective on the process.

The challenge that the more experienced counsellor, Imran, set himself is briefly stated in a fashion that belies its immensity:

> I had never actively accepted myself as 'homophobic', but I was. Joining the men's group soon blew that away.

Imran did a most difficult thing – he faced up to his prejudice rather than hiding behind it. He had some help; a gay member of his personal development group had helped him to approach the men's group, openly, about his problem and his wish to join the group to tackle it. We can only guess at the fear the other group members had to lay aside in order to support his agenda.

Many aspects of the personal agenda are not as frightening as Imran's and often the way to tackle them is not as extreme, as in Elizabeth's example:

> When I would come to the edge of meeting the depths of my clients' despair I would always pull back. I got over that edge, initially, through reading about people's experiences of despair. That would take me into my tears – and closer to my sense of my own existence.

People might be inclined to discount the value of reading because it offers secondary rather than direct contact with humanity – yet it can be effective in stimulating our imagination and expanding our consciousness. In his own autobiography one of the authors (Thorne) often refers to his study of literature as a constant source of inspiration in developing his knowledge of humanity and his empathic repertoire (e.g, Thorne, 2005: 128).

In a chapter devoted to the work over 72 sessions with a profoundly traumatised war veteran, one of the authors (Mearns) struggled to grasp the war context of his patients, so he sought an experience that might deepen his appreciation:

> An experience which helped me to sustain myself was attending an informal discussion group of veterans … I used that group to stay connected with the kinds of experiencing [my patients] spoke about. (Mearns and Cooper, 2005: 107)

There is a myriad of ways in which the person-centred counsellor might extend her life experience to become familiar with a broader range of humanity. None of this will tell her what her client is experiencing, but it puts the counsellor closer, so that she is not frightened by a lack of familiarity.

Expanding the Self we can Employ in the Counselling Room

If the counsellor is to become able to offer relational depth to a wider range of clients, then it helps if she can broaden the 'self' she can offer. This guidance runs counter to a tendency within the profession constantly to constrain the behaviour of the counsellor. Such a tendency can only result in the reduction of counselling to a set of prescribed interventions relating to specific client problems. While this may fit a medical model it flies in the face of the research evidence on the importance of relationship (Mearns and Cooper, 2005: chapter 1).

Expanding the self we can offer in the counselling room may take the form of becoming adept at employing more parts – or what we have called *configurations* of self – in response to the client and his parts (see Chapters 2 and 4). At a more accessible level for the newer practitioner we can also think in terms of various dimensions of our self that may not presently feature in the counselling room, but could, in due course, be useful to us in making 'bridges' into the lives and experiences of a range of other clients. These are termed *existential touchstones*, (Mearns and Cooper, 2005: Chapter 8) and are defined thus:

> Life events and self-experiences that have given us glimpses of different dimensions of ourself and which we can enter to put us into a feeling state that is closer to our client's present experiencing and thus act as a 'bridge' for us into a fuller meeting with our client.

An interesting feature of this phenomenon is that some of these existential touchstones may have started their life as negative or even damaging experiences for us, but we have gradually integrated them so that they can add to our therapeutic capacity rather than diminish it. Box 6.6 presents some examples of existential touchstones.

Box 6.6   Existential Touchstones: Vulnerabilities Turned into Strengths

Five counsellors give us glimpses of earlier, difficult, experiences that have become existential touchstones for them in their work.

- The memory of my own earlier *loneliness* is something I can touch to bring me closer to my lonely client.
- It took me years to get over my experience of *abuse* – but now it doesn't frighten me any more – now I can even use it as a way of getting closer to my client's experience of abuse.
- I don't think you ever 'get over' a major *bereavement* – but it gets to a point that it deepens you as a person and helps you to be with your client in the depth of their bereavement.
- My client's *anger* was frightening in its power. At first I shrank from it – but I got back close to it by touching how my old anger had felt. It was interesting to see me use that for the very first time.
- My client talking about his *suicide* was difficult for me – I found myself repeatedly tuning in but then fading out. I realised that what was affecting me was a resistance to touching my own much earlier thoughts about suicide. When I stopped resisting and touched the sense of my own experience, it calmed me, and deepened me, to meet my client.

An important point to note about using these very personal experiences is that they are *not* telling the counsellor anything about her client. The counsellor's own experiences of loneliness, abuse, bereavement, anger and suicidal ideation in Box 6.6 are *different* from those of her clients. The experiences are not empathy, but they help the counsellor *to get into an existential state that helps her to engage with the power of her client's experiencing.* More detail on the nature and power of touchstones is available in Mearns and Cooper (2005: Chapter 8) and Mearns and Schmid (2006).

Developing her congruence may be one of the more demanding objectives of the person-centred counsellor, but it carries an enormous dividend, not just for her clients but for the counsellor herself. Being congruent in counselling relationships is experienced by counsellors as *energising* rather than draining. Even if workers have not experienced this, they may recall its opposite: that working in a context where incongruence prevails is exhausting and debilitating. It takes energy to maintain illusions. As the counsellor gradually uses more of herself in her work, her client is offered a vibrant, experiencing human being who combines an acceptance of him with an ability to step into his world and move around in it without fear. It is little wonder that this combination is experienced as liberating and exhilarating by many clients.

The Three Conditions in Combination

At the conclusion of Chapter 3 we outlined the concept of *relational depth*, pointing to the fact that this is facilitated by the counsellor offering the core conditions of empathy, unconditional positive regard and congruence. We have proceeded since to describe these conditions separately. Such separate treatment, however, threatens to lead us into a field of theoretical abstraction. The power of the core conditions resides in the presence of all of them, in high degree, combining and intertwining to create something much larger than the parts. Other commentators have also observed this essential integrative nature of the core conditions. Bozarth, for example, says:

> … the interrelationship of the conditions of congruence, empathy and uncon-
> ditional positive regard is so high that they are inseparable in the theory.
> Rogers occasionally discussed the conditions separately, perhaps as a way to
> provide pragmatic guidelines to therapists and to clarify specific aspects of
> each dimension. (Bozarth, 1998: 83)

Indeed, Bozarth argues that 'the three conditions are really, ultimately and functionally one condition' (1998: 80).

Similarly, Freire regards empathy and unconditional regard as the same experience:

> This description leads us inevitably to the conclusion that empathic experi-
> ence and unconditional positive regard are ultimately the sole and same
> experience. With unconditional positive regard, the therapist accepts every
> aspect of the client's experience as she offers her *presence* to the client. With
> empathic experience, the therapist accepts every aspect of the client's frame
> of reference as she enters the client's world. (Freire, 2001: 152)

In the present chapter we have also developed the link between congru-
ence and empathy by suggesting that the main function of congruence is that it allows the counsellor to be an accurate rather than a shadowy and distorting reflector to the client. We could go further by regarding much of the counsellor's congruence as the product of her *attending to her own felt sense in relation to the client* in the moment and giving the product of that attention to the client. Gendlin spoke of this similarity between empathy and congruence:

> Congruence ... means responding from out of our own ongoing experiential process, showing the steps of thought and feeling we go through, responding not stiltedly or artificially, but out of our felt being ... As experiential processes, empathy and congruence are exactly the same thing, the direct expression of what we are now going through with the client, in response to him. (Gendlin, 1970: 549)

Unconditional positive regard and congruence are also related, with the existence of one facilitating the development of the other: when the counsellor accepts the client then it is easier for her to trust the client and feel free to use herself in a fully congruent way. Indeed, where counsellors experience difficulties with congruence in relation to a particular client, their person-centred supervisor will often invite them to consider how far they accept the client, since a lack of congruence can be a symptom of difficulties with trust and acceptance. Being congruent can also help to promote acceptance. This is referred to as *taking risks in the relationship*: for instance, the counsellor may be open about a difficulty she has in relation to the client and if the pair can explore and clarify that difficulty then their relationship and mutual acceptance may be enhanced in exactly the same way as occurs in any relationship.

Probably the most frequent challenge to the person-centred approach can be encapsulated in the question: 'What happens when your unconditional positive regard and congruence are in conflict – are you congruent about your lack of acceptance?' Carl Rogers was often asked this question, but rarely satisfied questioners, no matter what answer he provided! Part of the problem is that the questioner and the experienced person-centred practitioner endeavouring to respond are generally coming from quite different frames of reference. The questioner can readily imagine many contexts where she would experience that conflict, but the reality for the experienced person-centred counsellor is that, for the most part, this conflict simply does not arise. This may sound disingenuous in the extreme but it is none the less the reality. The developed and experienced person-centred counsellor does not have the kind of difficulty in valuing the client that is anticipated by the questioner. Many people have problems in valuing the other person when they are threatened by the position adopted by that person. But the major thrust of the person-centred counsellor's personal development has been such that they are less vulnerable within their own self – they are simply not threatened by the different value positions adopted by clients. They can consider the questioner's dilemma theoretically, but it is scarcely ever an issue in practice.

Nevertheless, we still need to consider this question for the developing person-centred counsellor. What does she do when she is confronted by a client who represents what she most fears? Should she endeavour to 'portray' some degree of valuing in the face of such a challenge? Actually, she might be able to do that because humans are so skilled at incongruence that they can be actors – a skill that is not observed in any other species. Should she, instead, immediately stop working with this client? Compared to the first option, this is an honourable choice, particularly if the counsellor *owns* her difficulty in the process and does not seek to project that on to the client. The third possibility is that the counsellor does not disconnect with the client but openly acknowledges her distress. This is a difficult choice and it is not one that trainers should seek to force upon trainees because, in making this choice, the trainee is actually opting, in that moment, to work beyond her personal limits. It is different for the experienced practitioner who has experience of entering these uncertain situations and functioning therapeutically. Nevertheless, it can be an important step for the trainee when she honours her own inadequacy and is honest with her client despite her own fear. One early trainee counsellor contributed a report of this kind of experience, which we reproduce in Box 6.7.

Box 6.7   Being Honest

I got to the point where I couldn't continue with Jan [the client]. She was so openly lesbian that it challenged me in every session. I didn't know what to do with that – I was scared. I couldn't 'pretend' with her – she would see through that. I talked with my supervisor about terminating with her. Looking back on it, I realise that I talked that out with my supervisor so that I wouldn't do it. In the end what I did was to 'come clean' with Jan. I made a 'speech' one day. I took a deep breath and said that I was scared of her; I knew this was more to do with me than her; I didn't want to 'put it on her'; but I always had had difficulty with her expressed affection for me and that I hadn't been honest about that up to this moment. Jan's reaction took my breath away. She thanked me for my honesty. She said that she was both sad and angry at my fear of her, but that it would have been much worse if I hadn't been honest. In that moment I remember wishing that I did not have this homophobic raft of fear within me, because I knew that, although we had been honest with each other, I could not go further with Jan until I had gone further with myself.

Congruence demystifies the counsellor's work because it shows simply and clearly what she is experiencing in response to the client. It shows that she is not harbouring complicated and threatening interpretations or theories about the client's pathology. It takes away the secrecy from counselling and ensures that the counsellor and the client share the same reality. Congruence is so basic to healthy human relationships and the development of trust that we must question any helping that minimises it. It is the professional responsibility of the counsellor to be fully and honestly present for her client, because her incongruence could certainly be *damaging* to someone who is already vulnerable. Early in this chapter we posed a question that might now be re-worded: 'Can I dare NOT to be me in response to my client?' We close this chapter with Box 6.8, which gives one client's view on the importance of his counsellor's congruence.

Box 6.8   Can I Dare *Not* To Be Me in Response to my Client?

Sometime after completion of counselling a client reflects back on his counsellor:

She was always *there* – always alive – always present. At the beginning I didn't trust her – like I didn't trust she was sincere – that she would *stay* interested in me. No-one had ever stayed interested in me. It took a long time before I trusted her. But every time we met she was so trustworthy – so real. She would get pissed off at me and she'd say so – and it was OK. Sometimes I'd get pissed off at her and that was OK too – like people do get fed up with each other from time to time – that's the way things are, isn't it?

In exploring the intricacies of empathy, unconditional positive regard and congruence we have drawn examples from many points in the therapeutic process. It now remains to work through that process, systematically highlighting the issues that arise at different stages. The logical place to commence such a journey is at its *beginnings*.

7

'BEGINNINGS'

The Power Game

Most of us at one time or another have been humiliated by our reception at the hands of someone from whom we are seeking help or information. The classically traumatic situation is one where we are kept waiting in an inhospitable room full of out-of-date magazines and are summoned – half an hour behind schedule – by a disembodied voice through an intercom which tells us to go to the second room on the right. We follow the directions and arrive in front of a closed door. We knock timidly and receive no response. We knock again and an irritable voice bids us enter. We go in to be confronted by a figure at a desk writing on a note-pad. We are ignored for a further minute and then a face looks up and an arm waves us towards an uncomfortable chair in front of the desk. By now we are so seriously intimidated that we can scarcely recall why we have come.

The process we have just described is an extreme example but it demonstrates in a stark form the abuse of power that, even today is disturbingly prevalent in some quarters of the helping professions. For the person-centred counsellor it is a matter of supreme concern that she does not

153

unwittingly fall into a similar trap. For her, as we saw in Chapter 1, her actions and attitudes are desirably determined by a belief that it is important to reject the pursuit of authority or control over others and to seek to share power. The implications of this belief for the reception of and initial encounter with clients are considerable and have a bearing on every aspect not only of the interaction between counsellor and client but also of the environment in which counselling takes place. Power games can be played with tables and chairs as much as with words and tones of voice. It is salutary for the counsellor to ask herself the question: 'What process does a client have to go through to get to me, and what messages does he receive along the way?' Box 7.1 summarises some of the questions such an examination might raise.

The Client Arrives with his Expectations

The counsellor who is awaiting a new client may well have difficulty in maintaining an openness to the experience of the first encounter. There can be many reasons for this but prior information often presents a major obstacle. Even if such information is limited its influence can none the less prove distracting and detrimental. It may be that the counsellor has had a phone conversation with the potential client and that this has sown the seeds of dislike or attraction or even the beginnings of a 'diagnosis'. The address of the client or, if the counsellor is institution-based, the client's work role or position in the hierarchy may evoke fantasies or stimulate attitudes in the counsellor. Most difficult of all can be the situation where the client has been referred by another person or agency so that the counsellor is in possession of a detailed referral letter or even a whole dossier of material about the client and his past life. In the face of such a welter of information the counsellor may experience grave problems in receiving the client with an open mind, and indeed of seeing him at all except through the distorting spectacles of other people's judgements and, not infrequently, of their impotence and frustration. Small wonder, then, that most experienced person-centred practitioners cultivate the art of deafness and blindness to other people's judgements about potential clients and even seek to hold at arm's length their own premature impressions which are usually based on fragmented and unreliable data. Referral letters and dossiers need to be treated with caution and read with skill. They could contain important information that the client would expect to be known. But the counsellor needs to develop the ability to distil the contents, separating fact from opinion – a more difficult task than it appears – and not allowing the content to create an impression before the first meeting.

Box 7.1   What Messages Does my Counselling Service Give?

- How warm and welcoming is the written material about my service?
- Does it over-emphasise my authority?
- How is my answerphone message received by others?
- If I have a website, does it convey friendliness as well as information?
- What does my waiting room say?

> Does it say that I am out of date like my magazines?
> Does it say that my service is shoddy like its furnishings?
> Does it say that we like the set-up well enough to put fresh flowers in the waiting room?
> Is my information board up to date and interesting enough to occupy the client who wants to be occupied?

- How does my receptionist respond to clients?

> Is he/she warm?
> Does he/she really help the client to feel that it is OK to be there?
> Is he/she equally sensitive to clients who need to be left alone and to those who need a bit of attention?
> Can he/she respond to the client in crisis?
> Does he/she know the kinds of situations when it is important that he/she interrupt me?
> Does he/she need more of my caring and attention?

- What does my counselling room say to clients?

> Does it convey warmth, or is it cold and clinical?
> Why is that certificate of mine on the wall?
> How far is it there for my clients or for me?
> Does it give confidence?
> Or does it remind clients that I am the expert?
> What else does my room divulge about me (through posters, paintings, books, etc.)?
> Is that OK?
> Is there a chair which is obviously 'mine' in the sense that it is more comfortable or higher than the others?
> Are there any tables or other obstacles between me and the client?
> Is the positioning of the furniture such that my client feels that I am not unduly close and yet close enough to hear every whisper and also able to touch without undue disruption?

The expectations that clients have of counselling and counsellors are many and varied and not a few will be at variance with the counsellor's own understanding of her task. Some clients may come expecting to be told what to do or be offered authoritative advice. Others, again, may expect a barrage of questions leading to a diagnosis of the problem. Yet others may be old hands at the therapeutic game and may come expecting little help but hoping against all the odds that this particular helper will be different. The counsellor can make no assumptions about her client's expectations but she can be sure that, unless these are to some extent revealed and explored in the early days of a therapeutic relationship, there will be grave difficulties later on. Everything, again, points to the desirability of the counsellor being able to be open, attentive, receptive and without assumptions, as she greets her new client for the first time and the door of the counselling room closes behind them.

The First Moments

The counsellor is on familiar territory, the client is not. She knows her room intimately, the client is there for the first time. The counsellor is well versed in the counselling activity, the client may be a complete novice. The counsellor is buttressed by her experience and knowledge, the client is likely to be vulnerable and in some distress. In short, at this opening moment this is a strikingly unequal encounter. The counsellor holds nearly all the cards in a game of which the client does not even know the rules. For the person-centred counsellor this clear imbalance of power will be something to address without delay. Somehow the client must be enabled to feel that he has not relinquished all control over his situation and put himself in an inferior position where he has no option but to be submissive and dependent. The counsellor will be at pains to do all she can to redress the power imbalance. Different counsellors develop their own individual ways of giving signals of warmth and equality. For instance one of the writers was influenced by his experience of a Japanese tea ceremony, and since then he has made a point of offering a hot drink to every client at the start of a session unless it is obvious that the client's crisis is too pressing. Pouring tea or coffee for a client has become an initial, unconditional gift and mark of respect. Having a glass of water to hand also shows forethought and care.

Pacing is important at the outset. An unhurried pace indicates that there is space in which to breathe, and it can induce a relaxation from tension. The counsellor's opening statement will be likely to reinforce further that it is the client's hour and that he has the freedom to use it for his own needs. The counsellor does not have a preconceived plan or structure into which the client must fit. The only structure may be the length of time which can be spent together on this first occasion and the counsellor may well make that explicit. Once, then, the client has chosen a chair and is sitting down with an air of expectancy the counsellor will begin:

Well, we have about fifty minutes together now. How can I be of help?

Sometimes, of course, no introductory words at all are necessary, for the client immediately bursts into tears or begins with a torrent of words which he has been holding back perhaps for days. Should this happen the counsellor will be content to give the client full attention and to follow where he leads. She will not attempt to intervene or to impose her own structure on the interaction. Some years ago one of the writers received a young female student who began to weep in the opening seconds of the first interview and who continued to cry for the following forty minutes. The counsellor merely waited attentively and after a few minutes gently took the client's hand and held it. At the end of the forty minutes the girl looked up, smiled through her tears and said: 'Thank you. I feel better now.' And she left without the counsellor having said a single word.

Sometimes the client's opening statements will reveal his expectations of the counselling process – or his lack of them. To the open-ended question 'How can I help you?' he may well reply, 'I'm not sure: perhaps you can't', or 'I would like you to give me your advice', or 'I just need someone who'll help me put things in perspective', or 'I've never been to a counsellor before. What do you do?', or 'I'm at the end of my tether. Someone's got to help me.' Whatever the reply the counsellor will be alerted to the client's expectations and needs and will be intent on understanding them so that she can relate to them and, if necessary, gently disabuse the client of inappropriate or unfulfillable expectations.

For the person-centred counsellor the task is always the same even if the response can take a hundred different forms. It is to 'level' with the client, to show him that he is worthy of absolute attention, that he merits every effort the counsellor can make to understand him, that he is perceived as a fellow human being who, for that reason alone, can be assured of the counsellor's acceptance and honesty. In the light of this overriding task it is instructive to track the varying responses that the counsellor might offer to the opening client statements quoted above. 'I'm not sure: perhaps you can't' might elicit: 'You're not really sure that I shall be of much use.' Or 'There's a real doubt in your mind about having come.'

Both these responses show that the counsellor's main concern is to indicate to her client that she really has heard what he has said and is not concerned to establish her own agenda or to offer what could only be facile assurance at such an early stage.

'I would like you to give me your advice' poses a more difficult problem for the counsellor. She knows that she is not in the business of advice-giving and that to be placed in such a role could be counterproductive. At the same time she may not wish to risk a response that could be seen by the client as an immediate put-down. She may opt for: 'You feel you need some guidance', or 'Perhaps, together, we can see what might be a way forward.' Or, most likely, she may regard the remark as simply an ice-breaker and merely nod or smile. Should it become apparent that the client really does expect her to offer authoritative instruction, or to tell him what to do, she will need gently to unravel this expectation as the session proceeds.

The client who opens with: 'I just need someone who'll help me get this in perspective' presents the counsellor with the dilemma of whether to respond to the role issue or to the veiled content implicit in the statement – or, indeed, to both: 'I shall be happy to help you see things more clearly', indicates the willingness of the counsellor to be the kind of mirror that the client seems to be requesting. 'You feel things have got somewhat out of proportion' acknowledges the client's fear that he has lost objective balance while: 'Perhaps together we can try to find the perspective you feel you've lost,' attempts to cope with both aspects of the client's statement.

Already in some of the possible counsellor responses the central issue of equality has been hinted at. As rapidly as possible the counsellor will wish, in the interests of honesty and clarity, to dispel the illusion that she will assume the role of expert in the client's life. The concept of coopera-tion and of 'coming alongside' in order that the necessary work be under-taken together needs to be established, although the counsellor, as always, must strive to be sensitive to the given moment and not allow a preoccu-pation with these role issues to ride roughshod over a client's more press-ing needs. It would be paramountly absurd, for example, to deliver a homily about working together if a client is shaking from head to foot and can scarcely string two words together.

The rare client who actually asks at the very beginning for a definition of roles and tasks is, in some ways, a counsellor's dream. Theoretically, of course, all clients should have addressed this issue before coming if they have read the agency's brochure or the counsellor's published statement about her work. In reality few do and those who have are unlikely to have internalised the implications for their own relationship with the counsellor. It is, therefore, worth reflecting on the likely response to the occasional client who says: 'I've never been to a counsellor before. What do you do?' As is almost invariably the case the counsellor has a number of options. She might decide to respond to the feelings behind the question: 'It's important to you to know how I work' or, as is likely at this opening moment, she might well take the question at its face value and try to answer it. Again, she might wish to check with the client whether he wishes to explore this issue thoroughly: 'Would you like us to talk about that at some length before we get started?' If she chooses the second option she is likely to say something like: 'I see my task as helping you to express what's on your mind so that you can perhaps begin to see things more clearly. And I really am concerned to try to understand what's going on for you.' Such a response is tackling a number of important issues in a highly concise way. In the first place the emphasis is placed firmly on the client's responsibility to move towards greater clarity with the counsellor's help. Second, there is an acknowledgement that to 'express what's on your mind' is not necessarily an easy thing to do and may require skilled help. Third, the counsellor's final remark stresses the paramount significance she attaches to understanding and indicates ('really am concerned') her preparedness to commit herself to this task. Should the client have made it clear that he really does want a kind of mini-seminar before beginning the counselling work, the likelihood is that the counsellor will talk at much greater length about the nature of the relationship that she hopes they may be able to achieve, and of her central belief in the capacity of individuals to find their own inner resources to cope with life's challenges. She may also explicitly state her willingness to stay alongside her client for as long as seems necessary and appropriate to both of them. Certainly there will be no reluctance on the counsellor's part to spell out to the client all those aspects of the counselling relationship and activities that require elucidation. She will be at pains to make it clear that she has no desire to retreat behind a professional smokescreen or to impress the client with psychotherapeutic jargon or mystique. On the contrary, her message will be that she wishes to be as honest and transparent as she can be about the counselling process, and that she is prepared to go to considerable lengths to convey this if that is what the client appears to want at the outset. One of the writers (Thorne) even found himself facilitating a discussion on a chapter from a previous edition of this book with a new client who was concerned to prepare himself adequately for the work ahead.

Establishing Trust

The duration of the *beginning* phase of counselling is directly related to the *readiness* of the client at the outset. Some clients arrive in counselling at a time when they are ready to take responsibility for their life and willing to trust an unknown process. Other clients may be embarking on this process before this sense of responsibility and trust is well-formed (see Box 7.2).

There is no magic formula and perhaps only two general rules, namely, that the process can never be hurried and that the counsellor's commitment is always to the consistent offering of the core conditions and to the equalising of power within the relationship. The client's 'readiness' will affect the speed with which trust develops in the relationship, and the establishment and maintenance of this trust is what will ultimately determine the level and quality of work that can be undertaken. In our case study, which begins later in this chapter, the client's 'readiness' was so great that, despite relatively poor work by the counsellor, both persons were swept into a depth of intimacy in only the second meeting. In other cases it may be weeks or months before sufficient trust is established to permit the first stumbling steps forward together.

There are some who would maintain that even the opening statement suggested earlier: 'Well, we have about fifty minutes together now. How can I be of help?' already colludes with a power imbalance. The very idea that the counsellor is there to help and that the client is the one to be helped has about it the whiff of a superiority/inferiority equation. There may well be something in this objection as far as certain clients are concerned, and Box 7.3 presents a range of other possibilities, all of which strive to avoid completely the trap of implying role definitions while at the same time offering a welcoming and unclinical invitation to an – as yet unknown – fellow human being.

All the responses presented in Box 7.3 share one element in common. They avoid small talk. No attempt is made to put a client at ease by discussing the weather, by alluding to the journey he may have made in order to be present or by discussing the state of the nation. Perhaps there may very occasionally be a case for resorting to such strategies, but in most instances a moment's reflection will reveal that a client's major concern is to embark at once on an exploration of his reason for coming. In such circumstances discussing the weather or other irrelevances usually heightens rather than alleviates anxiety and tension and sets an inappropriate norm of superficiality right at the beginning.

Box 7.2   The Client's State of Readiness for Counselling

Here are five elements that can denote a *low* 'state of readiness' in a client. None of these would make counselling impossible, but their presence or absence may lengthen or shorten the beginning of the counselling process.

Indecision about wanting to change: 'I'd like my relationship with my partner to be different but not if it creates too much upset.'

General lack of trust for others: 'People say they want to help me but really they want to help themselves.'

Unwillingness to take responsibility for self in life: 'It's nothing to do with me – it's this depression that makes me do these things.'

Unwillingness to take responsibility in counselling: 'It's your job to cure me – now get on with it!'

Unwillingness to recognise or explore feelings: 'Yes, I feel sad about it, but focusing on bad feelings never did anyone any good.'

Box 7.3   A Range of Counsellor Opening Statements

1   We have about fifty minutes now. How would you like to use the time together?
2   Well, what has brought you here? We have about fifty minutes now for us to use.
3   We have fifty minutes or so together now. Let me know what brings you here.
4   Well, where would you like to start? We have about fifty minutes now.
5   When you're ready please feel free to start where you want.
6   You have my full attention. It's over to you to let me know how you want to use the time we have.
7   [*Smiles*] Hello, then. It's all yours. Where would you like to begin?
8   [*Smiles*] How can I be of use to you?

The importance of starting immediately and avoiding all small talk is clear in the case of a client in crisis. The client response – 'I'm at the end of my tether. Someone's got to help me' – is just such an example of a client in crisis. In the face of such an opening statement the counsellor clearly needs immediately to move into a deeply empathic mode.

The client in crisis needs above all else to know that his feelings are received and understood, and that he is being taken with the utmost seriousness. This does not mean, of course, that the counsellor will be swept into the crisis herself. Indeed, the very activity of empathic understanding often has the effect of defusing a crisis, of slowing down the pace and relieving to some extent the crippling sense of anxiety and dread that the client may be undergoing.

The experience of being deeply understood and the sense of companionship that springs from this are in themselves powerful antidotes to the overwhelming feelings of panic and powerlessness that can be the concomitants of crisis. If the client in crisis is to endow the counselling process with trust he is more likely to do so if the counsellor's empathic ability is well to the fore from the opening seconds. Box 7.4 illustrates such an opening.

Box 7.4   The Crisis Client and the Empathic Beginning

Counsellor: How can I be of use to you?

Client: My sixteen-year-old son has been killed in a road smash – yesterday – I just can't face it. I feel I'm going mad. I'm caught in a nightmare.

Counsellor: [*puts her hand on the client's knee*] You just don't know how you are going to cope with what must be the most appalling thing that's ever happened to you. You feel you're going out of your mind.

Client: [*collapses sobbing into the counsellor's arms*]

It is likely that an opening session beginning with such a dramatic and empathic interchange will quickly develop an intensity of relationship leading to a high level of client self-disclosure. Indeed, the more the counsellor empathises accurately, the more likelihood there is of this occurring. There is a danger when a relationship accelerates at such breakneck speed that the client will subsequently feel that he has exposed himself too shamelessly and with indecent haste. The skilled counsellor will be alert to this possibility and may well attempt to forewarn the client of such feelings: 'We have shared a lot today and you have been very open with me. I want you to know that I feel fine about that just in case you feel later that you've said too much. I am sure it was right to jump in at the deep end.' The establishing of trust in a relationship is a delicate and complex process and inappropriate feelings of shame can be a major stumbling block to its consolidation.

In sharp contrast to the crisis client, the 'hardened' client who may well have visited a whole gamut of psychiatric and helping services challenges the counsellor in quite different ways. Such a person is likely to be swift to discern inauthenticity and to be well accustomed to the application of mechanistic counselling techniques. In short, he will be concerned to gauge the counsellor's genuineness and willingness to engage in a non-defensive way. Not surprisingly such clients can sometimes seem cynical and aggressive. Box 7.5 indicates the kind of – not untypical – opening exchange that can test the counsellor's congruence from the outset.

Box 7.5   The 'Hardened' Client and the Congruent Beginning

Counsellor: We have about fifty minutes now. How would you like to begin?
Client: The therapeutic hour, eh?
Counsellor: That's right.
Client: God knows where to begin. You people are all the same. You expect me to do all the bloody work.
Counsellor: I feel that's a bit rough. You've only known me for thirty seconds. But you reckon all counsellors are idle sods, do you, who force you to do all the difficult bits?
Client: Something like that, I suppose. But admit it, you aren't going to give me any answers, are you?
Counsellor: I doubt it, but I'm beginning to relish the prospect of wrestling around with you to find some answers. I'm game to have a go if you're willing to take the risk.

To such clients even genuine empathy may be seen as contrived and stilted, and the counsellor will do well to stay firmly in touch with her own feelings and to be ready to express them even if they seem combative or unaccepting. Hardened clients have often experienced helpers who had no real interest in them, or helpers who constantly ducked behind the helping role and disappeared into frightened anonymity. Above all they are seeking a counsellor who is prepared to be open and straight with them and whose identity is strong enough not to be shaken by their apparent aggressiveness or overt cynicism.

Some clients are so deeply self-rejecting when they first cross the counsellor's threshold that they are close to self-destruction. They feel worthless, rejected, without hope. In such cases it is the counsellor's attitude of unconditional positive regard that comes to the fore. This is not to say that empathy and congruence are irrelevant; simply that, for the deeply self-rejecting client, the most active ingredient for the fostering of trust is likely to be the counsellor's warm and unconditional regard. What is more, it may well be that such an attitude will have to be maintained over many weeks before the client can begin dimly to sense that it is strong and enduring. Such clients are often fearful that it is only a question of time before the counsellor's patience and warmth will run out, and they will be asked, politely, to seek help elsewhere. When it eventually dawns on them that this is not going to happen then the scene is set for them to make the first tentative move to climb out of the pit of self-negation. They begin to catch at least a germ or two of the counsellor's acceptance of them. One of the writers used to have on his wall – out of sight of all but the most inquisitive clients – a remarkable poem by Richard Church that begins 'Learning to wait consumes my life/Consumes and feeds as well', and this discipline of 'learning to wait' is a prerequisite in the face of the self-rejecting client. Without such a discipline, based on the deep belief in each individual's inner resources, there is little likelihood that the person-centred counsellor will be able authentically to maintain the consistent warmth and unconditionality of regard which alone can bring some of the most deeply distressed clients to the point of trusting the counsellor and the relationship she is offering.

'Disguises and Clues'

The inner world of a human being is a sanctuary, and it is therefore scarcely surprising that many clients grant admission only after much deliberation.

When the client hesitantly takes the initiative to move to a deeper level he may well do so in a somewhat ambiguous fashion. Especially in the early stages of a relationship, he may appear, in fact, to be giving double messages. Such behaviour is readily understandable, for the client can have no guarantee that the counsellor will be able to respond effectively to material not yet revealed. He does not know whether the more intense feelings, the raw needs and fears or the confusion or violence will drive the counsellor away. It is likely that such aspects of himself have driven other people away in the past. One strategy which the client may therefore choose to employ is to adopt a kind of 'disguise'. This behaviour indicates the need for the client to 'hedge his bets' so that in the event of the counsellor proving to be inadequate to respond at a deeper level he can readily retreat into the disguise without having suffered the consequences of rendering himself too vulnerable. Such a process is usually not wholly conscious on the part of the client – it falls just beyond the edge of his awareness.

In the early stages of a counselling relationship one of the most common 'disguises' is the cloak of humour when the client lets slip an important message but dresses the words up in apparent flippancy or accompanies them with laughter. In such an instance the counsellor is left with the choice of responding to the message or to the humorous packaging. An example of such a situation is the client who says, laughing as he does so, 'and I even get depressed about it sometimes – imagine that, me, depressed!' This kind of double message is telling evidence of how sophisticated the human being can be in his self-protection. If the counsellor proves unable to respond at the deeper level, or responds in an inadequate fashion, the client can readily fall back on the disguise and imply that it was the central message: 'Don't take me seriously; I was only joking.'

Another common strategy falling into the same category is for a client to convey a message of substance but to do so with a choice of words that makes it sound much less important. An example of this 'diluting' choice of words would occur if a severely depressed person spoke of himself as 'feeling a bit low sometimes' or a desperately lonely individual commenting 'but it's not so bad really because everyone gets lonely at times'. It is likely that we have all developed our own particular repertoire of preferred disguises and although a few, like those mentioned above, are very common, part of the counsellor's task at the beginning of a relationship is to discover the particular repertoire of the new client. This is an aspect of what we described earlier as appreciating the client's 'personal language' (see Chapter 5).

Sometimes it is not the client's actual words that indicate his desire to move to a deeper level but some non-verbal 'clue' which suggests that this important change could be made. The clue might be an unnaturally long pause, a change in the tone of voice, or a shift in eye contact. In just the same way as with disguises, the counsellor has the opportunity to accept the clue or not, and the client can acknowledge the existence of the clue or not. Sometimes the inexperienced helper may notice the clue but will decide not to go to a deeper level, perhaps for fear of entering terrain where she doubts her own ability to cope. More commonly, the inexperienced counsellor notices the clue but does not have the confidence to follow it up. She has not yet learned to trust her accumulated social experience, otherwise termed her 'sensitivity'. Or, again, it may be the client who decides that the counsellor's response is inadequate. In either case both may stay at the more superficial level. The social skill involved in exchanges such as these is truly marvellous: an invitation has been offered and either rejected or not accepted wholeheartedly enough, and all this has been conducted at a level of communication that neither needs to acknowledge. No matter what happens, both parties can save 'face', and this can be of particular importance for the client in the beginning stages of a counselling relationship.

The End of the Beginning

Much of this chapter has been concerned with first sessions or even opening moments in a counsellor–client relationship, but it will by now be clear that the beginning phase usually extends beyond the first session and cannot be expressed in terms of any particular time duration. We have made much of the establishing of trust in the relationship, and perhaps this must ultimately be the criterion that determines the point when the end of the beginning has been reached. At the stage when the client feels that he can trust the relationship sufficiently to take the risk of moving into unknown or half-known territory it can be said that the therapeutic journey is under way and the counsellor's companionship has been welcomed and endorsed. For some clients such a point, as we have seen, may be reached after thirty seconds, while for others it may be weeks before this critical phase is completed. It is this wide variation in the time required for trust to develop that has a crucial bearing on the structures that need to be agreed at the outset of the counselling relationship.

Structures and Contracts

As the end of a first session approaches, counsellor and client are faced with the problem of what to do next. It is, of course, possible that the only thing that needs to be done is to bring the relationship to a positive and satisfactory conclusion. After all there *are* some concerns and problems that can be appropriately explored and even resolved in the space of a fifty-minute interview! (Talmon, 1990.) Another reason for ending with the first session occurs where the client is not satisfied with the appropriateness of what the counsellor is offering. Perhaps the client has expected a more instantaneous 'solution', or seeks a relationship where the counsellor is a more powerful figure. Issues such as these can be important content during the initial session but they can also indicate a rapid ending even though the counsellor may regard it as premature (see Chapter 9). If the work is going to continue it is desirable that, at an early stage in the relationship, probably at the end of the first session, the implications of this are fully addressed. It is important for both client and counsellor that they have some sense of the nature of the commitment to each other on which they are about to embark.

There are likely to be a number of different options possible and, as always in the person-centred tradition, the counsellor will be concerned to ensure that she does not impose a structure on the client but that they work out a mutually acceptable arrangement for their work together. It is not uncommon for counsellor and client to agree on a provisional contract of a certain number of sessions. They might, for example, decide to meet weekly on four more occasions and then take stock. There is nothing intrinsically inappropriate about this kind of arrangement as long as it is clear from the outset that at the end of the agreed number of sessions it is the client and not the counsellor who will have the deciding say on whether or not to continue for a longer period. Many clients who present themselves for counselling have experienced much rejection and invalidation at the hands of others and it is only too likely that they will interpret the offer of a four-session contract as the counsellor's polite way of ensuring that she does not have to put up with them for more than a month. The policy of leaving the ultimate decision to the client about whether or not to continue does not, of course, mean that the counsellor forfeits her right to voice her own thoughts and feelings when the time comes to take stock. If she believes that the relationship is unproductive, or that little more is likely to be achieved she will say so, and her feelings will then become an important ingredient in the decision-making process. She will not, however, start from the basic assumption that she is right and that she knows better than her client. In our experience it has never happened that such provisional contracts end in a situation where the client wishes strongly to continue and the counsellor wishes strongly to terminate. If such an apparent impasse should ever arise it is our belief that the counsellor should attempt to continue at least for a while with all the support she can muster from her supervisor.

Instead of employing a provisional contract the counsellor and client may opt for a more open-ended arrangement whereby they agree to go on meeting for as long as seems necessary. It is likely that a somewhat imprecise time scale will be mentioned – a few weeks, a month or two, or, where the difficulties seem particularly severe, a few months perhaps. Such an arrangement is often much better suited to those clients who are highly anxious or fearful of rejection, or conscious that they have been sitting on a whole mass of distress for years. Again, however, it is essential that they know from the outset that the counsellor is not retaining the power to terminate the relationship when she feels it should end, but that they have the primary role in determining their own therapeutic need. Such open-ended arrangements can often benefit from periodic review sessions which will be much the same in nature as those occurring at the end of provisional contracts. These, too, can be agreed in principle at the outset and will become a natural part of the therapeutic process with either client or counsellor feeling free to introduce them.

The frequency of sessions needs also to be decided at an early stage, and here again the person-centred counsellor will be keen to avoid too much rigidity. It is likely that the weekly session of fifty minutes will be appropriate enough for most clients but there is nothing sacrosanct about this particular structure. The client who initially arrives in a state of dire crisis may well require more frequent meetings at first (possibly of a shorter duration), whereas there are others who may welcome a longer period between sessions. This tends to be the case with couples, where the processing they do between sessions is contained better by fortnightly rather that weekly meetings. Certainly there is every likelihood that as counselling proceeds the frequency agreed at the beginning will seem no longer appropriate. The duration of sessions, too, may change. Both writers have experienced some counselling relationships where clients have wanted and benefited from sessions lasting two or three hours or even longer. It is also not uncommon for a few clients to find themselves becoming more comfortable with longer sessions at less frequent intervals. At the beginning stage, however, what needs to be established is the willingness of the counsellor to be open about both the duration and the frequency of sessions no matter what structure is initially adopted. In practice, it is the exception rather than the rule for a client to desire a radical change of structure but the knowledge at the outset that such changes are at least *possible* is often of some importance to many clients. It is yet another sign that the counsellor is willing to share power and be responsive to her client's needs even if these change in ways which are potentially inconvenient to her.

It will be evident from much that has preceded that person-centred counsellors will find it difficult to work in agencies where policy dictates that clients can have a certain number of sessions and no more. Such a system takes away power from both counsellor and client, and it is only by acknowledging, accepting and transcending such shared impotence that a person-centred counsellor and her client could work constructively together. We do not believe this to be impossible but such policies certainly present formidable obstacles to person-centred work. Where they operate in order to cope with unmanageable numbers of clients it is clear that lack of resources is the real problem. When they are introduced on the grounds that short intensive therapeutic relationships produce good results we are unhappy. Clearly such short-term counselling can and often does prove highly beneficial, but we find it unlikely that this can be the case for all clients.

There is an important difference between 'short-term' and 'time-limited' counselling. Agency counsellors, particularly those working in primary care, have felt under pressure to conform to a 'time-limited' convention whereby they may offer no more than a fixed number of sessions, with no flexibility. This kind of policy pays no regard to individual difference among clients and is a crude and inefficient way of structuring a counselling provision. For a start, stipulating a limit of, say eight sessions, at the beginning of counselling can set that as a *target* in the mind of the client, where three or four sessions might otherwise have sufficed. Also, it can be uneconomic to end prematurely with a client when he is at a point of particular readiness. Disregarding points of readiness, where the client's condition is acute, is expensive when it results in later chronicity. The alternative, which is equally respectful of budgets, is to consider the work as 'short-term' but not time-limited. For example, in primary health care, nothing is time-limited, but everything is short-term. Under this system the counselling service might contract to offer an *average* of, say, six sessions per client. This system still allows the quantity of service to be contained and predicted, but it permits counsellors much more scope to sculpt their practice to invest 'savings' from those clients who required only two or three sessions in other clients with whom stopping at six sessions would represent an expensive waste of time. In a recent paper, McGeever (2006) reports on a major primary care counselling service, managed in this way, where the range of the provision is from one to forty sessions. This latter model is also better for counsellors, who can then garner a range of experience, comprising mainly short-term contracts but also some medium and even longer-term work (Mearns, 1998). Many of the issues raised by what is, in fact, a crucial matter with many financial and clinical implications were addressed in a keynote lecture given in 1999 by one of the writers at the annual training conference of the British Association for Counselling and Psychotherapy (Thorne, 1999).

Money Matters

For counsellors working in private practice or in fee-paying agencies the question of money has to be faced at an early stage with each new client. In some cases the agency absolves the counsellor from any responsibility in this area by determining the fee and by billing the account. Very often, however, the counsellor herself must incorporate the payment issue into the first session and this is not always easy, especially if the client is highly distressed or there has been some difficulty in sorting out times and frequency of subsequent meetings. The issue cannot, however, be dodged and it demands straightforward openness and directness. It is important that the client is not left with uncertainties and ambiguities. He needs to know exactly how much he has to pay (if there is some kind of sliding scale he needs to know the ramifications of this) and he needs to know what happens if he fails to turn up for an appointment without giving warning. The counsellor, for her part, will be concerned to understand the client's feelings about financial aspects of the relationship – especially if there are difficult feelings around – and she will be likely to offer whatever options are possible for the mode of payment. It is our experience that very often it is the counsellor who experiences great discomfort about the financial transaction rather than the client, and that such unease often springs from a lurking self-doubt about her competence or even a somewhat shaky faith in the effectiveness of the counselling process itself.

It is often these issues that the counsellor needs to address in supervision rather than other 'ethical' misgivings about charging for services which may be serving as a smokescreen for the more fundamental doubts about personal and professional identity. A final point to note about payment is the importance of the counsellor working for a fee which is neither so low that she feels 'used' or so high that she feels she has to 'perform' well to live up to that figure.

Summary

We make no apology for subjecting the beginnings of counselling relationships to such rigorous examination, or for dwelling on such apparently trivial matters as furniture and out-of-date magazines. It is well known that first impressions have profound significance for all of us in many different aspects of our lives, and it is therefore scarcely surprising that there are those who claim that the likely outcome of a therapeutic relationship can often be predicted from the quality of interaction which takes place during the first two or three sessions. For the person-centred counsellor everything she says and does, everything about the environment which she offers her client, everything about the structures that are agreed at the outset of the work together – all this will be attempting to convey the same unambiguous message: 'I welcome you, I accept and value you as a human being, I want to understand you, I want us to be able to be open and honest with each other and there is nothing in me that wants to take anything away from you. And my hope is that we shall be able to work together for as long as you feel it to be helpful and worthwhile.'

The Case Study (Part 1)

Introduction

We are arbitrarily defining the 'beginning' phase of the counselling process as the period during which the client develops sufficient trust in the counsellor and their relationship to explore the previously feared edges of his awareness. Developing sufficient trust to do this generally requires a degree of relational depth. Sometimes a client will attribute a high degree of trust to the counsellor *without* relational depth, but it is the kind of unquestioning trust of a child to the parent and has an ephemeral quality. It is vulnerable to sudden shifts of projection or the breaking of the transference spell as psychodynamic colleagues might view it. Only so long as the client can hold the counsellor in the position of 'perfect parent' can the unquestioning trust endure. In the person-centred approach to counselling we seek a trust that is adult–adult in nature rather than child–parent because the former offers a sounder basis for reaching more profound dimensions of the client's existential experiencing. There can also be a series of 'layers' to this developing trust. Sufficient trust is developed to make a start to the process but an enhanced level of relational depth becomes necessary in order to reach the more feared and private territory. This is discussed as part of the 'middle' process in Chapter 8.

In considering the beginning phase it is liberating for the trainee to appreciate that there is no single path which the therapeutic process must take in order to develop this trust; rather, there are many 'roads to success' as counsellor and client move forward towards the next phase of their therapeutic encounter. In the first part of the case study that follows we trace one such 'road' through the beginning of the counselling process. This is a single case and as such it cannot reflect all the points we have made in this book. None the less we hope it will highlight much of what it means for a counsellor and client to find sufficient courage and trust in each other to set out together on their unpredictable journey.

In describing a case a major problem is deciding what to leave out. In the account that follows we have tried to retain only material that both client and counsellor felt had been of particular significance. As a result, many meetings and events receive only brief comment to allow more space for exploring those moments that radically affected the process.

Data from a number of sources have been used in the case presentation, which is the outcome of work undertaken by both counsellor (Dave Mearns) and client some two years after counselling had ended and revised for this edition. First, audio-tape recordings were available for all sessions except the first. The second major source of information was the client, Joan. She had kept a diary during the period of counselling and was able to use this, together with the audio-tapes, to write detailed notes on how she had experienced the four-month counselling process. She was asked to comment on each of the seventeen sessions and also to take into account any insights that had occurred between meetings.

The third source of data was the counsellor's notes about the case. In this case study, as is usual in person-centred case studies, attention is given not just to the material the *client* brings and her behaviour in counselling, but also to the counsellor's experience of *himself* during the contact, as well as the counsellor's judgement on the quality and intensity of the therapeutic *relationship*. Hence case-notes of person-centred practitioners normally contain these three dimensions of 'client', 'self' and 'the relationship'. Such detailed case-notes were available for the first ten meetings but were more sparse thereafter. Some of the notes have been re-written in sentence form and are reproduced in the case presentation.

After Joan and the counsellor had reconstructed their individual experiences of the counselling process they came together to compare their perceptions and in this way created a further source of data. During this comparing experience Joan and the counsellor frequently referred back to the tape-recordings for clarification. These meetings threw up many examples of differences in understanding, including the discovery of assumptions the counsellor had made about the client's experience that turned out to be spurious. This close collaboration between counsellor and client ensures that the description of the counselling process that follows represents their agreed account and not simply the counsellor's gloss on events.

The Context

The setting for this case is a private counselling practice. At the time the counselling took place Joan was twenty-seven-years old. She was married to Roger, had no children, and was engaged in voluntary social work. Her mother was dead and she had lost contact with her father. Joan had been referred by a former client and made her appointment directly with the counsellor by telephone. During that telephone conversation Joan introduced the matter of fees. The counsellor had pointed to his normal policy, which was to have two fees: the higher for clients who could afford it and the other set somewhat lower for those in financial difficulty. The counsellor also mentioned that his policy was not to charge for the first session if the client chose not to continue. Joan decided to pay the higher fee and said that she wanted to pay for the first session regardless of whether they continued or not.

Another relevant part of the context is the state of being of the counsellor during the first session. This is of particular importance in the case under discussion because the counsellor was feeling drained and somewhat unsettled at the time. The addition of Joan brought his case-load up to its maximum and he wondered after the telephone call whether he should have been more cautious before accepting her. Another unsettling issue for the counsellor was his difficulty at that time with a client called Christine whose personal process was particularly demanding. Clients sometimes go through a period of being challenging and demanding, but the counsellor was having more difficulty than usual with the client Christine whose 'fragile process' (Warner, 2000a) led to her repeated demands to the counsellor to 'prove you can do a good job', combined with a seemingly constant stream of criticism. This difficulty was to exercise an undesirable influence on the opening sessions with Joan.

Meeting 1

It is interesting to note that in their reflections two years later the counsellor and client focused on exactly the same events as being particularly significant in the first meeting. We begin with Joan's account of the experience.

> When I came to his office I was very scared. I was putting a brave face on it, but this was really a matter of life or death for me … And he was a stranger … in a sense I was about to trust my life to a stranger.
>
> Just as I got inside the door and he moved towards me, he met my gaze with a flicker in his eyes as if he was nervous. I thought – 'Oh, God, he's not going to be strong enough for me!' In the first five minutes I wanted to run out of the door, but I just couldn't – so I kept on talking. I don't think I *showed* much feeling. That changed when he said, 'You look very tense – are you scared? … Is *this* scary?' I can hear on the tape that I let out a huge sigh of relief, and I remember I looked at him for the first time since I had sat down.

Much of the remainder of this meeting was devoted to Joan telling her story. She spoke about how she felt 'a prisoner' in her life – how she 'can't escape' – how she felt that she was 'dying in this marriage'. She referred to her husband Roger as 'feelingless' and she was intensely bitter at the fact that he seemed unable to respond to her emotion. She described the sado-masochistic practices that had begun early in their relationship. She felt that she had rushed into marriage because she had been 'scared to do anything else'. Two years previously she had had an affair, but had 'obeyed' Roger when he demanded that she end it. She said that she had felt 'paralysed by guilt' and the only possible course of action was to return to the marriage to 'try again'. In talking about this return to the marriage, she said, 'At one level I knew it wouldn't work, but I denied that to myself.'

Two years later Joan describes how it had felt to tell her story in counselling:

> By the end of the first session I had told most of my story. At times I went so fast that he [the counsellor] didn't have a chance to come in. I think that was the only way I could tell my story – I couldn't face the *feeling* that was involved in it. Also, I went fast and didn't look at him much, in case he put me off … in case I saw that he was disapproving or rejecting me.

Near the end of this meeting the counsellor quite firmly stopped Joan's flow of speech and took time carefully and deliberately to show his interest, warmth and understanding with a strongly *affirming* statement:

> You have told me an awful lot about yourself today. I have seen how scary it is to do that and also I've seen how important it is for you to do that. I have been in *awe* of your courage – you're sure not letting go without a fight.

In this account of the first meeting we have paid particular attention to the *client* and the material that she brought. However, as mentioned earlier, the person-centred counsellor is also concerned with monitoring *himself* and the development of his *relationship* with the client. Hence, we reproduce below the counsellor's reflections on these after this first meeting:

> SELF: As I focus on myself in this first session with Joan I am aware that I was quite nervous in the beginning. At first sight she seemed very intense and severe, with eyes that looked right through me. I was taken aback with her intensity and took some time to settle. Her long monologue at the beginning gave me the space to become more centred and to focus on *her*. It sort of feels like I actually felt *fear* towards her in the first moments and only when I focused on her did that slide and change to a real prizing of her in her struggle.

> RELATIONSHIP: I think the most important moment was near the end when I stopped her flow to strongly and clearly show her how much I admired her courage. That affirmation might be important for her in relation to her

struggle but I suspect it will also help to strengthen her trust and our relationship. I feel very positive about the potential for our relationship but I suspect that she is quite wary of making a commitment. It will be important for me to make a particular effort to *communicate* my respect and my understanding. I think she might not believe me unless I show it really strongly.

Meeting 2

This meeting began with the counsellor asking the question: 'What is most prominent for you just now?' Joan went on to talk about how much better she felt after the last meeting – all week she had felt stronger. She says: 'I hope it doesn't go away … I hope it works … ' We continue the account from the counsellor's notes:

At this point I made a mistake which was later recovered and ended in significant movement for our therapeutic relationship. As Joan said 'I hope it works' I was struck by her gaze, which seemed so penetrating. I became edgy and uncomfortable and I moved back in my seat as though I was under some threat. In a flash I thought about the hard time Christine had been giving me and how I was not coping at all well with that. I began to wonder if Joan was also desperately scared that I might fail her. Within a few moments I had become completely uncentred and found it difficult to put this theory to the back of my mind so that I could devote my full attention to listening to what Joan was saying. After a short silence I decided to face my uncertainty by commenting on what I saw in Joan's appearance in that moment. I did not reflect my deeper experiencing of her since I knew that was likely to be contaminated by the intrusion of my experience of Christine, so I said … [continued from tapes].

COUNSELLOR: I hope it works? … When you say that, you look so tense … and so *intense* … is there more to say on that … do you have any more feelings that go with that?
[*Long pause*]
JOAN: Yes … fear … no … *terror*! I'm terrified. I'm absolutely terrified. [*Pause*]
COUNSELLOR: [*in a soft, slow and warm voice*]: What are you terrified about, Joan?
JOAN: I'm terrified that you will desert me.

[Continued from the counsellor's notes]

This amazed me – I didn't see it coming at all. I was so contaminated by my experience with Christine that I had feared Joan might similarly be terrified lest I not be *powerful* enough for her. In fact Joan's terror was quite differently based – she was terrified I would *desert* her. I am glad that I was suspicious about my initial reaction and took care to check it out.

Joan continues the story of this second meeting by recalling that moment when she divulged her terror of desertion:

> This moment in our second meeting was critical for me. I remember that I was absolutely flooded with feelings after I said I was terrified of rejection. As well as feeling that this was my last chance for life and that I might be rejected, I also had a flash of realisation that the same terror of rejection ruled my relationship with Roger. There also seemed to be a strand which went further back (I later saw that this was to do with the issue of being rejected by my father). As well as all this, the very act of voicing the terror had a profound impact on my relationship with my counsellor. I felt much closer to him and much less scared when I realised that he was not going to turn me away as a hopeless case. This incident made it easier for me to tell him about my 'bridge' later in that meeting.

This incident seems to have contributed immeasurably to the trust between the counsellor and Joan, who was then able to share with him the details of her private suicide fantasy of jumping from a 'bridge' (see Chapter 8). The development of this significant trust is the point where we want to draw our arbitrary line to separate the 'beginning' and the 'middle' of the counselling process, because it is only when this trust develops that the client is prepared to take more risks in the relative certainty that the counsellor's acceptance and commitment will endure.

In this case trust has developed quite rapidly despite the counsellor's ineptitude at times. Two main factors contribute to the comparative speed of the process. First, it is clear that Joan is in a high *state of readiness* for counselling. Using the factors outlined earlier in this chapter (Box 7.2) as indicators of the client's state of readiness, it is clear that Joan was not dogged by indecision about wanting to change; that she did not suffer from a general lack of trust; that she was willing to take considerable responsibility for what happened in counselling; and that she was willing to recognise and explore her feelings. Where so many of these factors are present we would expect the beginning phase to be quite short. The counsellor also contributed to the speed of the process, because although he was in danger of over-identifying Joan with his other client, Christine, he was *aware* of that deficiency in himself and took care to *check* his perceptions of Joan. Although his was a clumsy beginning, the situation would only have been dangerous if he had been lacking in self-awareness or had been unwilling to check his assumptions.

The relative speed of the beginning phase in this instance should not mislead the reader into thinking that this is always the case. For example, in the case of 'Rick', described in chapter 6 of Mearns and Cooper (2005), the beginning phase lasts until the twenty-seventh meeting, when Rick utters his first words!

The trust in the relationship between Joan and her counsellor has now been established to the extent that significant progress can be made. They have concluded the 'beginning' and are about to enter the 'middle' phase of their counselling process.

8

'MIDDLES'

The Case Study (Part 2)

Meeting 2 (continued)

Towards the end of this meeting came one of those moments in counselling when the client takes a great risk and finds that her trust has not been misplaced. In the audio-tape of the meeting there is a long silence, which is eventually broken by Joan:

> JOAN: [*lowers her head and speaks with a slow but firm voice*] When I'm at my lowest I visit my 'bridge'. [*Pause*] It's a high bridge over the railway. [*Pause*] I do weird things like waiting for a train to come and then I imagine how my body would look if it was tumbling down towards the train – and I work out which carriage my body would hit … and how the pain would feel … and then the blackness … and nothingness. [*Pause*]
>
> COUNSELLOR: It doesn't sound weird to me … it sounds very important – like it's very important for you?
>
> JOAN: [*looking at counsellor*] It is crucial for me – it is what keeps me sane – in fact it's what keeps me alive in a funny kind of way … [*Pause*] I didn't think I would tell you about it because it's too important … too precious.
>
> COUNSELLOR: [*speaking slowly*] Yes, I see that – I think I see just how precious it is – it's incredibly important to you – it is actually the means by which you are coping with your life … it is so so precious – I feel honoured that you have trusted me with it.
>
> JOAN: [*smiles*].

The counsellor's understanding and acceptance in this exchange were experienced by Joan as offering a level of intimacy that added immeasurably to the depth of the relationship. Such experiences of relational depth are never lost, as Joan commented two years later:

> This was a most beautiful moment – and amazing that it should happen as early as our second meeting. I trusted him enough to make him the only person in the world to know about my 'bridge'. And he understood so well its meaning and significance … and indeed its beauty for me.

Of course, it is not just the quality of the counsellor's empathy that has created the relational depth. The client initiated the encounter by going to depth in her self revelation. The beauty of this experience for the client, Joan, provides a sharp contrast with what could happen if the counsellor felt bound by an agency protocol on suicide prevention. Such protocols generally call for special action from the counsellor (usually informing another party) if there is evidence of 'suicidal ideation' on the part of the client. Taken at face value, Joan could certainly be seen as fantasising her suicide, but from a phenomenological perspective her fantasy is actually part of her survival strategy. Protocols such as this are best analysed in terms of the 'politics of helping' – they exist under the pretence of protecting the client, but their real function is to protect the agency (Mearns, 2006b).

Meeting 3

The counsellor's notes explore the important elements for him in this third meeting:

> The *content* of this meeting is easy to describe. It was entirely devoted to Joan's growing feeling of disgust towards both her husband and herself in relation to the sado-masochistic practices in which they engaged. (Joan went into considerable detail on these practices and her feelings about them, past and present.) During this last week she has begun to refuse to take part in these activities. The *process* in the meeting seems to have been one of Joan 'unloading' some of the tension and guilt she feels about her SM sex – it seemed really important for her to tell me every bit of detail as though she was exorcising her guilt. It is also apparent that Joan is getting a little bit stronger already: I don't think that she could have refused her husband even two weeks ago … She's going very fast at present. But there was one strange thing about her today that I am only now aware of as I focus on her. I didn't really get the feeling that she was hugely disturbed by their sex life, and yet she seemed so very *intense*

when she was telling me about it. Is there something else behind it that we missed? It's too late for now to do anything about it – to begin the next session with that would not be a good idea since it would pre-empt whatever is important to her when she comes. But there does seem to be a difference in intensity between how she *was* in the session and what these practices *mean* for her. I shall store that up in case it arises in the future. Why did I miss this in the meeting itself? It seems so obvious now. I think I was a bit overawed by her SM experiences. I was blinded by them – I haven't had enough experience of the graphic details of SM – I was de-railed for a time and failed to sense the discrepancy between her content and her way of being.

Meeting 4

This extract from the counsellor's notes indicates the dominant theme of the fourth meeting:

Today Joan was as negative about herself and her situation as I have seen her since the first meeting. She repeated phrases like: 'It's no good'; 'I can't leave him'; 'I'm no good – I'm powerless.'

This was one of those meetings where the unskilled helper might have tried to take Joan out of her mood of depression with some version of *'there, there now, it'll be alright'*. However, a more fruitful response is to see this depression and regression as an integral part of the client's process: sometimes clients have to experience their position at its worst before they can move on through it. Also, the therapeutic process rarely progresses regularly. In fact, it more often describes the pattern of the rollercoaster, with peaks, troughs, loops and spirals (see later in this chapter). The task of the person-centred counsellor is to be a companion on all parts of the journey, even those that appear negative, depressing and at times irrational. Simply pointing out the irrationality of the regression does not stop it, and indeed can add to the client's experience of failure.

Twice during this meeting Joan said: 'I need to visit my bridge.' The counsellor went on to explore what that meant to her, but in doing that he later felt he had missed an opportunity, as he wrote in his notes:

I wish I had followed my intuition of suggesting that we might, literally, visit her bridge together. At the time I *knew* that that quick judgement of mine was soundly based and that I should follow it through. Our relationship is strong enough for her to have accepted me going with her to that most private place. Being with her there might have helped to loosen her present 'stuckness'.

In retrospect the counsellor was probably right to have erred on the side of caution on this occasion. It would have been a difficult suggestion to make because, although Joan has shared the significance of her 'bridge', it is still a private place for her. Also, in making such a suggestion, the counsellor needs to pay careful attention to the client's locus of evaluation. Is Joan in sufficient charge of herself by this point in the counselling process to be able to say 'No'?

Although caution is appropriate in this instance, the general issue of extending the therapeutic context is an important one. The person-centred counsellor should not feel confined to the physical boundaries of the counselling office. That room serves as a meeting place because it is convenient and private: sometimes these advantages are worth sacrificing for other benefits that might follow. Within the counselling profession there is a resistance to working outside the room – sometimes it is even elevated into a pseudo-ethical issue. This derives from earlier psychodynamic influences that have unfortunately restricted our exploration of the issues involved in widening the therapeutic context (Mearns and Cooper, 2005: 55–8).

Meeting 5

This meeting opened with the counsellor's question: 'What is happening for you this week?', to which Joan replied: 'Nothing very much.' Joan appeared very quiet and withdrawn during the first third of the meeting. The counsellor confronted this quietness and Joan's avoidance of eye contact, by being open about his experience of these:

> COUNSELLOR: It feels that you've been avoiding looking at me today ... and you seem much quieter ... how are you feeling?
>
> JOAN: [*bursts into tears*] It's so hopeless – I'm hopeless – I can't do it – I just can't leave him [*Roger*].
>
> COUNSELLOR: Is there any other feeling there as well?
>
> JOAN: I'm hopeless ... [*pause*] I feel that I'm letting you down.
>
> COUNSELLOR: Letting me down because you're not as strong as you have been?
>
> JOAN: Yes, I'm so embarrassed.
>
> COUNSELLOR: As though I'm probably not going to like you very much when you are this way?
>
> JOAN: [*still avoiding eye contact*] No – how could anyone like a crying little girl? [*She pulls her legs up under her on the seat and holds them with her arms, burying her head in her knees. Her crying becomes a deep sobbing.*]

COUNSELLOR: [*moves from his seat to sit beside Joan on the couch and gently puts his arm around her. They stay like that for nearly five minutes with Joan sobbing continuously.*]

For the remainder of the meeting the counsellor sat beside Joan who, once she had stopped sobbing, began to talk about the continual sadness she had felt in her life as a young girl.

The counsellor in this extract operated very fully as a person-centred practitioner. He was not only accurately empathic in relation to Joan's deepening unhappiness, indeed desolation, but he showed a consistently high valuing of Joan even while she was behaving in ways that *she* felt would be unacceptable. In all of this the counsellor was perfectly congruent with the quality and intensity of his own feelings and sensations; he was even willing to show the fullness of his response to Joan by moving towards her and holding her while she cried.

It might be difficult to judge the importance of an interaction like this without being in the situation. Joan was very clear on her view of the counsellor's behaviour in her later reflections:

It felt that he was willing to just *be with me* in my hopelessness and depression. He didn't try to take me out of it. That felt most important although it is difficult to describe *why* it was important. It is something to do with the fact that at the very time I expected him to *reject* me he actually came *towards* me and sat beside me – that meant that he really, genuinely was with me, and I could then face the full intensity of my desolation and somehow get through it.

The counsellor gives a similar view of this interaction in his notes:

Today was a critical session for Joan and also for our relationship. I was able to meet her on her very desolate ground, and share that with her. She certainly was going through powerful feelings, because the sensations which I experienced were incredibly charged: I was tingling with the sensation of her desperation and sadness. I could feel her with my whole body, and at the end of the session I felt both exhausted and enervated.

In this meeting there is another path the counsellor might have followed. Throughout this book we are at pains to emphasise that there can be many pathways through a therapeutic process – and all can be successful. An alternative response from the counsellor would be to explore whether

Joan was symbolising different parts or *configurations* within her self. Her response: ' … How could anyone like a crying little girl', while pulling her legs up under her on the seat and holding them with her arms, could be indicative of a self-configuration (Mearns, 1999; Mearns and Thorne, 2000). If that was the case, the dynamics among the different parts could be of considerable therapeutic significance. However, the person-centred counsellor would have to explore gently, taking great care not to insert any suggestion of self-pluralism because people are particularly vulnerable to the counsellor's direction at these edges of their awareness. However, bearing in mind the considerable emotionality currently being experienced by the client, the counsellor might well decide to stay with that, as in the present example, but take note of the possibility of parts so that he can hear their, often small, voices at some later opportunity. This issue, of whether the client is symbolising their self in terms of parts and how to respond, is considered later in the chapter.

Meeting 6

Joan arrived ten minutes early and since the counsellor was ready, the meeting began. Without waiting for an invitation, Joan started recounting the various half-forgotten memories and thoughts that had flooded into her consciousness during the past week. She spoke at length of the hitherto unmentioned fact that her father had regularly used her for sexual intercourse when she was aged between thirteen and sixteen. Sometimes the sexual intercourse would be preceded by various acts of physical cruelty. She spoke of these activities in just as much detail as she had earlier devoted to her sado-masochistic relationship with her husband. While speaking, she shook constantly, sometimes with 'hate', but also 'anger', 'fear', and later with 'desperation'. Near the end of the session she summed up her position with the rhetorical question: 'What do I do with all this feeling?'

As well as speaking of her father's cruelty Joan was bitter about the role her mother had played. The following extract from one of Joan's monologues sums this up:

> I kept quiet about it just like daddy said for ages and ages, but I kept hoping that mummy would find out. One time I thought she *must* have found out when she came in early and found me crying on the bed. I felt so bad – more than anything else I felt so guilty that she had found out – but I *wanted* her to find out. She left my room without a word and went downstairs. I kept waiting

for her to come up again but she never did and I fell asleep. The next day she acted like nothing had happened – and so did I.

Looking back on it now I am absolutely sure that she knew what was going on, but she covered it up ... and she didn't help me. Shortly after that time my father stopped doing it, and I was left totally alone. I remember feeling that I wanted to be dead all over because I had caused such terrible things to my daddy and mummy.

In the same meeting Joan made the connection between her relations with her father and those with her husband: 'it was almost as though I was picking another daddy and trying to get it right this time'. When the counsellor reflected on the apparent similarity in the sensations she seemed to experience as a sixteen-year-old 'wanting to be dead all over' and the 'blackness' and 'nothingness' which she found in her fantasy of jumping from the bridge, Joan recognised the parallels and went on to focus upon the other sensations, as well as 'comfort', which went along with this fantasy retreat into annihilation.

This meeting also highlighted a change in her relationship with Roger. As well as uncovering some of her reasons for picking him as a partner, she reported that in the previous week she had been able to tell him about the incest. She had cried a lot with him and he had responded better than she had expected: 'He didn't seem to know what was going on, but at least he held me and patted me – he showed as much concern as he could.'

In the account of this meeting we have not said very much about the behaviour of the counsellor. The truth of the matter is that it was the counsellor's behaviour in the *previous* session that facilitated the voicing of Joan's memories and her account of these in the present meeting. The events of the fifth meeting had added to the relational depth giving Joan the safety and confidence to enter new territory. Joan has developed a confidence in her counsellor, in their relationship and also in herself, that reflects what we call 'a continuing experience of relational depth' (see Chapter 3 and Mearns and Cooper, 2005: 52–3). Sometimes the term *mutuality* is used to describe this state of the relationship. The presence of the counsellor is important, but what he does is becoming less crucial since Joan is more able to take responsibility for herself.

Meetings 7, 8 and 9

Probably the most difficult thing to predict in the counselling process is its speed. Sometimes clients start slowly and later go very fast, while at other times the start is fast, only to be followed by a lull. As it transpired, the latter pattern fitted our present case. During meetings 7, 8 and 9 Joan faced and re-faced the material generated between meetings 5 and 6. She went round the issues time and again, processing and re-processing. This kind of apparently 'stuck' phase in a counselling process can be difficult for the counsellor. And yet such phases are often important facets of the client's process – it takes more than a few hours to change one's life. In Joan's case she had discovered much more than she had expected by the end of meeting 6. In a sense things had gone almost too fast for her in that time, and it is not surprising that it took her a few weeks to 'catch up' on herself. Two years later Joan was able to reflect on this phase of the counselling process:

> About the middle of our time together we went round in circles for quite a long time. It seemed that neither of us knew where to go next – and every-thing we tried drew a blank. I now realise that I was stuck because at some level I realised the enormity of what I had uncovered. I had come into counselling apparently hoping for help in making some changes in my present life, and suddenly I was coming to terms with the fact that my father used to torture me, then screw me, that my mother secretly colluded in all our denial of that and that I had married my husband because he was sexually cruel like my father!

Some extracts from the counsellor's notes show how difficult this phase can be, and how the person-centred counsellor will be concerned to try to detect the *locus* of the stuckness. If it is in the *client* then patient atten-tion is likely to bring reward, but if the locus of stuckness is either in the *counsellor* or in their *relationship,* then more direct action is required of the counsellor:

> As I suspected, we really do now seem to be well and truly stuck. I am convinced that the stuckness does not have to do with our relationship. Certainly our relationship is not stuck through lack of involvement. Also I don't think the stuckness is coming from me. I get no sense of withholding myself which would normally create stuckness. Nor do I feel that Joan is threatening any of my values which might cause me to become inhibiting towards her. I am aware that I am not surprised by her stuckness – perhaps I even expected it a little bit. When she came out with that mountain of stuff in our sixth meeting I remember thinking that she would take some time to process all that. I really do think that this is Joan's stuckness without pollution from myself. She seems blocked in herself, as she said today:'I feel I am choking inside … I feel I am stifling

myself.' As I am sitting focusing on it, I think that although I have not been creating the stuckness, I may actually have been contributing to it. I have felt so frustrated and I realise there have been a number of occasions when I have tried to help Joan find ways out of her stuckness. What I might do instead is to really try and *accept her in her stuckness.*

Meeting 10

When the person-centred counsellor uncovers, between meetings, a possible avenue for exploration, he would not normally *begin* the next session with this. Instead he would start with whatever was most prominent for the client and use the time to check on the persistency of his reaction to what was happening. In this particular case the counsellor waited some twenty minutes during which Joan seemed to be going over old ground, before he intervened to give his reactions as accurately and as fully as he could:

> I'm feeling pretty stuck – I've had this feeling on and off in our last few meetings. It's a funny feeling, because I feel OK about what we're doing and what we've done together. But after last week's meeting I realised that I hadn't really been listening to what was happening in you. I had got used to you steaming along like an express train and I seemed to be looking for ways of pushing you on and on. But I think I failed to realise that your express train has stopped in the station for the time being and that maybe we might look at what that means.

In this statement the counsellor is being absolutely congruent in his response to Joan. Congruent responses are sometimes quite lengthy, with the counsellor taking care to represent accurately, not just his dominant reaction in relation to his client, but all the details of that response – he 'shows his working'.

Although the counsellor's response was emphasising his impression that Joan was temporarily stuck, paradoxically it had the opposite effect of helping her to experience her present feelings more intensely and thereafter to move on. One of the marvels of human relationships is that if a helper tries to pull a client out of her feeling this often results in the client being stuck with it, while the alternative approach of endeavouring to understand and fully appreciate the client's experience frequently results in an intensification of the experience which is then the prelude to subsequent movement. One of the distinctive features of the person-centred approach is its capacity to capitalise on this process.

In focusing on her feelings about her history, anger first became prominent for Joan. While she was expressing her anger by screaming, she began to cry and slumped off her chair to squat on the floor. Her crying eventually changed to a deep sobbing and at that point the counsellor left his own chair to squat with her, still facing her. The counsellor takes up the account, not from his notes, but from memory two years later, prompted by the audio-tape of the meeting:

> I kept expecting her to stop, but she went on and on and eventually I realised that this sobbing came from the very kernel of her existence. This was sobbing which had been stored up for many years. As I sat with her I sensed that she was allowing that abused 'little girl' inside her to see the light of day and to do what had been forbidden many years before – to cry for herself. I remember thinking at the time that perhaps this was another beginning; the beginning of what would become her self-acceptance.

Joan also helps us to understand the process as she experienced it with this comment two years later:

> I think what happened was that very early in our meetings I opened the door to my feelings. A little came out, although it felt like a lot at the time, and then in terror at just how much feeling there was, I closed the door. I didn't do it consciously, it was as though at some level I knew I couldn't take it and my defences closed the door to my experience of the anger and most especially of the deep deep sadness at what my mother and father had done. I had been scared at the beginning, then I got less scared and some feeling came out, but then my fear returned. Only in this tenth meeting did my feelings fully uncork.

Meetings 11 to 14

Unfortunately, laziness on the part of the counsellor resulted in an almost total absence of notes following these sessions, so we have to rely on information from the audio-tapes along with the reflections of Joan and the counsellor some two years later. Joan begins by commenting on what happened to her after meeting 10:

> Once I had really opened up my anger and my sadness, they didn't just come out and then go away. They came back time and time again, but each time it was a little bit less. Even now I get angry and sad about it, and I guess I always will. But from that point onwards a lot of things changed quite suddenly. Well, it wasn't so much outside things which changed, but it was my way of looking at them that was different. Roger was no longer the ogre who totally

dominated my existence. Instead he was a rather weak guy who had his own problems. I knew now that I *could* leave him. Funnily enough that made me less desperate to leave though I knew it would happen when the time was right.

Listening to the tapes it is really obvious how my voice has changed in these sessions [11–14]. From being squeaky, brittle, and excited, it has become stable, calm, and mature. I have come out of my 'lost little girl' and suddenly I am able to be the woman who has choices in her life.

Joan's comment sums up quite well her state of being in these sessions. The issues to which she was attending centred on her taking control of her life. She knew that she had married Roger largely because he was similar to her father, and that their SM practices also reflected her relationship with her father, as she said in one session:

My aim in life became to have Roger love me while hurting me – unlike my daddy who had sex with me, and hurt me, but whom I felt never really loved me.

Her growing awareness of herself also uncovered the fact that she had behaved seductively towards most of her bosses, and had quite deliberately hidden her intellectual ability in previous jobs. She felt that this was all part of the pattern in which she repeatedly confirmed herself as 'an inadequate little girl'.

It is interesting that in her commentary on meetings 11–14 Joan says: 'I have come out of my "lost little girl".' This is the clearest indication yet that Joan is symbolising her self in terms of parts – at least she is doing this two years after the counselling ended. Had that symbolisation been so clear when the work was taking place the counsellor, at some point, would have explored the significance of the symbolisations for her – what did her 'lost little girl' mean to her? Following one part, or configuration (Mearns, 1999; Mearns and Thorne, 2000) can lead to others. Often the dynamics among the parts personifies the conflicts the person feels. Also, the person generally finds it easier to 'focus' on their experiencing (Gendlin, 1984; Purton, 2004) through the parts. Each of the parts has considerable life, but considered only together they may appear to neutralise each other. Configuration theory was developed as a person-centred way of understanding and working with people who experience their self as made up of different 'parts'. But we wish to emphasise again that the theory could potentially be grossly misused if it is taken to presume that all people must have parts and the task of the counsellor is to find them. The person-centred counsellor would approach the phenomenon with caution and, in a consistent person-centred fashion, would use only the terms the client employs to describe his self. (The person-centred discipline in relation to work with configurations is detailed in Mearns and Thorne, 2000: chapter 7.)

The 'end of the middle' of the therapeutic process comes during sessions 11–14, where it is clear that Joan has largely faced and overcome the emotional blockages that have been inhibiting the process of her life; she has begun to achieve self-acceptance and she is now freer to make changes in her life.

Our discussion of meetings 11–14 continues at the beginning of Chapter 9, as Joan and her counsellor move through the final period of their counselling process. There are, however, a number of general issues which warrant discussion before we leave this middle part of the therapeutic process, and to these we now turn.

'Middles' – An Overview

The person-centred counsellor does not conceptualise her work as following a clearly definable series of steps. Instead she recognises that each client is unique, and that the therapeutic process which he experiences will be different from that of any other individual. This emphasis on the uniqueness of each client does not mean, however, that it is meaningless to investigate the counselling process. There are some issues – the development of *relational depth* and the consequent growth of trust, for example – which are so fundamental that they will play a major part in work with most clients. In this middle period moments of relational depth may be experienced as *intimacy* and the more continuing form of relational depth will develop to create an experience of *mutuality*. Also common in this middle period is the client's achievement of *self-acceptance*. Furthermore, there are some events that only occasionally occur within a therapeutic process, but none the less warrant examination because they can present profound problems if the counsellor is not aware of their importance. This last group includes the question of the boundary between the counsellor's full therapeutic involvement and her *over-involvement.* The remainder of this chapter will explore all these aspects of the counselling process.

The counsellor in the case study paid attention to three dimensions: the development of the therapeutic relationship, the client's process and the counsellor's process. We shall consider the issues relevant to this middle period of the therapeutic process under the same three headings.

The Development of the Therapeutic Relationship

The establishment of a degree of *relational depth* and consequent trust between client and counsellor was a crucial part of the 'beginning' of the counselling process, but this does not mean that relational depth ceases to be an important issue as the work continues. We would expect the relationship to deepen and to be reinforced as the counsellor and client experience each other more fully.

In the latter part of meeting 2 there is a powerful moment of relational depth when Joan took the risk of speaking of her fear of rejection and again when they shared the importance that Joan's 'bridge' played in her life. In meeting 5 when, in Joan's words, the counsellor was 'willing to just be with me in my hopelessness and depression' we see a similar moment of relational depth. At times such as these, understanding between client and counsellor exists at many levels, as does acceptance. The outcome is a profound sense of sharing. Such moments, which may be marked simply by a gentle touch, a brief reciprocated glance, or even just sitting silently together, tend to stand out and to be remembered by both client and counsellor long afterwards. For the client whose history of relationships has been disturbed and whose self-acceptance is weak, such moments may be unique and powerfully instrumental in the development of his self-regard. Moments of relational depth tend to be experienced as *intimacy* by both client and counsellor. They are powerful experiences of two human beings encountering the full humanity of each other. For most clients these would be wholly warm and 'positive' experiences – but not for all clients. The client whose earlier development has been characterised by an inconsistent and unpredictable loving may have developed a healthy suspicion of expressed warmth by the other and also warmth that he experiences in himself. This system of self-protection, described in Chapter 2 as 'ego-syntonic process', leads the person to have a strongly ambivalent reaction to moments of relational depth. Like any other human being, a part of them values and craves the intimacy, but another part is fundamentally threatened by it and responds with suspicion or even with hate and anger. This does not mean that relational depth is contra-indicated in such a case – far from it – since 'relationship' was the basis for the damage it is potentially the most healing context. We mention it here merely as a caution against presuming that all our clients will wholly value the experience of intimacy. There are illustrations of challenging work with clients who fear intimacy in Mearns and Thorne (2000) and Mearns and Cooper (2005).

Moments of relational depth add to the confidence that both counsellor and client have in their relationship and thus contribute to the establishing of a *continuing experience of relational depth* (as described at the end of Chapter 3 and in Mearns and Cooper, 2005: 52–3). In previous editions of this book we have described this process as the development of *mutuality* (Mearns and Thorne, 1988, 1999). With this sense of continuing relational depth, both counsellor and client experience their work as a truly shared enterprise and they can trust each other's commitment to achieve and maintain genuineness in relation to each other. Neither is fearful of the other, and intimacy comes easily in ways appropriate to the counselling setting. The various forms of human defensiveness that characterise everyday relationships are largely absent between the counsellor and client who have developed this continuing relational depth – they have nothing to fear in each other in the counselling context. Increasingly they become so transparent that they cease to be symbols for each other and they can dare to see each other clearly. The counsellor now has no difficulty in releasing her empathic sensitivity in whatever ways are most congruent for her. The client, too, becomes more active in making suggestions as to how they might proceed – he might even make rather unusual requests of the counsellor in the certain trust that the counsellor will respond honestly. (For instance, at the end of our case study, Joan makes the unexpected request that the counsellor accompany her on a visit to her mother's grave.)

The Client's Process

In a video-taped interview shortly before his death, Carl Rogers said: 'There are some very special moments in a person's life when they feel able to change. Hopefully more of these happen in therapy' (Bennis, 1986). This is in fact a very simple statement of what person-centred counselling aims to do: it seeks to create more of those 'special moments' when the client will feel able to change.

Essentially, person-centred counselling endeavours to create such moments by *freeing the natural healing process within the client*. As discussed more fully in Chapter 1, the person-centred approach assumes that people basically want to be 'healthy' in the psychological as well as the physical sense and that they have the potential to develop such positive mental health. With problems that have a long history, often the difficulty the person is experiencing is actually related to the systems of self-protection they had developed to survive damaging situations – usually damaging relationships – earlier in life. They developed ways of seeking to protect the self that helped them to survive their earlier life, but those earlier protections become dysfunctional in later life, particularly in the ways they inhibit the person in relationships. The task of the counsellor, through the counselling relationship, is to help the client to free his natural healing process so that his development can progress beyond present blocks. Social and emotional isolation, fear, denial, lack of clarity, lack of awareness of feelings, paralysing self-doubt and self-rejection are typical examples of such blocks. Through the relationship that the two create, the client is no longer so isolated socially and emotionally, and his fear diminishes as his trust increases, for fear and trust are opposite sides of the same coin. The reduction in fear is the key that unlocks other doors; when the client is less fearful he can face the difficulties that, up till then, he has had to deny. The world of his feelings becomes less threatening and more accessible to him. Experiencing a relationship with the counsellor where he is deeply valued makes it increasingly difficult for him to deny his own value, and begins the dismantling of the barrier of self-doubt or self-rejection. This gradual freeing of the healing process within the client, sometimes called *movement* in counselling, is beautifully described by Goff Barrett-Lennard (1987) as 'the passage from woundedness to hope'.

It is interesting to reflect more closely on what actually happens when a client 'changes' in a therapeutic process. We tend to use that word 'change' rather glibly, without really considering what it means. In another book, Mearns refers to '*seismic*' change and exemplifies this with the present case study of Joan:

> it is as though the pressure towards change has been building up under the surface and then quite suddenly a major shift takes place. (Mearns, 2003: 92)

This can be compared to '*osmotic*' change, described thus:

> In this form of change it is as though the client has not been aware of the self-concept change which has slowly developed. The process has taken place so gradually that each element of the change was imperceptible, but there has come a time when the client notices the effects of the accumulated change. (Mearns, 2003: 92)

In 'osmotic' change the counsellor may have been seeing the change long before the client. The experience is encapsulated by one client as: 'It feels really strange … nothing has changed, yet everything is different.'

Since movement in person-centred counselling depends upon the removal of blockages such as those mentioned earlier, it is unlikely to be an even and regular process. The trainee counsellor can be grossly misled by writers and trainers who over-simplify the process into a series of neat and ordered stages. Such 'stages' present the trainee with the welcome illusion of an understandable and predictable process. But it is a fiction and one that leads the trainee away from the central activity of tracking the client. Once the trainee is expecting, and waiting for, the client to follow a pattern that has been laid down for him by theoreticians he has abandoned the person-centred perspective.

The experienced person-centred counsellor knows and feels comfortable with the fact that her client's movement is likely to include periods of stuckness or regression and that there will be many plateaux and lulls. Furthermore, the counsellor will know that most often these apparent 'hiccups' are natural aspects of the freeing of the client's healing process. Such phases are often indicative of the fact that the client needs to gain further strength before moving on, and they require the counsellor's attentive companionship just as much as at times of rapid movement or dramatic change.

Experienced counsellors are well aware that clients often *appear to get worse* before they get better, but this can be difficult for the new practitioner who may be confused when she sees her client apparently deteriorate despite what seems to her to be a good working relationship. One way of understanding this phenomenon is to remember that before he seeks professional help the client will have been doing the best he can to protect himself against his difficulties. He may have denied many of his fearful feelings, tried to avoid situations which would arouse his sadness or anger, restricted his way of relating with others to minimise emotional contact and risk – in short he will have constructed many barriers to protect himself. As the counselling process begins and the client's fear diminishes he will begin to take more risks by facing situations that he might previously have avoided and by being open to feelings of which he had earlier been afraid. To those around him, he may cause distress by breaking down and crying more often, or showing the anger which was earlier suppressed, or becoming more emotionally needy or demanding. In that beautiful and ageless book by Virginia Axline, devoted entirely to the case study of her play therapy work with one six-year-old boy, Dibs (Axline, 1971), we see that when Dibs really began to make progress in therapy he appeared to his parents to be 'more disturbed'. He was in fact feeling stronger and more able to show his anger and his sadness, whereas previously he had suppressed these feelings. In our own case study Joan shows some strength after the second meeting, as she begins to initiate changes at home, but by the fourth and fifth meetings she has apparently slumped down into profound feelings of powerlessness and negativity. We see later, in meetings 5 and 6, however, that it has been of crucial importance for Joan to have got to the bottom of her pit of desolation and to share that with the counsellor. She had been able to experience fully the deep desperation she had known as a young girl. Previously it had never been safe enough to allow that feeling into full awareness, and the result was that she had always been blocked by it. An important part of the healing process released in the client is that he begins to 'accept himself' in the sense that he starts to cherish himself as a person of worth; a person who assuredly has weaknesses and strengths, but one who is fundamentally of value.

A number of factors in the person-centred relationship contribute to the development of *self-acceptance*, including the counsellor's consistent valuing (see Chapter 5), and the releasing of emotional blocks that have locked the client, perhaps for years, in a negative view of himself – in Joan's case, for example, she was released from the fear and guilt associated with her abuse as a child. The growth of self-acceptance enables the client to value himself and to trust his valuing process: his *locus of evaluation* in the therapeutic relationship moves from the counsellor to himself. Such a shift is certainly apparent in our case study, where meeting 10 seems to be the focal point by which time this shift is clear. After that time Joan's whole attitude and approach to her life have changed: she is clearer about the value of aspects of her life, such as her marriage; she has greater certainty about her own value; and she is able to be much more effective in initiating change in her life where it is necessary. From this point onwards her *need for the counsellor* is lessened, though her valuing of him is still high. Sometimes it is awe-inspiring how rapidly a client can move from the pit of depression to a state of basic self-acceptance in which everything seems different. As we shall see in the next chapter on endings, the client may still have much to do to reshape his life, but when the core of self-acceptance is established the most important part of the counselling work is accomplished and the change for the client is *irreversible*. One client described how this emerging self-acceptance felt:

> It feels as though nothing has changed, but everything has changed. I came into counselling thinking that what I wanted to do was to make a number of changes in my life. So far I haven't made any changes in my life, and my whole

life has changed. The change has happened to *me*: for the first time in my life I can say that I have good points and bad points, but basically I am OK as a human being. Although nothing else in my outside life has changed, this will change it all: this will allow me to be loving as a partner, it will allow me to show my love to my children; it will allow me to look at the work I do and decide what parts I want to keep, and it will allow me to meet people and not be afraid of them.

This achievement of basic self-acceptance is usually followed by a sharp increase in the client's *personal power*. Analogies with physics are more poetic than scientific, but it is as though the fusion within the person through his self-acceptance releases a huge amount of energy. This is just as well, because once self-acceptance is established a client often wishes to make many changes in his life, as we shall see in Chapter 9, and he will need all the energy he can command to be able to do this.

The Counsellor's Process

The person-centred counsellor also goes through a process during the course of the counselling relationship. The main theme of that process is her struggle to offer a relationship at depth to her client. This struggle within each therapeutic relationship recapitulates the same kind of struggle throughout her working life. The struggle is simply stated but supremely challenging – it is to become able to offer relational depth to every single client who comes through her door. She is expecting herself to become both deeper and broader as a person, such that she is undeterred by whatever systems of self-protection the client may have developed, protections that generally inhibit relationship. She can offer all the core therapeutic conditions, completely, to every client. Of course, this represents a developmental process that has barely begun during basic training. During that early development she will become familiar with the therapeutic conditions and the challenges they pose for her. She will experience moments of relational depth with clients and a continuing experience of relational depth with only some. Initially she may be self-critical – after all, everyone expects to be perfect when they start! A key part in her process will be when her self-criticism gives way to self-curiosity, with the attendant gain in self-acceptance that accompanies that shift. Self-curiosity, backed by self-acceptance, is a sufficient objective for basic training because it provides the platform for her lifelong developmental process whereby she will be able to access her existential depths and also the breadth of her humanity in order to offer an encounter at relational depth to an ever-widening range of clients.

The above paragraph summarises the developmental process described in Chapter 3 (and in Mearns and Cooper, 2005: chapter 8), but it also mirrors the kind of process the counsellor goes through with each client. Early in the process the counsellor may well be struggling with aspects of her self that are not at peace. That was well illustrated in the work with Joan by the intrusions for the counsellor of his difficulties in relation to the other client, Christine. Essentially, in the early part of the process, the counsellor is struggling for congruence – struggling to become able to use her self fully and fluidly in relation to her client. She will make 'mistakes', especially early in the process. In all the case material we offer in various books, we are careful not to edit out the 'mistakes' (Mearns and Thorne, 2000; Thorne, 2002; Mearns, 2003; Mearns and Cooper, 2005), because the 'mistakes' are part of the process of struggling to encounter our client at depth. We find that our empathy fails or is only partial; we struggle with our valuing of our client – failing at times; and, probably more than anything, we struggle to step out of the normal responses of our 'presentational self' (see Chapter 3) to respond congruently to the other from greater depths within our self. 'Making mistakes', in the sense of 'missing' the encounter with the other in some way, is part of our humanity. Our failings are to be cherished rather than vilified. Vilification leads to avoidance and defensiveness. Our client cannot learn from these, or, what they 'learn' is that their own mistakes are also to be judged, or, worse, that they are probably responsible for *our* mistakes. A more constructive response to mistakes is to be *responsible to the client*. That will mean we must struggle to be aware of our own vulnerabilities; being aware of our client's experiencing of our actions; being open with the client about our own process; and, not infrequently, tendering our client an apology.

Sometimes quickly, sometimes slowly, as the process unfolds the counsellor will become more fully involved with her client. She becomes more adept in offering herself as a mirror to her client and utilising the full potential of her congruence, as detailed in Chapter 6. In our case study we note the counsellor doing this as early as meeting 3. In reflecting on that meeting afterwards he drew on his own felt sense of the client in coming to the hypothesis that there might be more behind Joan's feelings about her husband and their SM practices. There was no adequate space to make use of this hypothesis at that time, but its validity was later realised when Joan's abuse emerged. Similarly, in meeting 5, when the counsellor sat beside Joan, he was able to tap his own bodily sensations as a reflection of her experience: 'I was tingling with the sensation of her desperation. I could feel her with my whole body.' Another clear example came in meeting 10 when the counsellor squatted in front of Joan on the floor and felt the depth of her sadness. There were many other examples of the counsellor's use of his self in relation to Joan, but these were among the most striking in the case study notes we have used.

In exploring the full involvement of the counsellor in the counselling process we must address the question of the difference between such full involvement and *over-involvement*. Like most other counselling practitioners we recognise the counsellor's 'over-involvement' as potentially damaging to the therapeutic process, as well as sometimes being unethical. Indeed, because such a high degree of personal involvement is required of the person-centred counsellor, over-involvement is regarded even more seriously because it threatens the very basis of person-centred work by undermining the client's trust in the integrity and professionalism of the counsellor. When that trust is abused by a counsellor it damages not only the therapeutic relationship in question, but the integrity of the whole approach and its underlying rationale.

Over-involvement takes different forms but generally involves the counsellor's needs becoming too prominent in the relationship. A common form is where the counsellor uses her relationship with the client as a means of confirming her own importance by exerting power over others. The person-centred approach is not the most fertile ground for the power-oriented counsellor, who might be more suited to counsellor-centred approaches. But in the context of the person-centred approach the symptoms of this abuse of power might include the creation of excessive dependency among her clients; repeated and strong instances of unresolved feelings of love and/or hate; and a failure ever to reach a state of mutuality with a client.

Another form of over-involvement is where the counsellor gets her own process mixed up with her client's process. So, for example, she does not hear her client's actual experience of bereavement, but imagines it to be similar to her own; or she allows her own anger towards her client's abuser to intrude; or she gets lost in her own internal desolation when trying to meet her client in his. If the counsellor's experience of bereavement, abuse or existential desolation is still too raw for her the danger is that over-involvement will replace full-involvement. The worst response to the danger of this form of over-involvement is to make sure that it can never happen. The only way that can be achieved is by the counsellor withdrawing most of her humanity. Only if the counsellor is distinctly uninvolved can she be sure that this form of over-involvement will not happen. Of course, that is not the choice in a relationally oriented approach such as person-centred counselling. Rather than fearfully avoiding any possibility of this form of over-involvement, we want the developing counsellor to become more aware of it. The developmental agenda becomes one of understanding those areas of our own process that carry considerable power, reviewing where we are with them, noting the ways in which they could encroach negatively, and monitoring our ongoing practice for dangers of our over-involvement. Our supervisor and, during training, our personal development group can be powerful supports to us in our monitoring process. But the process is not simply one of monitoring dangers – it is developmental – it will support our efforts to reclaim these powerful self-experiences in order that they may convert into future resources ('existential touchstones'). It seems clear that this form of over-involvement should not be feared, for it is part of our developmental agenda.

A counsellor who seeks sexual gratification with a client is unquestionably over-involved and, regardless of the intricacies of the client's or her own motivation, is deemed to be behaving unethically. There are no exceptions or qualifications.

Having stressed the dangers of sexual over-involvement, while having earlier in this chapter placed great value on intimacy in the therapeutic relationship, we cannot fail to address the important question of what place, if any, the counsellor's *sexuality* can have in the therapeutic relationship. Texts on counselling usually ignore the issue of sexuality completely. However, we consider it extremely important for the counsellor to come to recognise, understand, and feel comfortable with her sexuality. Counsellors should know that at times they may find that their strong positive feeling for a client has that same edge and quality as a loving response to a sexual partner. Sexuality is a normal part of human responsiveness and as such there will be occasions when the counsellor will recognise sexual feelings as an aspect of her attraction to the client.

The counsellor's sexuality carries danger only if she *over-reacts* to it in any of the following three ways:

- If the counsellor engages in sexual activity with her client;
- If the counsellor, unaware of her attraction, sends sexual *signals* to the client;

- If the counsellor reacts to her own sexuality by *rejecting* the client: often this would take the form of the counsellor becoming a little colder or withdrawing slightly from the client, without explanation. This is one of the more common reactions to sexual feelings, and might be disturbing to the client for whom issues of acceptance and rejection are critical.

Sexuality is a normal and life enhancing part of being human. Far from pretending that sexuality does not exist, we would encourage person-centred counsellors to reflect upon and discuss the issue of their sexuality, and for this to be a particular focus of attention in training and supervision. Sexuality becomes less threatening when it does not have to be denied and when the counsellor is confident in the knowledge that she will not exploit a client for her own sexual gratification.

We left our case study at a point when Joan had opened herself to the full extent of her earlier experiences, As a young person she had 'survived' these experiences but they had seriously restricted her later emotional and relational life. Now she was in a position to do more – she was about to *survive her survival.*

9

'ENDINGS'

The Case Study (Part 3)

Meetings 11–14 (continued)

During these four meetings Joan reviewed her professional life and determined to resume the studies that she had previously dropped upon protestations from Roger. She also started dancing classes for the first time since she was fourteen-years-old, and arranged a holiday with a female friend. She felt sorry for Roger but not regretful about the fact that emotionally at least she had deserted him (although she was very shaken when he threatened suicide).

It soon became apparent that, once freed of the fear from feeling her own anger and sadness, Joan was able to internalise her *locus of evaluation* (see Chapter 1). It was clear, too, that she was building up her self-esteem faster than would usually happen in a person who had earlier arrived at such a profoundly negative self-appraisal: perhaps in the early years of her life she had been able to lay down strong foundations for positive self-esteem.

There would be a long process of personal growth to follow Joan's awakening if her movement towards positive psychological health was to be maintained. In many counselling relationships the counsellor would assist some way along that path, but in our case Joan and the counsellor parted quite early. Near the end of the fourteenth session the counsellor commented on how easily Joan had taken up the restructuring of her life.

She began to cry – a bubbling kind of crying that seemed to represent a mixture of relief and joy. In the review two years later, Joan observed that this was the moment when she knew she could do the rest herself. She knew she had rediscovered a happy child who went back beyond her teenage years of abuse and humiliation.

Meeting 15

The ending came quite suddenly. At the beginning of the fifteenth meeting Joan said that she could end very soon, although she would like a little support as she resolved the problem of 'being a new person in an old life'. This phenomenon is well described in Joan's words:

> I have changed dramatically, and suddenly. I suppose it has been happening for a long time, but it is only now that I'm seeing the full effects of the change. The turn-around is simple to describe – I've started to feel OK about myself. Easy to say, but the consequences are traumatic – it is likely that I am now going to have to quit my husband, restart college, be alone with myself, give up failing at things, be less guarded about expressing my feelings with others and give up manipulating and deceiving people (well, *most* of the time!). The problem is that the whole edifice which is my life is built on these things. It is *all* going to change because I now look on myself differently. *I am a new person in an old life.*

Meetings 16 and 17

These last two meetings were devoted to the following:

- Helping Joan to work out the strategies she would adopt to change those parts of her life that she wanted to change
- Reviewing the process of their counselling time together, and
- Considering whether there was any *unfinished business* between them.

During the last two meetings the counsellor became more assertive about some of the issues that should be considered and how that could be done. For instance, he was quite forceful in encouraging Joan to review every area of her life, to uncover all the implications occasioned by her change in self-concept. The counsellor also initiated the idea of reviewing the counselling process and the question of unfinished business.

In her exploration of what she might do in the immediate future, Joan paid most attention to the possible ending of her relationship with Roger; the extra voluntary work she would undertake in preparation for her application to a social work degree course; and how she wanted to explore further not just her feelings for her parents, but how they actually had behaved towards her. A fourth issue Joan introduced took the counsellor completely by surprise, but on reflection made perfect sense. Joan's words describe this best:

> I woke up one morning last week and knew that I now could have children. The realisation took my breath away: I had always seen myself as someone who could never be bothered with children. Now I know that what was behind that was a *fear* of having children – a fear that I was so messed up that I would mess them up. Roger never showed any interest in children either, so that was another way in which we were suited – maybe again that was another reason why I picked him.

A little time was spent outlining the possibility of later 'reviews' and even 'restarts'. And after devoting space to 'reviewing the counselling process', the last main item that the counsellor introduced was the question of whether there was any unfinished business between them. For his part he began with a detailed account of his uncertainties and confusion during the beginning of their time together. He had never really explained what had been going on with him at that time, including his difficulties with the other client, Christine, and how these had affected him with Joan. Joan reacted to this information with interest and told him that it would have been quite helpful to her if he had been more frank at the time. She had indeed been very confused by his behaviour: he had seemed 'distracted' and somewhat 'detached' and she had misinterpreted this as a rejection of her. To have had more honest information from the counsellor would have helped.

The only other issue under this heading of 'unfinished business' came from Joan, who admitted that early in their time together she had felt quite a strong sexual attraction towards the counsellor. Her main comment on this was:

> I'm sure this must happen often in this situation. At the beginning of our time together I was extremely vulnerable, and also I was taking a lot of risks. The fact you were showing me a lot of caring was so unbelievable and exciting. As I

grew stronger, that attraction diminished in importance for me, but it is really, really important that you were solid. It feels that that attraction was a really natural thing for me to feel, but if you had responded to it, it would have been terrible – it is really really important that you were solid.

At the very end of the seventeenth and last formal session Joan took the stage for the last time and said:

It is difficult to know what to say, but I want to say something at the end. I find it amazing to see where I am now compared to four months ago. It's almost incomprehensible – I've tried to work out how it happened. It feels complicated – like it feels that *I did it, but that I couldn't have done it without you.* Also, what I treasure is how you were with me. At the times I was most ugly, you moved even closer. And there have been so many times when … what we've been doing together has felt like … has felt like … a kind of loving.

Postscript

One month after this last meeting Joan telephoned the counsellor and asked if he would go with her to visit her mother's grave. Joan said that she did not know what she would do there, but that it felt really important for her to go. She did not want to make the visit alone, and would like the counsellor to go with her since she could trust him to cope with whatever happened. The counsellor agreed to this request without difficulty, and the visit took place. During the ten minutes they stood silently at the graveside Joan looked cold and expressionless. However, at the end of this time she screamed and gave her mother's gravestone an almighty kick. She cried a little after that, but seemed more upset by the fact that she had hurt her foot quite badly.

At their review two years later Joan was able to complete this part of her story. For about three months she had continued weekly visits to the graveside on her own. At first she went to the grave to give her hate and then, after talking with an aunt, she went with a tentative understanding of her mother's own vulnerability and finally, on her last visit, she went with forgiveness. Joan never forgave her father, nor did she seek any contact with him.

The End of the Counselling Process

The case study of Joan and her counsellor illustrates the fact that the end of the counselling process is characterised by *action*. Such action is the outcome of three important developments: the therapeutic movement has occurred leading to the rapid enhancement of the client's self-acceptance; the various emotional factors preventing a more active life have been reduced; and there is a gradual recognition of a new freedom to make choices and changes that earlier would have seemed impossible. During meetings 11–14 Joan's developing self-acceptance had enabled considerable movement: she had re-evaluated her attachment to her husband; understood more about her behaviour towards her bosses; and begun to re-evaluate her abilities and interests. These psychological adjustments enabled Joan to take actions in her life like deciding to resume her studies, beginning to dance again, arranging a holiday with a friend and behaving quite differently in relation to Roger. Instead of being the tormented, conflicted and essentially subservient wife, Joan had quite suddenly been able to withdraw the emotional dependence that she had placed on Roger. She was able to speak and behave more confidently towards him. She could even talk to him about her growing detachment from the relationship without being paralysed by guilt or fear.

These rapid changes towards the end of the counselling process are characteristic of what happens when self-acceptance has been achieved. It is as though the floodgates which had been holding up the client's personal growth are now open, and all the pressure for change that had been building up over many years surges through and settles quite quickly into its new pattern.

Joan described this phase of the process as one where she was 'a new person in an old life'. This experience is common for clients who have achieved a turnaround in their attitude to their self. Previously they will have built a life around them that reflected their lack of self-acceptance. They may have been self-defeating, over-submissive and under-valuing of their own abilities. When self-acceptance is achieved all these things can now change, but sometimes at the cost of considerable turmoil. Perhaps the client's relationships at home and at work can be nourished and strengthened by his personal growth but it is possible that these relationships have relied upon the client being weak. Being a new person in an old life can even present a challenge to the client in relation to his children. They will have developed strategies for handling a parent who seemed troubled and conflicted much of the time, and who may have found it difficult to show his love for them. A client who has released himself from the oppression of self-rejection is potentially a much more exciting and loving person to be with, but the client should not be surprised if his children are cautious in their acceptance of this new person whose rapid change they may at first find difficult to trust.

'I never promised you a rose garden' is the title of a famous song and book (Green, 1967). This title is most descriptive of the experience of many clients after counselling. While they are pleased with the new self that has emerged, there may also be a tinge of disappointment that their successful progress through counselling does not mean that life is easy thereafter. Sometimes the client has built up a fairy-tale image of what life would be like 'if only I were well'. Such a fairy-tale ending, with its theme of 'living happily ever after', does not bear much resemblance to the reality of having to construct a new life to fit the newly-emerged self. The counsellor can play an important part in helping the client to adjust the lack of fit between his new self and his old life. Joan was able to do much of this for herself, but often the counsellor remains an extremely important person for the client at this time. The counsellor may now be the only person in the client's life who understands the change which has taken place and how positively that change is experienced by the client.

One of the tricky things that can happen at an ending is that the client misjudges his 'balance' with respect to movement in counselling. He exhibits a level of change within counselling that is more than he later wants or can cope with, as one client reflected some months after ending:

> At the end of counselling I was going to change everything about me. I had succeeded in killing the whining little girl in me and, boy, I wasn't going back there! Everything was going to change – my partner could put up with my changing or she could get out – and I was finally going to tell my mother what I thought of her before she died.

The experienced counsellor will probably be cringing as she reads this. It is indicative of a partial change process which will be re-balanced once the social mediation dimension of the client's actualising process re-establishes its voice. Often this incomplete process is a function of the counsellor's inability to be alive not only to her client's striving for growth but also to the now quieter voice of her social mediation imperative. Person-centred counsellors who are themselves 'hooked on growth' can do this disservice to their clients.

In meetings 16 and 17 of our case study the counsellor also appeared more active in the sense that he initiated activities such as reviewing the process, looking at unfinished business and pressing Joan to consider every detail of her life after the end of counselling. This kind of 'action' on the part of the counsellor can extend to making suggestions on strategies the client might consider, and helping the client to gather information concerning such matters as jobs, legal issues, welfare benefits and resources. This more active role is partly related to the fact that the client is becoming more active, but it also stems from the fact that the client has substantially internalised his 'locus of evaluation'. In this circumstance the counsellor can trust the client to exert his own power in their relationship. This frees the counsellor to offer information, suggestions and even advice, in the knowledge that the client is not overawed by the counsellor's presence and that he will take what is useful to him and reject what is not. This issue of the fluctuating 'power dynamic' within the therapeutic process is explored in Mearns (2003: 77–9).

Endings that the Counsellor regards as 'Premature'

When a client terminates suddenly without warning or explanation it is appropriate that the counsellor reflects on her own functioning in order to seek understanding, but it is not appropriate for her to assume that the responsibility must necessarily be hers. Sometimes the client simply decides that the counselling process is not for him at this time in his life.

Occasionally a client announces his decision to terminate, but stays long enough to explain the reasons. This can give invaluable feedback to the counsellor, who might otherwise only have had fantasies about the client's reasons, but at other times it is more difficult to trust the veracity of the client's statement. For instance, there is what is referred to as the client's *flight into health*. This applies where the client pretends that all his problems have been solved since last week, and no further counselling support is needed! The counsellor should challenge such a statement, but would be wise to do so gently, since the client's trust in her may be low.

Another difficult ending for the counsellor is where the client retains a narrow definition of his problem and judges that the process is finished, either when this problem is solved or when it becomes obvious that it is not going to be solved quickly. For instance, the client who sees his problem as one of failing to attract a partner may be confused by the counsellor who seeks to help him explore the ways he sees *himself*; or the client who feels 'a bit down' following the death of a close family member may be discouraged when the process appears to take longer than the customary consultation with his doctor. The person-centred counsellor would want to invite the client to explore the wider implications of his presenting problem, but if the client does not acknowledge these, then it is not appropriate for the counsellor to try to enforce her own perception. Clients, after all, have the right to remain at the level of functioning they choose without being coerced by counsellors who are bent on producing fully-functioning persons and nothing less.

Preparing for Endings

In person-centred counselling the client generally dictates the end-point. This is as true in short-term services linked to health provision as it is in open-ended private practice work. In short-term services the client, as well as the counsellor, knows the parameters of the provision and can assess when they have had enough, for now at least. But the counsellor should not feel that they must not initiate an 'endings' discussion. It is perfectly appropriate for the counsellor to introduce tentatively the question: 'Have you any thoughts on when we should stop?' It is important that the counsellor raises this issue in such a way that the two of them can discuss it openly, without the client feeling that he is expected to be ready to stop. Just as it is difficult for the counsellor to appreciate the significance of the therapeutic process for the client, it is not easy for the counsellor to make judgements on how able the client feels to continue on his own. Sometimes a client has made enormous progress in counselling but finds it difficult to imagine how he will continue on his own. 'Ending' for this client may take a little longer while he becomes accustomed to being on his own. Near the end of a lengthy counselling process a client of one of the authors (Mearns) commented: 'Sometimes when I am unsure about something that is happening in my life I sit back and say to myself: "What would I say about this if I was with Dave right now?"' This client was finding a way of becoming her own counsellor.

From our case study it appears that Joan first became aware of a natural ending when she realised in meeting 14 that she had rediscovered a happy child who existed before her teenage years of abuse and humiliation. Many changes had happened to her, but this one seemed to carry particular significance. At the beginning of meeting 15 Joan announced that she could end 'very soon'. A useful question to the client at this juncture is what he feels he would want to *do* before the end. In our case study Joan was clear that she wanted to look at the changes she would make in her life. However, as well as undertaking this task, we find that three other matters were raised by the counsellor. He mentioned the possibility of *reviews* or even *restarts*. It is important to mention these since the client might well assume that counselling is a once-and-for-all offer. Although a major thrust of person-centred counselling is to enable the client to develop the personal strength and self-perception to help him negotiate future difficulties in life, this is not to suggest that he will never again enter into a counselling relationship. On the contrary, if his initial counselling process has been successful it will have equipped him with the ability to use future counselling support efficiently.

The second issue introduced by the counsellor was the idea of *reviewing the counselling process*. One of the benefits of 'reviewing the process' is that it can help both client and counsellor to check their cognitive understanding of the events and process they have been through. Understanding, on a cognitive (thinking) as well as an affective (feeling) level, can also be important for the client as he approaches difficulties in the future; he is able to *think* about his life as well as experience his feelings. However, reviewing the process while it is ending may still not yield complete understanding. The events, the feelings and the relationship may be still too fresh to comprehend fully. Rogers reports the words of a client who has reached the end of a successful counselling process. Even then, this client cannot fully understand the active ingredients of that process:

> I can't tell just exactly what's happened. It's just that I exposed something, shook it up and turned it around; and when I put it back it felt better. It's a little frustrating because I'd like to know exactly what's going on. (Rogers, 1961: 151)

It is interesting that Joan, in our case study, reflects a similar uncertainty at the very end in a statement we quoted earlier:

> It's almost incomprehensible. I've tried to work out how it happened. It feels complicated – like I did it, but I couldn't have done it without you.

It may be that clients, and indeed counsellors, can only understand the therapeutic process fully once they have had some time to be separate from it and to experience its longer-term impact. In compiling the case study for this book, Joan and the counsellor were able to achieve an understanding of their counselling process, which would not have been possible at the point where counselling had ended. Perhaps other clients would value the opportunity to spend some time reviewing their process some two years later.

The third and final element which the counsellor introduced to the ending process was the question of whether they had any *unfinished business* that they might like to complete together. For this question to be effective it must be asked with plenty of time left, and in such a way that it is regarded as considerably more than a formality. This question is an opportunity for the client to voice questions, uncertainties, or confessions that are usually quite important to him but which would otherwise have gone unsaid. This is the counsellor's last therapeutic intervention, but like all the rest it is not a demand, as evidenced by one client who responded to the question in such a way as to leave the counsellor ever more in mystery: 'Unfinished business … yes … and I think I'm going to keep it that way [smiles]!'

After the End

We have already said that the end need not be final in the sense that the client can arrange reviews or even restarts of the counselling process, but a much more important question is of concern to person-centred practitioners: 'Can clients and counsellors become friends?' In other counselling approaches, which create a large power difference between counsellor and client, this question would be a complete non-starter. However, within the person-centred tradition there is a range of opinion on the question of whether clients can become friends. Some person-centred counsellors would assert that 'once a client, always a client'. This is a safe position which preserves integrity, and as such must be respected. However, it does not address the inevitable questions raised by the concept of mutuality. If mutuality is experienced as we have presented it, then the two persons are freely sharing responsibility for the process that takes place between them. Why then are they not free to continue a relationship as friends once the counselling process is ended? In most cases, for the present writers, this question is scarcely contentious: former clients can and do become friends, and even colleagues in the future.

Underlying our question lurks the much more difficult issue of whether client and counsellor could at any time in the future become sexual partners. In person-centred counselling, as we have described it, the relationship between counsellor and client is one where the counsellor is present as a person and not just as a role. With the development of mutuality this personal relationship is strengthened and becomes more reciprocal. Nevertheless, during the course of counselling we have argued that the nature of the counsellor's responsibility rules out sexual behaviour. We want to go a little further and suggest that even upon completion of counselling the counsellor should for some time thereafter, even perhaps for some years thereafter, consider that the counselling relationship may not be permanently closed and should therefore conform to the usual ethical principles as far as sexual behaviour is concerned. The reason for this caution with respect to sexual relations is prompted by two considerations. First, neither counsellor nor client can be sure that the ending they mark for the process is indeed final – clients sometimes return to complete a process they had earlier thought was finished. Our second argument for caution relates to the point we made earlier in this chapter concerning the difficulty for the client of understanding fully the counselling process immediately it has ended. We believe that such understanding is a very important ingredient and precedent to relationships that are to change their character so profoundly. The cautious stance we have taken on this issue further reinforces our view that sexual relations in the context of a power difference between the partners represents sexual abuse of a most insidious kind.

Another question appropriate for the counsellor after the end of a counselling relationship is 'How have I been affected by this experience?' We would not expect the counsellor to be so malleable as to be significantly changed by every counselling contact. Equally, the person-centred counsellor who does not change and grow through her experience might question the extent to which she is being fully present in her counselling relationships, and wonder about the nature of the climate she is creating for her clients.

This question takes us back to Chapter 6, where we explored the developmental agenda for the person-centred counsellor. Some readers might have closed the book at that point because it is so demanding an agenda. It invites the person-centred counsellor to regard their initial training as merely the start of her development. It may disappoint her by pointing out that her development is not about learning *how to* counsel but about becoming a person who can counsel. It treats her early experience of establishing relational depth with a client as something to celebrate, but it then invites her to become able to offer that to every single client. It invites her to explore her catalogue of feared self-experiences but does not settle for mere awareness – for if she can truly integrate these experiences they may become existential touchstones that can broaden as well as deepen the person she offers to her clients. Furthermore, it does not say that her 'development' will be over a period of two, five, or even ten years, but that it will be life-long. So, why do so many people willingly embark upon that pathway? Perhaps because experiencing our humanity and offering it to others takes us to those places for which we yearn, where meaning, purpose and fulfilment are to be found.

Appendix

Questions and Responses

There are some questions about person-centred counselling that arise repeatedly. Sometimes these come from practitioners allied to other disciplines who have picked up on certain aspects of the approach but who cannot be expected to have studied it at depth. At other times these questions come from person-centred counsellors in training as they discover the particular challenges of the approach. Questions such as these are addressed across the nine chapters of the book, but we thought that it would be useful to lay out and respond to some of the most common ones here.

Question 1: Is it possible, in your opinion to combine the person-centred approach with other therapeutic approaches?

We are alarmed when we read in an entry in the *Directory of the British Association for Counselling and Psychotherapy* that a practitioner is describing herself as psychodynamic, person-centred, gestalt and rational emotive behavioural – or some other unlikely combination. We cannot even begin to conceptualise what such a self-description might indicate. Does it mean that the counsellor combines all these approaches in some amazingly integrated or eclectic fashion, or does it suggest that on a certain day, at a certain hour, she dons one mantle and the next another – psychodynamic for this client but person-centred for the next? We would be similarly alarmed if we were grounded in a therapeutic approach other than our own. During the development of the national body's individual and courses accreditation schemes the thinking was the same as ours – that counsellors could operate from any specialism – but it was important that they *had* a specialism. The rationale behind this is that the depth and coherence of the counsellor is critical. The counsellor will be placed under varied and at times dramatic demands, and the depth of their grounding will give a coherence as well as a stability to their working. When courses presented themselves as 'integrative', it was not acceptable that this integration simply reflected the variety in their trainers' interests, the courses were expected to have developed a strong basis, structure and rationale defining that integration and were required to address in writing specific questions about their integrative model (BAC, 1993: 1–2; Dryden, Horton and Mearns, 1995: 38–40).

Looking specifically at the person-centred approach, there are key aspects that we would regard as inherent in using the label. Most particularly these concern our understanding of the individual's resourcefulness, the operation of the actualising process and his or her ability to be self-directing; our belief in the importance of the therapeutic conditions and the centrality of the counsellor's non-directive attitude at the level of content; and our refusal to embrace the role of expert on the client's life and experience. These key aspects alone rule out for us the possibility of combining the approach with other orientations that are based on quite different or even contrary assumptions. It is possible, we believe, for the person-centred counsellor to become an expert in facilitating the *process* of therapy but even then great care has to be taken to ensure that the client's essential autonomy and right to self-determination are not violated. It has become highly fashionable in recent years for practitioners to describe themselves as 'integrative', without the discipline demanded by the national body in the early years, but our experience suggests that when person-centred counsellors adopt this label they are often in danger of abandoning fundamental principles of the approach without quite realising that they have done so. This is not to say that person-centred practitioners should refrain from becoming knowledgeable about other approaches or from familiarising themselves with the theory and practice of other orientations. At the very least, such knowledge may prove important in cases where referral to other practitioners is indicated but, at a deeper level, fresh insights can enrich the person-centred counsellor's fund of wisdom and experience and sharpen her appreciation and understanding of the person-centred approach itself through such comparative study.

Question 2:   How do you refute the accusation that person-centred counselling encourages selfishness and disregard for the feelings of others?

This kind of question springs from the idea that the person-centred approach, with its emphasis on valuing the client's experiencing of his world and finding his power to become more active in his world, makes clients self-inflated and prone to trample on the lives of others. The sense of liberation from oppressive conditions of worth, it is claimed, can lead clients to assert themselves and their own needs and desires in such a way that others are hurt and even abandoned. There are stories of clients of person-centred practitioners who, given the chance to hear their own voices for the first time, have rejected parents, walked out on marriages and engaged in outrageously selfish and irresponsible behaviour. There is truth in these stories. It is undoubtedly the case that when an individual begins to change and to assume responsibility for his or her own life the disruption in the lives of those around them can be considerable and seldom welcomed. Some of this social disturbance will relate to the 'partial change process' described in Chapter 9, where the client, once released from an oppressed psychological position, can initially swing to the opposite position before finding a middle ground. Of course, the client is not the only person who carries responsibility for his social relations – those around him might reasonably be asked to take responsibility for their own positions.

Interestingly, there is some evidence to suggest that clients of person-centred counsellors not only demonstrate increasing autonomy but also 'catch' some of the empathic ability of their counsellors. Far from becoming selfish, clients often demonstrate an increasing sensitivity to others and the confidence to enter more positively into social interaction. The ability to confront those who have previously been sources of unhappiness can also lead to changes in the dynamics of a relationship which are wholly positive. Research carried out in Germany showed that the greatest gain made by participants in person-centred group therapy was in their ability to offer empathic understanding to fellow group members and to other significant people in their lives. This gain was greater even than their progress in regard to self-exploration and self-awareness (Giesekus and Mente, 1986: 163–71). In our experience many clients in individual therapy make similar strides in empathic ability and social skills. Far from becoming more selfish, clients who are in a person-centred counselling relationship for any length of time are likely to become more socially involved and more capable of stretching out to others constructively. Our revision of Rogers' original theory (see Chapter 2) to include the concept of social mediation as a buffer to the actualising tendency is also relevant to this question.

Question 3:   Does not the person-centred approach's attitude towards boundaries inevitably lead to questionable and even unethical behaviour on the part of the counsellor?

Person-centred counsellors, like their colleagues from other orientations, subscribe to the ethical principles of their professional organisations and associations. In this sense they are working within structures and guidelines that themselves provide certain boundaries. However, as well as these undisputed ethical boundaries, there are others that are more approach-specific. These would be seen as 'good practice' in one model, but should not be generalised to other models without discussion. These 'boundaries' might include strict adherence to time and place, an avoidance of physical contact with clients, a veto on self-disclosure on the part of the counsellor and other unwritten rules conditioning the therapeutic relationship. As was discussed in Chapter 8 in relation to the therapeutic context, such boundaries emanate, historically, from a classical psychodynamic approach. They are relevant to the kind of authority position sought by that approach but not to a person-centred approach. For the person-centred counsellor the attempt to 'equalise' the relationship is paramount. The counsellor's task is to create an environment where the client feels increasingly empowered to discover his own resources, find his own sense of direction and take charge of his life. Boundaries are established to facilitate these outcomes and it is self-evident that they must at all times be respectful of the client's needs and therefore be open to re-negotiation. For the counsellor to impose boundaries without a consultative process with the client would be a denial of the essential equality of the relationship which it is hoped to establish. In practice, much that goes on in person-centred counselling will not, to all outward appearances, differ much from what happens in other orientations. The client will probably come week by week for a fifty minute session, at the same time and on the same day of the week. The counsellor will be unlikely to reveal much of herself during the therapeutic process and there will probably be little if any physical contact. The significant difference from some other approaches lies in the fact that all this is susceptible to change. For the person-centred counsellor attentiveness to the process of the relationship is of fundamental importance both in terms of the client's emerging autonomy and of the movement towards reciprocity. In the light of this process new boundaries may need to be negotiated and agreed. Perhaps sessions become less frequent or more frequent. Their length, too, may change for there is nothing sacrosanct about the 50 minute hour. The developing relationship may lead naturally to respectful physical contact and the counsellor's openness may result in greater self-revelation. The important and fundamental principle is that boundaries are not set in stone but are open to renegotiation in the light of the client's needs and of the therapeutic process. Boundaries, like so much else in the person-centred tradition, are not simply imposed but explored and agreed. As a result the practice of person-centred counselling is in its very essence a deeply ethical activity and is utterly at variance with a rule-bound or manual dictated practice which places inflexible regulations or procedures above the emerging needs of persons in relationship.

Question 4: Doesn't person-centred counselling, with its heavy emphasis on subjective experience, ignore social and political issues and thus reinforce the status quo?

This is a tremendous question. It echoes the suspicion that counselling, because it permits people to get things off their chests, defuses potential rebellion or agitation and is therefore a form of subtle social engineering. This does not ring true to our experience nor does it make much sense in Carl Rogers' own life. The older he became, the more concerned he was with the state of the world. The last decades of his life were dedicated to the pursuit of world peace, the development of cross-cultural communication and the creation of new forms of community. He described himself as a 'quiet revolutionary' and saw the whole person-centred approach as subtly subversive. As we think of ourselves and of many of our clients over the years we see a process whereby the experience of relationship, characterised by deep understanding and interpersonal honesty, provokes not only distress but sometimes rage at the rampant injustices and shameless hypocrisy that all too often characterise our political or social environment.

In another fundamental way the person-centred approach is politically radical. It is a constant opponent to the societal influences of *social control* over the individual. While even some counselling approaches, notably cognitive behaviour therapy, accept an implicit, if not explicit, agenda to work towards symptom reduction as the only evaluated goal of intervention, person-centred counselling works with the whole person and is oriented towards the goals of that person rather than the agenda society has for the person. This creates a continual uncomfortable dissonance for the person-centred counsellor working in the health service or in education, both heavily determined by social control politics. Yet there is an interesting irony in this, because, at their core, both the professions of medicine and education are also about the whole person and their development. For a fuller consideration of these political issues see Mearns (2006b).

Question 5: Person-centred counselling seeks not to form a dependent relationship between client and counsellor. But surely there are circumstances where the client is *so* vulnerable that the counsellor needs to allow a degree of initial dependency? When the client grows stronger they can then be weaned off that dependency.

Under *no* circumstances would the person-centred counsellor encourage the client's dependency. The whole object of the work of the person-centred counsellor is to facilitate the client's *agency* – his ability and willingness to take responsibility for himself. While it might seem logical – caring even – to believe that with the very vulnerable client we might start with a dependency that offers the client a kind of comfort, it is fool's gold. The problem with dependency is that it is not as easy as one would think to 'wean the client off it'. In a classical psychodynamic approach the same kind of thinking applied as is voiced in this question – that the dependent transference relationship could be developed and later in the analysis the transference would be unpacked and the autonomy of the client established. The reality is better depicted by the 21 victims of long-term analysis represented in the book by Rosemary Dinnage (1988). Even after lengthy analyses these clients were still in a dependency relationship with their analysts and former analysts. In person-centred counselling, especially with a person whose locus of evaluation is highly externalised, the client may seek the security of a dependent relationship but the person-centred counsellor's task is to offer the therapeutic conditions in high degree while not developing dependency.

Question 6: The person-centred approach is stronger in Britain than in many other parts of the world. Why is that?

Because we have been prepared to engage with the various institutions that are stakeholders in regard to the practice of counselling. In this regard, for example, we have done a good job in staying connected with the universities. At the time of writing 70 per cent of the counselling professoriate in Britain are person-centred specialists. Also, during the first 30 years of the development of the counselling profession in Britain we stayed close to the main professional association, the *British Association for Counselling and Psychotherapy*, dialoguing with colleagues from other approaches on the development of individual accreditation, the accreditation of training courses and the nature of ethical practice. Similarly, we have worked hard to dialogue with state institutions such as the health service as well as secondary and tertiary education, so that a person-centred approach to counselling could be accepted within those contexts. In the USA this dialogue was largely ignored during the enormous popularisation of the approach in the 1960s. By contrast in Austria the same attention was paid – as in Britain – to dialogue with institutions and as a result the person-centred approach is well established there.

Question 7: Where does each of you think person-centred counselling might go in the future?

Dave Mearns responds: One possibility is that the person-centred approach might help the counselling profession to widen rather than narrow its relevance. There is a tendency for developing professions to draw ever-tighter boundaries around their practice. While that may afford considerable security for the practitioners, it is not particularly useful in taking the profession to a wider group of clients. However, the person-centred approach as we have described it in this book, in terms of the power of relationship, could continually prompt the profession to look in more expansive directions. For example, at present, counselling is probably only seen as a relevant possibility by about 10 per cent of troubled people. We need to be looking at why that is the case and actively exploring creative models for taking the profession to the other 90 per cent. Probably the person-centred approach is best placed to provide the lead in responding to that radical challenge because it is set within negotiated rather than pre-set boundaries and could be consultative as well as creative with respect to forging different contexts for counselling.

Brian Thorne responds: There is growing evidence that for many clients their experience of person-centred counselling has enabled them not only to find more satisfaction in their work and relationships but also to discover a new sense of purpose and meaning in their lives. It is becoming clear that the approach has much to offer at a time of great political, intercultural and ecological crisis, when despair is an increasingly common response. It may only just be beginning, however, to embrace the implications of modelling a way of being which can directly address the existential and spiritual malaise of a world on the brink of disaster.

References

Alexander, R. (1995) *Folie à Deux: An Experience of One-to-One Therapy.* London: Free Association Press.

Asay, T.P., and Lambert, M.J. (1999) 'Therapist relational variables', in D.J. Cain and J. Seeman (eds), *Humanistic Psychotherapies: Handbook of Theory and Practice.* Washington, DC: American Psychological Association. pp. 531–57.

Axline, V. (1971) *Dibs in Search of Self.* Harmondsworth, Middlesex: Penguin.

Balmforth, J. (2006) 'Clients' experiences of how perceived differences in social class between counsellor and client affect the therapeutic relationship', in G. Proctor, M. Cooper, P. Sanders and B. Malcolm (eds), *Politicizing the Person-Centred Approach.* Ross-on-Wye: PCCS Books. pp. 215–24.

Barrett-Lennard, G.T. (1962) 'Dimensions of therapist response as causal factors in therapeutic change', *Psychological Monographs,* 76: 43 (Whole No. 562).

Barrett-Lennard, G.T. (1987) Personal Communication. Third International Forum on the Person-Centered Approach, La Jolla, California.

Barrett-Lennard, G.T. (1998) *Carl Rogers' Helping System: Journey and Substance.* London: Sage.

Barrett-Lennard, G.T. (2005) *Relationship at the Centre: Healing in a Troubled World.* London: Whurr.

Bates, Y. (ed.) (2006) *Shouldn't I be Feeling Better by Now? Client Views of Therapy.* Basingstoke: Palgrave Macmillan.

Beahrs, J. (1982) *Unity and Multiplicity.* New York: Brunner/Mazel.

Bennis, W. (1986) *Carl Rogers Interviewed by Warren Bennis.* Video-tape produced by University Associates Incorporated, San Diego.

Bergin, A.E. and Jasper, L.G. (1969) 'Correlates of empathy in psychotherapy: a replication', *Journal of Abnormal Psychology,* 74: 477–81.

Bergin, A.E. and Solomon, S. (1970) 'Personality and performance correlates of empathic understanding in psychotherapy', in J.T. Hart and T.M. Tomlinson (eds), *New Directions in Client-Centered Therapy.* Boston: Houghton-Mifflin. pp. 223–36.

Bergin, A.E. and Strupp, H.H. (1972) *Changing Frontiers in the Science of Psychotherapy.* Chicago: Aldine-Atherton.

Berne, E. (1961) *Transactional Analysis in Psychotherapy.* New York: Grove Press.

Bettelheim, B. (1987) 'The man who cared for children', *Horizon*. London: BBC Television (video).

Beutler, L.E., Malik, M., Alimohamed, S., Harwood, M.T., Talebi, H., Noble, S., et al. (2004) 'Therapist variables', in M.J. Lambert (ed.), *Bergin and Garfield's Handbook of Psychotherapy and Behavior Change,* 5th edn. Chicago: John Wiley and Sons. pp. 227–306.

Bohart, A.C. (2004) 'How do clients make empathy work?', *Person-Centered and Experiential Psychotherapies*, 2: 102–16.

Bohart, A.C., and Tallman, K. (1999) *How Clients Make Therapy Work: the Process of Active Self-Healing*. Washington: American Psychological Association.

Boyles, J. (2006) 'Not just naming the injustice – counselling asylum seekers and refugees', in G. Proctor, M. Cooper, P. Sanders and B. Malcolm (eds), *Politicizing the Person-Centred Approach*. Ross-on-Wye: PCCS Books. pp. 156–66.

Bozarth, J. (1984) 'Beyond reflection: emergent modes of empathy', in R.F. Levant and J.M. Shlien (eds), *Client-Centered Therapy and the Person-Centered Approach*. New York: Praeger. pp. 59–75.

Bozarth, J. (1998) *Person-centered Therapy: a Revolutionary Paradigm*. Ross-on-Wye: PCCS Books.

Bozarth, J. (2001) 'Client-centered unconditional positive regard: a historical perspective', in J. Bozarth and P. Wilkins (eds), *Rogers' Therapeutic Conditions: Unconditional Positive Regard*. Ross-on-Wye: PCCS Books. pp. 5–18.

Bozarth, J. and Temaner Brodley, B. (1986) 'The core values and theory of the person-centered approach'. Paper prepared for the First Annual Meeting of the Association for the Development of the Person-Centered Approach, Chicago.

British Association for Counselling (BAC) (1993) *The Recognition of Counsellor Training Courses Scheme: Guidelines for Integrative and Eclectic Courses*. BAC/CRG Information Sheet. Rugby: British Association for Counselling.

Brodley, B.T. (1999) 'The actualizing tendency concept in client-centered theory', *The Person-Centered Journal*, 6 (2): 108–20.

Brodley, B.T. and Schneider, C. (2001) 'Unconditional positive regard as communicated through verbal behavior in client-centered therapy', in J. Bozarth and P. Wilkins (eds), *Rogers' Therapeutic Conditions: Unconditional Positive Regard*. Ross-on-Wye: PCCS Books. pp. 156–72.

Brown, M. (1979) *The Art of Guiding: the Psychosynthesis Approach to Individual Counseling and Psychology*. Redlands, CA: Johnston College, University of Redlands.

Burns, D.D. and Nolen-Hoeksema, S. (1991) 'Coping styles, homework compliance, and the effectiveness of cognitive behavioral therapy', *Journal of Consulting and Clinical Psychology*, 59: 305–11.

Cain, D. (1987) Personal Communication. Third International Forum on the Person-Centered Approach, La Jolla, California.

Carkhuff, R.R. (1971) *The Development of Human Resources*. New York: Holt, Rinehart & Winston.

Chantler, K. (2006) 'Rethinking person-centred therapy', in G. Proctor, M. Cooper, P. Sanders and B. Malcolm (eds), *Politicizing the Person-Centred Approach*. Ross-on-Wye: PCCS Books. pp. 44–54.

Cooper, M. (2003) '"I-I" And "I-Me": Transposing Buber's interpersonal attitudes to the intrapersonal plane', *Journal of Constructivist Psychology*, 16(2): 131–53.

Cooper, M., Mearns, D., Stiles, W.B., Warner, M.S. and Elliott, R. (2004) 'Developing self-pluralistic perspectives within the person-centered and experiential approaches: a round table dialogue', *Person-Centered and Experiential Psychotherapies*, 3(3): 176–91.

Coulson, W. (1987) 'Reclaiming client-centered counseling from the person-centered movement'. Copyright: Centre for Enterprising Families, P.O. Box 134, Comptche, CA 95427, USA.

Coulson, W. (2000) Personal communication.

Davies, D. and Neal, C. (eds) (1996) *Pink Therapy: a Guide for Counsellors and Therapists Working with Lesbian, Gay and Bisexual Clients*. Buckingham: Open University Press.

Davies, D. and Neal, C. (eds) (2000) *Therapeutic Perspectives on Working with Lesbian, Gay and Bisexual Clients*. Buckingham: Open University Press.

Dinnage, R. (1988) *One to One: Experiences of Psychotherapy*. London: Viking.

Duncan, B.L. and Moynihan, D.W. (1994) 'Applying outcome research: intentional utilization of the client's frame of reference', *Psychotherapy*, 31: 294–301.

Dryden, W., Horton, I. and Mearns, D. (1995) *Issues in Professional Counsellor Training*. London: Cassell.

Elliott, R. and Greenberg, C. (1997) 'Multiple voices in process-experiential therapy: dialogues between aspects of the self', *Journal of Psychotherapy Integration*, 7: 225–39.

Fairbairn, W.R.D. (1952) *Psychoanalytic Studies of the Personality*. London: Routledge.

Festinger, L. (1957) *A Theory of Cognitive Dissonance*. Evanston, IL: Row, Peterson.

Fiedler, F.E. (1949) 'A comparative investigation of early therapeutic relationships created by experts and non-experts of psychoanalytic, non-directive, and Adlerian schools'. Unpublished doctoral dissertation, Chicago: University of Chicago.

Fiedler, F.E. (1950) 'A comparison of therapeutic relationships in psychoanalytic, non-directive and Adlerian therapy', *Journal of Consulting Psychology*, 14: 436–45.

Freire, E. (2001) 'Unconditional positive regard: the distinctive feature of client-centered therapy', in G. Wyatt (ed.) *Rogers' Therapeutic Conditions: Unconditional Positive Regard*. pp. 145–55.

Gaylin, N.L. (1996) 'Reflections on the self of the therapist', in R. Hutterer, G. Pawlowsky, P.F. Schmid and R. Stipsits (eds), *Client-Centered and*

Experiential Psychotherapy: a Paradigm in Motion. Frankfurt-am-Main: Peter Lang. pp. 383–94.

Gendlin, E.T. (1967) 'Subverbal communication and therapist expressivity: trends in client-centered therapy with schizophrenics', in C.R. Rogers and B. Stevens (eds) *Person to Person: the Problem of Being Human.* Lafayette, CA: Real People Press. pp. 119–28.

Gendlin, E.T. (1970) 'A short summary and some long predictions', in J. Hart and T. Tomlinson (eds), *New Directions in Client-Centered Therapy.* Boston: Houghton Mifflin. pp. 544–62.

Gendlin, E.T. (1981) *Focusing.* New York: Bantam.

Gendlin, E.T. (1984) 'The client's client: the edge of awareness', in R.F. Levant and J.M. Shlien (eds), *Client-Centered Therapy and the Person-Centered Approach.* New York: Praeger. pp. 76–107.

Gendlin, E.T. (1996) *Focusing-Oriented Psychotherapy.* New York: Guilford.

Gergen, K.J. (1972) 'Multiple identity: the healthy, happy human being wears many masks', *Psychology Today,* 5: 31–5, 64–6.

Gergen, K.J. (1988) 'Narrative and self as relationship', in L. Berkowitz (ed.), *Advances in Experimental Social Psychology. Vol. 21.* New York: Academic Press. pp. 17–56.

Gergen, K.J. (1991) *The Saturated Self.* New York: Basic Books.

Giesekus, U. and Mente, A. (1986) 'Client empathic understanding in client-centered therapy', *Person-Centered Review,* 1(2): 163–71.

Green, H. (1967) *I Never Promised You a Rose Garden.* London: Pan.

Gurman, A.S. (1977) 'The patient's perception of the therapeutic relationship', in A.S. Gurman and A.M. Ragin (eds), *Effective Psychotherapy.* New York: Pergamon. pp. 503–43.

Heider, F. (1958) *The Psychology of Interpersonal Relations.* New York: Wiley.

Hermans, H.J.M. (1996) 'Voicing the self: from information processing to dialogical interchange', *Psychological Bulletin,* 119: 31–50.

Hermans, H.J.M. and Dimaggio, G. (eds) (2004) *Dialogical Self in Psychotherapy.* Hove: Brunner-Routledge.

Hermans, H.J.M. and Kempen, H.J.G. (1993) *The Dialogical Self: Meaning as Movement.* San Diego, CA: Academic Press.

Hermans, H., Kempen, J. and Loon, R. van (1992) 'The dialogical self', *American Psychologist,* 47 (1): 23–33.

Honos-Webb, L. and Stiles, W. (1998) 'Reformulation of assimilation analysis in terms of voices', *Psychotherapy,* 35 (1): 23–33.

Hovarth, A.O. and Bedi, R.P. (2002) 'The alliance', in J.C. Norcross (ed.), *Psychotherapy Relationships that Work: Therapist Contributions and Responsiveness to Patients.* Oxford: Oxford University Press. pp. 37–69.

Howe, D. (1993) *On Being a Client.* London: Sage.

Hubble, M., Duncan, B.L. and Miller, S.D. (1999) *The Heart and Soul of Change: What Works in Therapy.* Washington, DC: American Psychological Association.

Ide, T., Hirai, T. and Murayama, S. (2006) 'The challenge for "fully functioning community": the school counselor bridging the gap between a family and a school'. Paper presented at the 7th World Conference for Person-Centered and Experiential Psychotherapy and Counseling. Potsdam, Germany; July.

Inayat, Q. (2005) 'The Islamic concept of self', *Counselling Psychology Review*, 20: 2–10.

Jourard, S.M. (1971) *The Transparent Self*. New York: Van Nostrand Reinhold.

Keijsers, G.P.J., Schaap, C.P.D.R. and Hoogduin, C.A.L. (2000) 'The impact of interpersonal patient and therapist behaviour on outcome in cognitive-behaviour therapy', *Behaviour Modification*, 24 (2): 264–97.

Keil, S. (1996) 'The self as a systemic process of interactions of "inner persons"', in R. Hutterer, G. Pawlowsky, P. Schmid and R. Stipsits (eds), *Client-Centered and Experiential Psychotherapy: a Paradigm in Motion*. Frankfurt am Main: Peter Lang. pp. 53–66.

Kessel, W. van and Lietaer, G. (1998) 'Interpersonal processes', in L.S. Greenberg, J.C. Watson and G. Lietaer (eds), *Handbook of Experiential Psychotherapy*. New York: The Guilford Press. pp. 155–77.

Keys, S. (ed.) (2003) *Idiosyncratic Person-Centred Therapy: From the Personal to the Universal*. Ross-on-Wye: PCCS Books.

Khurana, I. (2006) 'Person-centred therapy, culture and racism: personal discoveries and adaptations', in G. Proctor, M. Cooper, P. Sanders and B. Malcolm (eds), *Politicizing the Person-Centred Approach*. Ross-on-Wye: PCCS Books. pp. 195–7.

Kiesler, D.J. (1982) 'Confronting the client–therapist relationship in psychotherapy', in J.C. Anchin and D.J. Kiesler (eds), *Handbook of Interpersonal Psychotherapy*. Elmsford, NY: Pergamon. pp. 274–95.

Kiesler, D.J. (1996) *Contemporary Interpersonal Theory and Research: Personality, Psychopathology and Psychotherapy*. New York: Wiley.

King, M., Sibbald, B., Ward, E., Bower, P., Lloyd, M., Gabbay, M. and Byford, S. (2000) 'Randomised controlled trial of non-directive counselling, cognitive behaviour therapy and usual general practitioner care in the management of depression as well as mixed anxiety and depression in primary care', *British Medical Journal*, 321: 1,383–8.

Kreitemeyer, B. and Prouty, G. (2003) 'The art of psychological contact: the psychotherapy of a mentally retarded psychotic client', in *Person-Centered and Experiential Psychotherapies* 2 (3): 151–61.

Krupnick, J.L., Sotsky, S.M., Simmens, S., Moyer, J., Elkin, I., Watkins, J., et al. (1996) 'The role of the therapeutic alliance in psychotherapy and pharmaco-therapy outcome: findings in the national institute of mental health treatment of depression collaborative research program', *Journal of Consulting and Clinical Psychology*, 64 (3): 532–9.

Kurtz, R.R. and Grummon, D.L. (1972) 'Different approaches to the measurement of therapist empathy and their relationship to therapy outcomes', *Journal of Consulting and Clinical Psychology*, 39 (1): 106–15.

Lafferty, P., Beutler, L.E. and Crago, M. (1991) 'Differences between more and less effective psychotherapists: a study of select therapist variables', *Journal of Consulting and Clinical Psychology*, 59: 305–11.

Lago, C. (2006) *Race, Culture and Counselling*, 2nd edn. Maidenhead: Open University/McGraw-Hill.

Lago, C. and Haugh, S. (2006) 'White counsellor racial identity: the unacknowledged, unknown, unaware aspect of self in relationship', in G. Proctor, M. Cooper, P. Sanders and B. Malcolm (eds), *Politicizing the Person-Centred Approach*. Ross-on-Wye: PCCS Books. pp. 198–214.

Lambers, E. (2000) 'Supervision in person-centred therapy: facilitating congruence', in D. Mearns and B. Thorne, *Person-Centred Therapy Today: New Frontiers in Theory and Practice*. London: Sage. pp. 196–211.

Lambers, E. (2002). Personal Communication.

Lambers, E. (2003) 'Psychosis', in D. Mearns, *Developing Person-Centred Counselling*. London: Sage. pp. 113–5.

Lambers, E. (2006) 'Supervising the humanity of the therapist', *Person-Centered and Experiential Psychotherapies*, 5: 266–76.

Lambert, M. J. (1992) 'Implications of outcome research for psychotherapy integration', in J.C. Norcross and M.R. Goldstein (eds), *Handbook of Psychotherapy Integration*. New York: Basic Books. pp. 94–129.

Lietaer, G. (1984) 'Unconditional positive regard: a controversial basic attitude in client-centered therapy', in R. Levant and J. Shlien (eds), *Client-Centered Therapy and the Person-Centered Approach*. New York: Praeger. pp. 41–58.

Lietaer, G. (2001) 'Being genuine as a therapist: congruence and transparency', in G. Wyatt (ed.), *Rogers' Therapeutic Conditions: Congruence*. Ross-on-Wye: PCCS Books. pp. 36–54.

Lietaer, G. (2002) 'The client-centered/experiential paradigm in psychotherapy: development and identity', in J.C. Watson, R.N. Goldman and M.S. Warner (eds), *Client-Centered and Experiential Psychotherapy in the 21st Century: Advances in Theory, Research and Practice*. Ross-on-Wye: PCCS Books. pp. 1–15.

Lorr, M. (1965) 'Client perceptions of therapists', *Journal of Consulting Psychology*, 29: 146–9.

McGeever, K. (2006) 'A long-standing commitment: providing a managed counselling service in Lanarkshire', *Healthcare Counselling and Psychotherapy Journal*, 6 (4): 36–9.

McMillan, M. and McLeod, J. (2006) 'Letting go: the client's experience of relational depth', *Person-Centered and Experiential Psychotherapies*, 5: 277–92.

Mearns, D. (1985) 'Some notes on unconditional positive regard'. Unpublished paper produced for Glasgow Marriage Guidance Service.

Mearns, D. (1986) 'Some notes on congruence: can I dare to be me in response to my client?' Unpublished paper presented to the first Facilitator Development Institute (Britain) Therapy Training Course.

Mearns, D. (1996) 'Working at relational depth with clients in person-centred therapy', *Counselling*, 7 (4): 306–11.

Mearns, D. (1997a) *Person-Centred Counselling Training*. London: Sage.

Mearns, D. (1997b) *The Future of Individual Counselling*. The Ben Hartop Memorial Lecture, 7 May. Published as an Occasional Paper by the University of Durham.

Mearns, D. (1998) 'Managing a primary care service', *Counselling in Medical Settings*, 57: 1–5.

Mearns, D. (1999) 'Person-centred therapy with configurations of self', *Counselling*, 10: 125–30.

Mearns, D. (2002) 'Further theoretical propositions in regard to self theory within person-centered therapy', *Person-Centered and Experiential Psychotherapies*, 1(1&2): 14–27.

Mearns, D. (2003) *Developing Person-Centred Counselling*, 2nd edn. London: Sage.

Mearns, D. (2006a) 'Person-centred therapy: a leading edge', Masterclass presented at Metanoia, London and elsewhere (see www.davemearns.com).

Mearns, D. (2006b) 'Psychotherapy: the politics of liberation or collaboration? A career critically reviewed', in G. Proctor, M. Cooper, P. Sanders and B. Malcolm (eds), *Politicizing the Person-Centred Approach*. Ross-on-Wye: PCCS Books. pp. 127–42.

Mearns, D. and Cooper, M. (2005) *Working at Relational Depth in Counselling and Psychotherapy*. London: Sage.

Mearns, D. and Schmid, P.F. (2006) 'Being-with and being-counter. Relational depth: the challenge of fully meeting the client', *Person-Centered and Experiential Psychotherapies*, 5: 255–65.

Mearns, D. and Thorne, B. (1988) *Person-Centred Counselling in Action*, 1st edn. London: Sage.

Mearns, D. and Thorne, B. (1999) *Person-Centred Counselling in Action*, 2nd edn. London: Sage.

Mearns, D. and Thorne, B. (2000) *Person-Centred Therapy Today: New Frontiers in Theory and Practice*. London: Sage.

Merry, T. (1995) *Invitation to Person-Centred Psychology*. London: Whurr Publishers.

Merry, T. (1999) *Learning and Being in Person-Centred Counselling*. Ross-on-Wye: PCCS Books.

Milgram, S. (2004) *Obedience to Authority: an Experimental View*. New York: Harper Collins.

Morita, T., Kimura, T., Hirai, T. and Murayama, S. (2006) 'The approach to the relationship based on a "way of being" of the school counselor'. Paper presented at the 7th World Conference for Person-Centered and Experiential Psychotherapy and Counseling. Potsdam, Germany; July.

Moustakas, C.E. (1959) *Psychotherapy with Children – the Living Relationship*. New York: Harper and Brothers.

Mullen, J. and Abeles, N. (1972) 'Relationship of liking, empathy and therapist's experience to outcome of therapy', in *Psychotherapy 1971, an Aldine Annual*. Chicago: Aldine-Atherton. pp. 256–60.

Müller, D. (1995) 'Dealing with self-criticism: the critic within us and the criticized one', *The Folio: Journal for Focusing and Experiential Psychotherapy*, 4: 1–9.

Neal, C. and Davies, D. (eds) (2000) *Issues in Therapy with Lesbian, Gay, Bisexual and Transgender Clients*. Buckingham: Open University Press.

O'Connor, R.C., Sheehy, N.P. and O'Connor, D.B. (2000) 'Fifty cases of general hospital parasuicide', *British Journal of Health Psychology*, 5: 83–95.

O'Leary, C. (1999) *Couple and Family Counselling: a Person-Centred Perspective*. London: Sage.

Orlinsky, D.E., Grawe, K. and Parks, B.K. (1994) 'Process and outcome in psychotherapy – noch einmal', in A.E. Bergin and S.L. Garfield (eds), *Handbook of Psychotherapy and Behavior Change*, 4th edn. New York: Wiley. pp. 270–378.

Patterson, C.H. (1984) 'Empathy, warmth and genuineness in psychotherapy: a review of reviews', *Psychotherapy*, 21(4): 431–8.

Pörtner, M. (2000) *Trust and Understanding: the Person-Centred Approach to Everyday Care for People with Special Needs*. Ross-on-Wye: PCCS Books.

Prouty, G. (1994) *Theoretical Evolutions in Person-centered/Experiential Therapy: Applications to Schizophrenic and Retarded Psychosis*. New York: Praeger.

Prouty, G. (2001) 'A new mode of empathy: empathic contact', in S. Haugh and T. Merry (eds), *Rogers' Therapeutic Conditions: Empathy*. Ross-on-Wye: PCCS Books. pp. 155–62.

Prouty, G., Van Werde, D. and Pörtner, M. (2002) *Pre-Therapy: Reaching Contact Impaired Clients*. Ross-on-Wye: PCCS Books.

Purton, C. (2004) *Person-Centred Therapy: the Focusing-Oriented Approach*. Basingstoke: Palgrave/Macmillan.

Raskin, N. (1974) 'Studies on psychotherapeutic orientation: ideology in practice', *American Academy of Psychotherapists Psychotherapy Research Monographs*. Orlando, Florida: American Academy of Psychotherapists.

Rennie, D.L. (1998) *Person-Centred Counselling: an Experiential Approach*. London: Sage.

Rogers, C.R. (1951) *Client-Centered Therapy: its Current Practice, Implications and Theory*. Boston: Houghton Mifflin.

Rogers, C.R. (1959) 'A theory of therapy, personality and interpersonal relationships as developed in the client-centered framework', in S. Koch (ed.), *Psychology: a Study of Science* (Vol. 3). New York: McGraw-Hill. pp. 184–256.

Rogers C.R. (1961) *On Becoming a Person*. Boston: Houghton Mifflin.

Rogers C.R. (1963a) 'The concept of the fully functioning person', *Psychotherapy: Theory, Research and Practice*, 1(1): 17–26.

Rogers C.R. (1963b) 'The actualizing tendency in relation to "motives" and to consciousness', in M. Jones (ed.), *Nebraska Symposium on Motivation*. Lincoln, NE: University of Nebraska Press. pp. 1–24.

Rogers C.R. (ed.) (1967) *The Therapeutic Relationship and its Impact. A Study of Psychotherapy with Schizophrenics*. Madison, Wisconsin: University of Wisconsin Press.

Rogers, C.R. (1973) 'Some learnings from a study of psychotherapy with schizophrenics', in C.R. Rogers and B. Stevens (eds), *Person to Person: the Problem of Being Human*. London: Souvenir Press. pp. 181–92. (Abridged from a paper in Pennsylvania Psychiatric Quarterly, Summer, 1962).

Rogers, C.R. (1974) 'In retrospect: forty-six years', *American Psychologist*, 29(2): 115–23.

Rogers, C.R. (1977) *The Right to be Desperate*. Video produced by the American Association for Counseling and Development, Washington D.C.

Rogers C.R. (1979) 'Foundations of the Person-Centered Approach,' *Education*, 100(2): 98–107.

Rogers, C.R. (1980a) *A Way of Being*. Boston: Houghton Mifflin.

Rogers, C.R. (1980b) 'Growing old – or older and growing', *Journal of Humanistic Psychology* 20(4): 15–16.

Rogers C.R. (1986) 'Reflection of feelings', *Person-Centered Review*, 1(4): 375–7.

Ross, C.A. (1999) 'Subpersonalities and multiple personalities: a dissociative continuum?', in J. Rowan and M. Cooper (eds), *The Plural Self*. London: Sage. pp. 183–97.

Rowan, J. (1990) *Subpersonalities: the People Inside Us*. London: Routledge.

Rowan, J. and Cooper, M. (eds) (1999) *The Plural Self: Multiplicity in Everyday Life*. London: Sage.

Sachse, R. (1990) 'Concrete interventions are crucial: the influence of the therapist's processing proposals on the client's interpersonal exploration in client-centered therapy', in G. Lietaer, J. Rombauts and R. Van Balen (eds), *Client-Centered and Experiential Psychotherapy in the Nineties*. Leuven: Leuven University Press. pp. 295–308.

Sanders, P. (2000) 'Mapping person-centred approaches to counselling and psychotherapy', *Person-Centred Practice*, 8(2): 62–74.

Sanders, P. (2006) *The Person-Centred Primer*. Ross-on-Wye: PCCS Books.

Sands, A. (2000) *Falling for Therapy: Psychotherapy From a Client's Point of View*. London: Palgrave Macmillan.

Schmid, P. (2003). 'The characteristics of a person-centered approach to therapy and counseling', *Person-Centered and Experiential Psychotherapies*, 2(2): 104–20.

Schmid, P.F. and Mearns, D. (2006) 'Being-with and being-counter: person-centered psychotherapy as an in-depth co-creative process of personalization', *Person-Centered and Experiential Psychotherapies*, 5: 174–90.

Schwartz, R. (1987) 'Our multiple selves', *The Family Therapy Networker*, March/April: 25–31 and 80–3.

Schwartz, R. (1997) *Internal Family Systems Therapy*. New York: Guilford.

Schwartz, R. and Goulding, R. (1995) *The Mosaic Mind*. New York: Norton Press.

Selfridge, F.F. and Kolk, C. van der (1976) 'Correlates of counselor self-actualisation and client-perceived facilitativeness', *Counselor Education and Supervision*, 15(3): 189–94.

Sembi, R. (2006) 'The cultural situatedness of language use in person-centred training', in G. Proctor, M. Cooper, P. Sanders and B. Malcolm (eds), *Politicizing the Person-Centred Approach*. Ross-on-Wye: PCCS Books. pp. 55–9.

Shoaib, K. (2006) 'Unveiling the unspoken: working transparently with South Asian communities', in G. Proctor, M. Cooper, P. Sanders and B. Malcolm (eds), *Politicizing the Person-Centred Approach*. Ross-on-Wye: PCCS Books. pp. 183–94.

Slack, S. (1985) 'Reflections on a workshop with Carl Rogers', *Journal of Humanistic Psychology*, 28: 35–42.

Stern, D.N. (2003) *The Interpersonal World of the Infant: a View from Psychoanalysis and Developmental Theory*. London: Karnac.

Stiles, W. (1999) 'Signs and voices in psychotherapy', *Psychotherapy Research*, 9: 1–21.

Stiles, W.B. and Glick, M.J. (2002) 'Client-centered therapy with multi-voiced clients: empathy with whom?', in J.C. Watson, R. Goldman and M.S. Warner (eds), *Client-centered and Experiential Psychotherapy in the Twenty-First Century*. Ross on Wye: PCCS Books. pp. 406–14.

Stinckens, N. (2000) 'De innerlijke criticus in beeld gebracht: Een typologie van verschijningsvormen', *Tijdschrift Cliëntgerichte Psychotherapie*, 38: 201–15.

Stinckens, N., Lietaer, G., and Leijssen, M. (2002) 'The valuing process and the inner critic in the classic and current client-centered/experiential literature', *Person-Centered and Experiential Psychotherapies,* 1(1&2): 41–55.

Talmon, M. (1990) *Single Session Therapy*. San Francisco: Jossey-Bass Publishers.

Tausch, R., Bastine. R., Bommert, H., Minsel, W.R. and Nickel, H. (1972) 'Weitere Untersuchung der Auswirkung und der Prozesse klienten-zentrierter Gesprächs-psychotherapie', *Zeitschrift für Klinische Psychologie*, 1(3): 232–50.

Tausch, R., Bastine, R., Friese, H. and Sander, K. (1970) 'Variablen und Ergebnisse bei Psychotherapie mit alternieranden Psychotherapeuten', *Verlag für Psychologie*, 21(1).

Thorne, B. (1985) *The Quality of Tenderness.* Norwich: Norwich Centre Publications.

Thorne, B. (1991a) *Person-Centred Counselling: Therapeutic and Spiritual Dimensions*. London: Whurr Publishers.

Thorne, B. (1991b) *Behold the Man*. London: Darton, Longman and Todd.

Thorne, B. (1992) *Carl Rogers*. London: Sage.

Thorne, B. (1996) 'The cost of transparency', *Person Centred Practice*, 2: 2–11.

Thorne, B. (1999) 'The move towards brief therapy: its dangers and its challenges', *Counselling*, 10(1): 7–11.

Thorne, B. (2002) *The Mystical Power of Person-Centred Therapy*. London: Whurr Publishers.

Thorne, B. (2004) *The Quality of Tenderness*, Revd edn. Norwich: Norwich Centre Occasional Publications.

Thorne, B. (2005) *Love's Embrace*. Ross-on-Wye: PCCS Books.

Thorne, B. (2006) 'The gift and cost of being fully present', in J. Moore and C. Purton (eds), *Spirituality and Counselling: Experiential and Theoretical Perspectives*. Ross-on-Wye: PCCS Books. pp. 35–47.

Tolan, J. (2003) *Skills in Person-Centred Counselling and Psychotherapy*. London: Sage.

Truax, C.B. and Carkhuff, R.R. (1967) *Toward Effective Counseling and Psychotherapy*. Chicago: Aldine.

Truax, C.B. and Mitchell, K.M. (1971) 'Research on certain therapist interpersonal skills in relation to process and outcome', in A.E. Bergin and S.L. Garfield (eds), *Handbook of Psychotherapy and Behavior Change*. New York: John Wiley. pp. 299–344.

Tudor, K. and Worrall, M. (2006) *Person-Centred Therapy: a Clinical Philosophy*. London: Routledge.

Vaillant, L.M. (1994) 'The next step in short-term dynamic psychotherapy: a clarification of objectives and techniques in an anxiety-regulating model', *Psychotherapy*, 31: 642–55.

Van Werde, D. (2003a) 'Dealing with the possibility of psychotic content in a seemingly congruent communication', in D. Mearns, *Developing Person-Centred Counselling*. London: Sage. pp. 125–8.

Van Werde, D. (2003b) 'An introduction to client-centred pre-therapy', in D. Mearns, *Developing Person-Centred Counselling*. London: Sage. pp. 120–4.

Warner, M.S. (2000a) 'Person-centred therapy at the difficult edge: a developmentally based model of fragile and dissociated process', in D. Mearns and B. Thorne, *Person-Centred Therapy Today: New Frontiers in Theory and Practice*. London: Sage. pp. 144–71.

Warner, M.S. (2000b) 'Person-centered psychotherapy: one nation, many tribes', *Person-Centered Journal*, 7(1): 28–39.

Warner, M.S. (2002a) 'Psychological contact, meaningful process and human nature', in G. Wyatt and P. Sanders (eds) *Rogers' Therapeutic Conditions: Contact and Perception*. Ross-on-Wye: PCCS Books. pp. 76–95.

Warner, M.S. (2002b) 'Luke's dilemmas: a client-centered/experiential model of processing with a schizophrenic thought disorder', in J.C. Watson, R.N. Goldman and M.S. Warner (eds), *Client-Centered and Experiential Psychotherapy in the 21st Century: Advances in Theory, Research and Practice*. Ross-on-Wye: PCCS Books. pp. 459–72.

Warner, M.S. (2006) 'Toward an integrated person-centered theory of wellness and psychopathology', *Person-Centered and Experiential Psychotherapies*, 5: 4–20.

Warner, M. and Mearns, D. (2003) In discussion. 6th World Conference for Person-Centered and Experiential Psychotherapy and Counseling. Egmond, Holland; July.

Watson, J.C. and Steckley, P. (2001) 'Potentiating growth: an examination of the research on unconditional positive regard', in J. Bozarth and P. Wilkins (eds), *Rogers' Therapeutic Conditions: Unconditional Positive Regard*. Ross-on-Wye: PCCS Books. pp. 180–97.

Watson, J.C., Goldman, R.N. and Warner, M.S. (eds) (2002) *Client-Centered and Experiential Psychotherapy in the 21st Century: Advances in Theory, Research and Practice*. Ross-on-Wye: PCCS Books.

Wilkins, P. (2003) *Person-Centred Therapy in Focus*. London: Sage.

Zinschitz, E. (2001) 'Understanding what seems unintelligible', in S. Haugh and T. Merry (eds), *Rogers' Therapeutic Conditions: Empathy*. Ross-on-Wye: PCCS Books. pp. 192–205.

Author Index

Subject Index